UNDER A FEATHERED SKY

THE UNTOLD STORY OF NATO'S ROLE IN NEWLY INDEPENDENT KOSOVO

By

ADE CLEWLOW

MentonBlackbush
ISBN-13: 978-1-8381564-0-4
eBook: 978-1-8381564-1-1

To the people of Kosovo.

"In a highly charged and often dangerous environment, peace is frequently bought by a few quite junior, yet talented people, given disproportionate responsibility. Their courage, initiative and judgement is what allows the big international bureaucracies that send them into harm's way to succeed, despite those organisations often displaying a bewildering inability to support and give clear direction to the very people on whom they depend. Ade Clewlow was one such individual. His candid account of his experiences in Kosovo makes for great reading. It ranges from acute observations on the highest levels of international incompetence, that blithely ignores ground level reality, through to daily encounters with people actively and cunningly conspiring to thwart well laid plans. I thoroughly recommend it. Military and diplomatic professional, or lay person with an interest in what lies behind the headlines, they will all thoroughly enjoy and learn from this page-turning, stimulating and very human tale."

General The Lord Richards of Herstmonceux GCB CBE DSO

June, 2020

CONTENTS

LIST OF ABBREVIATIONS

1* General – Brigadier General (in the UK it is simply Brigadier)
2* General – Major General
3* General – Lieutenant General
CIA – Central Intelligence Agency
Col – Colonel
EFI – Expeditionary Forces Institute (pronounced 'Effy')
EU – European Union
EULEX – European Union civilian mission
FRY – Former Republic of Yugoslavia
HQ – Headquarters
HRH – Her Royal Highness
ICO – International Civilian Office
IOM – International Organisation for Migration
JFC – Joint Forces Command
KFOR – Kosovo Force
KIKPC – KFOR Inspectorate of the KPC
KLA – Kosovo Liberation Army
KPC – Kosovo Protection Corps
KSF – Kosovo Security Force
LNO – Liaison Officer
MA – Master of Arts
MA – Military Assistant
MAT – Ministry Advisory Team
MCAD – Military Civilian Advisory Division
MoD – Ministry of Defence
NAT – NATO Advisory Team
NATO – North Atlantic Treaty Organisation

NATO's New Tasks –establishing a civilian-run Ministry of the KSF, dissolving the KPC and standing up and training the new multi-ethnic, civilian run Kosovo Security Force, or KSF.

NGO – Non-Governmental Organisations

NSE – National Support Element

OKPCC – Office of the KPC Coordinator

OLA – Office of the Legal Authority

OSCE – Organisation for Security and Cooperation in Europe

PM – Prime Minister

PZ – Protection Zone

Q&A – Question and Answer

RAF – Royal Air Force

RSS – Recruiting, Screening and Selection (of personnel)

R&R – Rest and Recuperation

SASE/FOM – Safe and Secure Environment/Freedom of Movement

SOSAB – Senior Officer Selection and Appointment Board

SUV – Suburban Utility Vehicle

TRADOC – Training and Doctrine Command

UN – United Nations

UNDP – United Nations Development Programme

UNMIK – UN Mission in Kosovo

Montenegro

Serbia

Protection
Zone 4

● Mitrovice

PRISTINA ■

● Peje

Protection
Zone 1

Protection
Zone 3

KOSOVO

Protection
Zone 5

● Gjilan

Protection
Zone 6

● Ferizaj

● Prizren

Protection
Zone 2

Albania

Macedonia

KPC Protection Zones 2008/09

PART ONE

CHAPTER ONE

'No Time to Waste'

I was in the centre of Mitrovice, on the ethnic Albanian side of Kosovo's most divided town, together with Major General Rahman Rama, the Deputy Commander of the Kosovo Protection Corps, commonly known as the KPC, and Simi, my interpreter. Dressed in civilian clothes, surrounded by local residents inside a smoke-filled café, with British troops patrolling on the street outside, we were waiting for a member of the KPC to arrive. He had agreed to meet us even though he did not know the reason why.

When he walked through the door we all got up from our table, Major General Rama leading the greetings. The man shook our hands in turn and we waited for him to sit down. After much scraping of chairs, a silence quickly filled the space between us. He looked confused, as well he might. His Deputy Commander had travelled from Kosovo's capital city, Pristina, at short notice, specifically to see him. This didn't happen every day.

Major General Rama explained that he wanted to talk to the man about his son. His look deepened as concern spread across his face. With Simi translating quietly to me on the opposite side of the table, Rama told him what we knew. The man said little but his shock was tangible. After finishing his explanation, and to my surprise, Rama turned and asked me to speak to him.

I had been in the country for barely 5 days but it was not difficult to find the right words to reinforce Rama's message. Thinking quickly, I looked him in the eye and spoke carefully.

I urged him to use his influence to avoid something terrible happening that would likely stir up tensions in the town, and potentially across the country. There was no time to waste. Acting now was crucial to avoid the world changing for many people, including his family and friends.

When I finished, my words translated through Simi, I sat back. The meeting was brief, the man excused himself and we stayed to finish our coffees. My mind drifted as I reflected on the significance of what we had just done. It was a situation that I had never expected to have to deal with. At least not so soon.

Only a week earlier I had been pushing my daughter on a swing in a local play park in England, enjoying the last few days with my family before deploying on a 6-month tour of duty in Kosovo. Within a few days I was already playing my part in shaping the future of the Balkans' newest independent country.

It only occurred to me later that the British Army soldiers who had patrolled past the café that afternoon had done so to provide protection, a visible deterrence in the immediate vicinity of our crucial meeting. Their presence was no coincidence.

Nothing happened by chance in Kosovo.

CHAPTER TWO

'Flying the Flag'

It was the summer of 2008 and I was again packing my gear into a hire car, parked outside our house on a military base near Swindon. After spending much of 2004 away from my family I was about to disappear again to a little known part of the world for 6 months. Whilst my daughter, who was 3 years old, was unlikely to be too affected, my son at nearly 7 was going to miss me. As I walked round to the driver's seat I looked back for a final time and waved. As ever, my family looked on, left behind at home, standing on the doorstep, unsure when we would see each other again, my wife doing her best to distract the kids as their father left for a long tour abroad. I was excited by what lay ahead but I knew I was going to miss my family terribly. It was a bittersweet moment.

I had just emerged from a year-long course at the Defence Academy, during which time I had completed an MA in Defence Studies through King's College, London, brushed up my international relations theory and developed my analytical and military planning skills.

Part of my course had involved studying for a Special Subject of my choice. I had always been fascinated by the geopolitical strategies employed by Great Britain and Russia in 19th-Century Afghanistan, known as the 'Great Game'; choosing this subject provided me with the opportunity to discover more about this period of military history. The extraordinary role played by British army officers made a strong impression on me, deploying on missions lasting months, knowing the desired strategic outcome but acting entirely independently without any recourse to higher authority or a support network.

I was inspired by the approach to what was a complicated and ever changing environment. I admired the high degree of autonomy gifted to the individual officers to make decisions that would have long-lasting geopolitical implications. Whilst in reality I was clearly unlikely to emulate this scenario in my next posting, the ability to act alone, to display resourcefulness and to make a difference, very much resonated with my personality.

During my second term I had to choose what job I wanted to do after the course finished. I had 8 months to fill before taking command of my regiment. Scrolling through the list of potential operational tours overseas I looked for somewhere off the beaten track; where the spirit of the Great Game could be adapted to the 21st Century, within reason. There were lots of roles in Afghanistan but they failed to meet my brief. There were a few opportunities in Iraq but I had already served in Baghdad and the operation was winding down. So with very few British officers deployed in unfashionable and newly independent Kosovo, and a vacancy in Pristina, Kosovo's capital city, I knew where I wanted to go. I applied for and was appointed to be the 19th British Liaison Officer to the Kosovo Protection Corps, the KPC.

Following a long line of British Lieutenant Colonels, I deployed to Kosovo to provide the eyes and ears for NATO's International Military Presence in the country, known as Kosovo Force, or more colloquially KFOR. Commanded by French, Italian and German 3* Generals on an annual rotation, there were 16,000 troops deployed in Kosovo in 2008, a country tucked away in the southern Balkans, with an indigenous population of around 2 million people, approximately 90% of whom were ethnic Albanian. The remaining ethnic groups were largely made up of Kosovo Serbs and Roma.

The UK had provided the NATO Liaison Officer, locally known as the LNO, to the KPC since 1999. That year had seen an increase in ethnic cleansing of entire Kosovo Albanian villages at the hands of Serbian paramilitary police. On 24th March 1999, under pressure to act, NATO authorised Operation Allied Force, an air campaign against the Former Republic of Yugoslavia (FRY) and its forces deployed in Kosovo. After 78 days, sufficient pressure had been brought to bear on President Milosevic in Belgrade to admit defeat and agree to the withdrawal of his forces from the territory of Kosovo. Sitting together in Macedonia, representatives of NATO and FRY signed a military technical agreement on 9th June 1999 that led to the total removal of Yugoslav and Serbian forces from Kosovo within 10 days.

The Kosovo Liberation Army, known as the KLA, had been engaged in a guerrilla war against Serbian paramilitary forces since 1994 but the conflict escalated significantly throughout 1998 and into 1999. The KLA, men and women, numbered many thousands of volunteers, who had either fought against or supported the guerrilla war against the Serbs. In the immediate post war period, during the summer of 1999, as displaced Kosovo Albanians were finally allowed to return to their shattered homes, under the watchful eyes of the newly deployed KFOR troops, the question of demilitarising the KLA personnel was a pressing problem for the NATO leadership.

On the initiative of the KFOR Commander, British General Sir

Mike Jackson, a new organisation was established, under a UN mandate, in September 1999, called the Kosovo Protection Corps, the KPC. Its role was to support the government in times of civil emergency. De-mining became a key staple of their role, they developed an internationally recognised urban search and rescue capability, and the KPC offered other civil emergency activities such as supporting the local population during natural disasters. Uniformed and highly respected for their previous role fighting against the Serbs, the KPC came to embody the spirit of Kosovo and developed into one of its most important and revered institutions; some described it as an alternative government.

Having a British LNO was a metaphorical badge of honour worn proudly by KPC members and over the 9 years preceding my arrival, a profound respect had developed between the UK military and the KPC, exemplified through the LNO's position at the heart of the organisation. Fully embedded in the KPC headquarters in central Pristina during the working day but accommodated in the KFOR barracks at night, the LNO spent hours in the company of the KPC 3* commander and his 2* deputy, travelling with them to meetings, acting as a mentor, advisor and confidante. It was a unique role and much cherished by those who had been fortunate to fill it. I was both intrigued and excited by what lay ahead of me.

As I drove east along the M4 towards the airport, a familiar sense of adventure began to grow. With a boot full of personal and military equipment, my mind began to think about what lay in store. Fresh from reading Noel Malcolm's *Kosovo: A Short History*, a new chapter in my life was about to begin.

And with the exploits of the Great Game fresh in my memory, I deployed to Kosovo determined to make a difference.

Walking down the aircraft steps, the late afternoon heat at once focused my mind on what was to come. Within a few days of being in Kosovo, I began to get a sense of what my role would be and how I could add value to the KPC and its members. As the LNO, being trusted to pass information in many directions was vital to the credibility of my position. I knew that I would have to write a weekly report for the KFOR command team, and others in KFOR's higher headquarters, NATO's Joint Force Command in Naples, Italy. I was expected to note what I had observed, adding personal comments as appropriate. I would be filling a key function for the KFOR leadership team, joining the dots of an organisation's thinking and behaviour. I would be KFOR's main point of contact in the KPC, and the KPC's conduit into KFOR. It was going to be a fascinating role.

Fortunately I had a very early opportunity to demonstrate that I was going to be bringing a new approach to the role.

During my handover period I was introduced to many of the key people within KFOR headquarters who I would be working closely with. In one discussion with a British Colonel, a Reservist acting as the intelligence chief, I was told about a potential inter-ethnic attack that was actively being planned and which had been picked up by various sources. It was serious enough to warrant an intervention by KFOR. The timing was imminent and the location was the divided town of Mitrovice in the north of Kosovo. One of those suspected of being involved was the son of a member of the KPC.

Although unorthodox, we decided on a less high-profile approach by agreeing that the individual's father should be spoken to by the KPC Deputy Commander. It was hoped he could exert some influence on the man, and in turn his son, to convince him not to go through with the attack. This approach was designed to tap into the Albanian medieval honour system, or 'bessa', which was still very much in place in Kosovo at that time.

The first person I contacted via Simi was General Rama, who would lead the conversation and who would become a key ally for me throughout my tour. Despite barely knowing me, the institutional respect for the British LNO was enough for him to trust me and the plan was initiated. The arrangements were put in place, the man was told to report to a café in Mitrovice and we prepared to drive north from Pristina.

Our efforts that day were successful; the attack never took place. The Mitrovice meeting was the first taste of what life was to become as I attempted to steer the KPC through the next 6 turbulent months.

CHAPTER THREE

'Military Operations; Kosovo style'

Not only had the unexpected deployment to Mitrovice given me an opportunity to spend some time with General Rama, I also had a chance to talk at length with my interpreter, Simi. It was only on the drive back from Mitrovice that he finally opened up to me in the relative quiet of our official vehicle, a Toyota Landcruiser, equipped with siren and blue lights for escorting the KPC command team on official journeys. While Kasper, my armed Danish driver and bodyguard, was taking us back to Pristina, Simi gave me a run through of the previous 6 months since Kosovo's declaration of independence had been made by Prime Minister Hashim Thaçi. He explained the impact on the KPC.

It was clear that I was going to need to reach out and create a lot of relationships within the KPC, and probably in many other directions that I was unaware of at that time. The prospect of a difficult and politically sensitive security sector transition happening on my watch was the perfect way to establish my credentials. I had hoped to make a strong first impression and I was taking over at a time when much help, advice and guidance was needed by the KPC from the LNO; the Mitrovice meeting had been the ideal way to start my tour.

During those first few days of my handover, I also had a chance to observe the country as a whole. Kosovo had a naturally beautiful and dramatic landscape, with snow-capped mountains, rolling hills, lakes, forests and deep gorges hiding rivers that looked as if they would burst into life at the first sign of rain. It was stunning scenery. However, it was also a country that looked in dire need of help, with poverty evident in the towns and more remote villages that we drove through. The most striking sight was the amount of litter that was piled up along the roadside and that had blown into the fields as far as the eye could see. Before arriving in the country, people had said to me that Kosovo is only beautiful in the winter when the ground is snow covered, masking the rubbish like a white blanket; I now understood. Quite why the litter problem had become so bad remained a mystery throughout my tour. In fact I became immune to it, as did most people who lived in Kosovo at that time.

The Kosovo that I had seen on the television, during the extensive coverage of the war in 1999, suddenly came to life. As I was being driven around the country visiting remote KPC bases, I was given a running commentary by Simi about incidents that had happened at the end of the 1990s. KLA memorials regularly appeared on the roadside, commemorating the deaths of local volunteers where they fell during the fighting. They varied in size, from small gestures, featuring two or three photographs of fallen fighters alongside bunches of faded flowers laid on top of the gravestones, to lavish cemeteries with large murals depicting images of KLA martyrs painted onto concrete walls. Every location was accompanied by red Albanian flags, featuring the black eagle emblem, fluttering in the late summer breeze, their presence a constant reminder of the sacrifice from a decade earlier.

At one point in our whistle-stop tour, we parked up in Prekaz, a small village north west of the capital. A shrine had been constructed commemorating the murder by Serbian forces in 1998 of the Kosovo Liberation Army founder Adem Jashari and 57 members of the wider Jashari family. After spending some time looking at the graves, the trees providing shade from the heat of the late summer sun and a sense of protection for those interred in the ground, I laid a wreath at the memorial and marked my departure with a salute. It had become a tradition for the new LNO to pay his respects this way. We then drove a short distance to the nearest KPC base in Skenderaj where one of the few remaining survivors of that massacre was the KPC officer in charge, Brigadier General Jashari. A quiet and thoughtful man, meeting General Jashari was a powerful reminder of why I was in Kosovo.

So why was my 6 months going to be any different to the 18 LNOs before me? The answer was not straight forward. From 1999, Kosovo had been under the daily control of a UN Interim Administration, called UNMIK, which had been authorised under UN Security Council Resolution 1244. The KPC had been established under UNMIK's oversight. The resolution also authorised the deployment of an 'International Military Presence', otherwise known as KFOR, to provide security within the UN administered region.

Fast forward 8 years.

In 2007 the UN's Secretary General, Ban Ki Moon, had appointed a Special Envoy to find a long-term solution to Kosovo's future status. Former Finnish President Martti Ahtisaari, had written a document called the Comprehensive Proposal for the Kosovo Status Settlement, known as the 'Ahtisaari Plan', which opened the door to independence for Kosovo. It also recommended the drawing down of the KPC and creating a new professional, civilian-led, multi-ethnic security force with 2,500 members and 800 reserves called the Kosovo Security Force, the KSF. It added that KFOR in conjunction with the International Civilian Representative and the state of Kosovo, would exercise *executive authority* over the dissolution of the KPC and the establishment of the KSF.

The 'Ahtisaari Plan' stated that after a 120-day transition period, during which Kosovo would attempt to gain recognition as an independent nation state from the international community, the country then had 12 months to dissolve the KPC and establish the KSF. Published in March 2007 and endorsed by Ban Ki Moon 4 months later, the Kosovo Status Settlement led to the writing of Kosovo's constitution and then, on 17th February 2008, in line with the 'Ahtisaari Plan', the Government of Kosovo declared independence. This was the trigger for the transition period to begin.

So far so good.

Up until this time, NATO's force in Kosovo, KFOR, had been focused on providing a 'Safe and Secure Environment' and 'Freedom of Movement', colloquially known as SASE/FOM, for Kosovo's ethnic groups to live in relative harmony. The newly independent country was predominantly ethnic Albanian apart from the area north of the River Ibar in Mitrovice and a couple of Kosovo Serbian pockets; a town in the east and a village in the south. With the exception of a major breakdown of security in 2004, during which an incident in Mitrovice was the catalyst for a few days of deadly inter-ethnic violence resulting in loss of life, KFOR had been doing a good job of keeping the peace.

As the guarantor of a secure environment, under the 'Ahtisaari Plan', NATO had been directed to exercise *executive authority* over what would become known as the 'New Tasks' in Kosovo; establishing a civilian-run Ministry of the KSF, dissolving the KPC and standing up and training the new multi-ethnic, civilian-run

Kosovo Security Force. In response, by the end of 2007 NATO had set up a Ministry Advisory Team, the MAT, in Pristina which was directed to set up a new Ministry for the KSF from scratch. This involved writing new laws, establishing regulations and developing policies and processes for the Ministry and the KSF. NATO had also begun thinking about the remaining two tasks; how to deactivate the KPC and concurrently stand up the new security force, the KSF, before 14th June 2009.

A small NATO team under the command of a German officer, Colonel Karl Habel, had already deployed to Kosovo by late 2007 with this task in mind. Joining Colonel Habel a few months later in early 2008 was a British officer, Colonel Stuart Roberts. The growing team was called the Military Civilian Advisory Division, known locally as MCA Division or MCAD. At a press conference in Brussels in June 2008, NATO officially announced the 'New Tasks'.

There was only one problem, NATO had changed the language. Rather than exercising *executive authority* over the three tasks, a phrase which was very clear in the UN's 'Ahtisaari Plan', the NATO Secretary General announced that they would *supervise* the tasks instead. It was a subtle change in language but one that would allow KFOR considerable wriggle room to choose to what degree it wanted to commit to the tasks related to closing the KPC and setting up the KSF; one word made the highly interdependent process far more difficult for those, like me, who were at the heart of the transition. So NATO, through KFOR, had unilaterally changed the language to suit its own agenda. For NATO, pacifying its member states who had refused to recognise Kosovo for fear of encouraging their own national separatist movements had become the priority.

KFOR as an organisation didn't recognise Kosovo, the UN didn't recognise an independent Kosovo despite the UN Secretary General,

Ban Ki Moon, endorsing the 'Ahtisaari Plan' that recommended its independence, and NATO, as the provider of a 'Safe and Secure Environment' with 'Freedom of Movement' through the deployment of the International Military Presence, or KFOR, had managed to wriggle out of exercising executive authority over its 'New Tasks'.

It was a complete mess.

The issue of Kosovo's recognition soon turned to farce. Shortly after the 'New Tasks' press conference in Brussels by the NATO Secretary General De Hoop Scheffer, back in Kosovo the Ministry Advisory Team, the MAT, had to change its name. Even though De Hoop Scheffer explained at the press conference that the decision for NATO to take on the 'New Tasks' reflected a *consensus* within the North Atlantic Council, which consisted of representatives from all NATO member states, a sense of collective agreement in NATO's mission in Kosovo was very clearly absent. Within KFOR one or more nations had clearly objected to the use of the word Ministry in the title *Ministry Advisory Team*. Presumably the logic was that by using the word Ministry, the countries that made up KFOR were effectively recognising a Ministry within the Government of Kosovo, and therefore by extension, Kosovo's independence. Overnight the title changed to NATO Advisory Team, the NAT, in order to please those NATO member states who had troops deployed in KFOR but who refused to recognise Kosovo as a nation state.

Not only had the MAT become the NAT, it was now the turn of the Kosovans themselves to feel thoroughly undermined by their 'security partner'. Documents distributed by KFOR, internally and externally, only ever referred to the *Institutions* of Kosovo, the IoK. This mirrored the language used by the 'Ahtisaari Plan' written before Kosovo declared independence from Serbia, rather than the *Government* of Kosovo, the GoK, now that it was a sovereign country.

It seemed extraordinarily petty behaviour by the world's foremost security organisation.

Just when KFOR's political correctness looked like it had reached its zenith, there was still room for one more insult to the Kosovans. In planning documents and on power point presentations, even the new Kosovo Security Force – the KSF – became a victim of the politically correct environment that consumed KFOR headquarters. The Kosovo Security Force, referred to in the 'Ahtisaari Plan' and in Brussels by NATO, started to change its abbreviated version from the KSF to *a Ksf*. Every time I saw a small 's' and small 'f' I would correct it back to capitals, assuming it had been a typo by a non-native English speaker. I did this repeatedly, but it wasn't a typo at all. It was another attempt by those countries who chose not to recognise Kosovo – but who were happy to remain in country enjoying their tax-free status while at the same time fulfilling their commitment to an overseas NATO deployment – to impose their views on the situation in Kosovo. I learned that the act of writing *security force* in capitals, was to *de facto* recognise that Kosovo was going to have its own Security Force and hence was an independent sovereign state, which of course KFOR did not recognise. And what about the Kosovans? The few who witnessed this behaviour shrugged it off, knowing that they were an unequal partner with KFOR and could do nothing about it. And they had much bigger issues to contend with than worrying about words and letters.

Every time I saw this I shook my head in bemusement.

Of the three 'New Tasks', I had little to do with the now renamed NATO Advisory Team. The international team within the NAT was staffed with young, talented lawyers and other constitutional experts, led by a senior British civil servant, Andy Lennard, whose office in KFOR headquarters was close to the main entrance. His team had a mammoth task ahead of them and they worked all hours. Bright, intelligent and committed to making Kosovo a better place, they epitomised the phrase 'work hard; play hard'. I often saw Andy's team in town, making the most of their time off. During working hours, I kept in close contact with Andy, escaping to his office to discuss the latest developments in our respective areas.

Settling into life in Film City, the local name for the KFOR headquarters on a hill above Pristina, was a surreal experience. Based on what used to be home to the local film studios, the KFOR base was filled with representatives from every nation deployed in Kosovo, which included non-NATO forces. Along with the usual 'ISO' container accommodation units, stacked one on top of each other, similar to those seen at countless building sites across the world, there were paths criss-crossing the base with neatly painted white stones bordering perfectly manicured patches of grass, well-tended bushes and flowers planted symmetrically throughout. Exploring the base was like walking around an international holiday resort, with a range of restaurants, cafés and shops available for the thousands of troops who either lived in the base or who were bussed in at weekends from outlying KFOR military bases.

Most contributing nations had their own NSE – or National Support Element – housed in elaborate buildings designed in the style of that country. The Italian NSE was a mock three-storey Dolomite-style ski lodge, the Norwegian NSE was a large log cabin big enough for 100 people, with a long bar, its own pool table, sun deck and sauna. The French NSE had a large bar close to my accommodation which I discovered offered entertainment until late into the night, with live bands and discos most weekends. The Spanish had a tapas bar, the Irish their very own pub, with Guinness on tap, which was always full. Across the camp there was no shortage of entertainment for KFOR's troops; it was never ending.

Then there was the British NSE. Rather than an ostentatious demonstration of national pride, we had a 'living room', tucked away behind the Slovenian NSE and across the road from the Irish bar. The handful of Brits on the base were very proud of the small space. With satellite TV piped in from the UK, which was the only place that offered Six Nations International Rugby coverage in Film City, a fridge full of beer, a few cases of wine and a pile of 'stickies' – the military colloquial name for chocolates – all available on a honesty basis, together with day-old British newspapers, it was a home from home. It was not designed to host many guests, in fact if there was another member of the Brit community already there it began to get crowded. But it was snug and an ideal place to escape from the madness of living on the camp.

It didn't stop there. There was a large multi-vehicle servicing bay to rival any local Kwik Fit, a petrol station, a helicopter landing site, outdoor sports pitches and volleyball courts dotted throughout the base, all surrounded by an impregnable perimeter fence that I think was designed to keep people in, as much as to keep the locals out. There was a one way road system with a maximum speed limit of 10kph; life entered slow motion when you had to drive for any distance inside the camp. With a speed limit to enforce, international military police personnel deployed on the streets with speed guns. The only features missing to make it a 5-star resort were a golf course, a swimming pool and access to a local beach.

Being a NATO mission, there was an obsession with identity. Everyone had badges on their uniform, normally sewn onto shirts and jackets at €1 each; I shelled out a lot of money in the first few days so that I could become a fully trusted member of the KFOR family. The laundry facilities were on an industrial scale, the gymnasium was more suited to a university campus. There was a library, education centre, conference centre, and if I ever tired of eating in the official dining facility, known as the 'defac', there was a range restaurants and take-away food outlets as an alternative, including Chinese, Italian and burger bars. I learned that the main street, which housed many of the different shops and restaurants, had been coined the 'walk of shame' by my predecessor; the inference being that any self-respecting British military officer on operations would never be seen on it. I have to admit I broke that rule within days. Containing the only shops that sold whisky, it was hard not to go there.

The facilities were perfect for the many international troops who were sent to Kosovo every year. Yet the comfortable surroundings were also symptomatic of a wider malaise within KFOR's approach to Kosovo. It was as if KFOR had become entirely self-serving. It appeared to have abandoned any pretence of trying to support Kosovo's development as a nation state; rather it retained a stifling influence in its role as the NATO-led International Military Presence. For most of the military inhabitants in Pristina, Film City was all they saw for 6 months, barring the occasional tourist trip to a recognised landmark in the country. Emphasising the military nature of this strange world I had landed in, everyone had to wear uniform inside camp, unless people were just heading to the gym or returning from taking part in sport. Wearing civilian clothes was not permitted. Walking around the camp on a Friday night with the vast majority of the men and women dressed in their national combat uniform, beer in hand, took some getting used to. Only NATO civilians who were employed in other functions were allowed to wear normal clothes, and they stood out. Even during the day, walking across the base was akin to walking through a bizarre militarised café culture, where every seat was taken with troops idly passing their time. This only became more pronounced when the Italian command team took over the leadership of KFOR a week into my tour of duty.

By contrast to Film City, the British camp, situated a couple of minutes away at the bottom of the hill, called Slim Lines, was what you would expect of a UK military base. Orderly, austere and functional. There was accommodation for the resident infantry unit, a large classroom converted into a self-equipped gymnasium, a well-stocked medical centre, administration blocks and a war memorial. Focused on an entirely different element of the mission in Kosovo, having British troops around was always a reassurance, and going to Slim Lines was a breath of fresh air. There was a combined mess, for Officers and Sergeants, a shop for the basics and a café called the 'EFI', offering a few home comforts. Sharing the camp with the British was a Portuguese Battalion. With their own combined Officers' and Sergeants' Mess, they also manned the front gate and I quickly established a rapport with them because of my ability to speak Portuguese. If ever I needed some favourite Portuguese delicacies, I knew where to go.

Going to Slim Lines became an integral part of my weekly routine. Not only was my administration managed by the British troops inside the camp, for example approving my leave requests and booking flights for me in and out of the country, it was also great to be in an environment that had a sense of purpose. Slim Lines was a bolt hole for me; after only a week in Kosovo I had succumbed to the temptation to eat a cooked breakfast every morning, with the resultant dip in my energy levels. I quickly realised that I needed to eat a more healthy breakfast every morning in the 'defac', which catered for hundreds of KFOR troops each day. I soon dispensed with a hot food option and chose a mug of tea and a bowl of cereal every day, a habit I maintained throughout my tour. To compensate I decided to treat myself to a full English breakfast every Saturday morning at the EFI. Hardly original but it was a lifesaver, especially after a Friday night out in Pristina. The EFI, manned by British civil servants and offering high street café food, stocked British favourites, with a great range of ice creams and other staple hot meal options. With British Forces radio playing through the speakers, UK troops meeting together for coffee and a game of darts, it was an important reminder of home.

With 16,000 troops deployed across the country in a number of multinational task forces, and with a modest level of security incidents reported every day, there was a sense that the force numbers were way too high for the relatively peaceful security environment that existed. And it was those troops, who were based in the furthest reaches of the country, who would descend on Film City every Saturday on organised coach trips. Even the main road, the 'walk of shame', was cordoned off to traffic on Saturdays to prevent injury to the hundreds of troops, many of them armed, who came to Film City to spend their money, go shopping, drink in the cafés or bars and return back to their bases at the end of the day. The shops not only enjoyed significant footfall every weekend, but with a near cartel on prices between each outlet, they must have been making a significant profit. It certainly wasn't the type of military operation I was used to. And I could not imagine a more soul-destroying existence than being barred from leaving the camp.

Fortunately this was not the case for me.

Most military personnel based in KFOR HQ were confined to camp. Whether this was on security grounds, where an irrational mistrust of the local population permeated KFOR's corridors, or whether it was for reasons of prudence, to prevent inevitable alcohol-related incidents happening in Pristina by KFOR troops who had been let out of base, I was never sure. For some there was an official pass that allowed individuals to leave the base in uniform, issued to staff officers from inside KFOR headquarters for meetings with local Kosovan officials or members of the sizeable international community based in and around Kosovo.

And then there was an even more special pass, an SFEC, which allowed the bearer to not only leave camp, but to do so in civilian clothes. I had been given this pass during my handover and it was, quite literally, my very own get-out-of-jail card. Issued to very few people, mainly those involved in intelligence roles or to NATO civilians, I quickly appreciated the value of this official document and kept its existence to myself. I would be able to explore Kosovo in ways that thousands of KFOR military personnel would never see.

And it didn't take me long to use my pass. I realised that I had to be extremely discreet over my use of the official car at weekends while wearing civilian clothes. I began parking the car close to my accommodation on a Friday evening so that I was less visible when going out during the weekend. Keeping a low profile was important when it came to my out-of-hours activities. Losing the privilege would have been catastrophic. Having the ability to leave the base in civilian clothes not only became vital for my role but it also provided a lifeline for me when I needed to find some peace and quiet during what became an intense 6-month tour.

What I found in downtown Pristina was a thriving social scene, with an excellent service sector; cafés comparable with any western town, bars which were always busy and restaurants with a high standard of service and food. Reflecting on this discovery, I shouldn't have been surprised. After 1999 the international community had deployed to Kosovo in large numbers; the UN, EU, many other international NGOs and the wider diplomatic community were all based in Pristina. And with thousands of Euros metaphorically burning a hole in their collective pockets, they went out to spend their money.

Driving around the city, it looked as if every third vehicle was from KFOR, the UN or one of the many other international organisations that had made Pristina home. It felt as if Kosovo was sinking under the weight of international supervision, but this in turn had spawned an excellent social scene for the thousands of civilians for whom Pristina was a temporary home. I started to make myself familiar with the best places to go for a coffee, for dinner and where to meet people in town. As a former Gurkha officer, I also found a genuine Nepalese restaurant. Simi, my interpreter, took me to a few places in the first few weeks with his wife, Valbona, who was studying to be a lawyer. One evening Simi and Valbona invited me to go to Pristina's ABC cinema to watch an Albanian film with English subtitles called 'Time of the Comet', a tragi-comedy that contributed to my understanding of Albanian culture. It was the first and probably my last visit to a Kosovan cinema.

Downtown Pristina offered everything you would expect; I discovered smoke-filled nightclubs packed with drinkers, bars and restaurants where people just didn't care who you were or where you were from, and I got to know the places where more private conversations could be held. I was led astray on more than one occasion by international colleagues on the streets of the capital. I ventured out to Germia Park, a large area of forest covering a series of hills east of Pristina, where it was possible to walk for hours without seeing any litter or other people, as long as you avoided the taped-off areas that had still not been cleared of mines by the UN 9 years after the end of the war.

I found myself being invited to official dinners with senior officers from KFOR, the UN and within the British community. I met diplomats, spooks and the media; the latter were fascinated by my role, the shadowy British figure who accompanied the commander of the KPC on every trip. It started to become a defining time in my life and I was hungry to experience everything. Pristina was a cosmopolitan city; I liked it.

Unusually I also knew someone who lived in the city. Alexandra was the sister of a family friend who was living and working in Pristina and had been in the country for a number of years. She was fluent in Albanian and was volunteering for a political organisation called Vetevendosje – or the English translation, the Movement for Self Determination. What little I knew about Vetevendosje, whose political roots lay in the removal of Serbian sovereignty over Kosovo, suggested I needed to be cautious. I was godfather to Alexandra's niece, and to me that was a pretty innocent connection. For Alexandra, who was working with a political movement that, amongst other things, opposed KFOR's mandate in Kosovo, it was clear from the start that it may be a difficult relationship.

However, soon after arriving in Pristina I called Alexandra and we arranged to meet within a few days; I was looking forward to it. So after attending a Saturday morning meeting on my second weekend in Kosovo, I drove into the city and parked in the local KPC barracks. We had arranged to meet outside the Hotel Grand. There was no danger of not recognising her as the family likeness was strong. It was actually great to spend some time with someone who I was connected to via long standing friends; we didn't know each other at all but through her sister's connection we got on well. After giving me a brief tour of the centre of Pristina, we dived into her favourite bookshop then headed for a coffee. It was good not to be immersed in KPC business for a couple of hours and I enjoyed listening to her views on Kosovo. Alexandra was studying for a PhD and was doing a range of things with Vetevendosje, including translating its publications into English. I think Alexandra found our meeting quite bizarre; as one point she asked me directly:

'Are you a Colonel?'

'Of course,' I replied.

This set her off into a fits of laughter. 'The activist and the army officer,' she declared.

I think she was still a bit unsure about the risks associated with seeing me but she offered to take me to her office and introduce me to the leader of Vetevendosje, Albin Kurti. I am not sure I would have taken that step; in all likelihood Vetevendosje was under surveillance and walking into their offices would have compromised me pretty quickly.

We had enjoyed each other's company and we parted; within days she headed out of Kosovo for 6 weeks, but we had promised to meet up again when she returned. As I drove back up to Film City I was playing the whole meeting over in my mind, trying to decide whether, in the circumstances, it was prudent to keep this friendship going. On balance I decided that I needed to take some advice, so I made a mental note to visit a colleague in the British Embassy before she returned to Kosovo.

As I became more familiar with the city in particular I started venturing out much more, using my pass to great effect. The weather was still very warm and nothing I had seen so far in Pristina gave me cause for concern from a security perspective. The day after seeing Alexandra I took my camera out with me and walked through the city. It was a quiet Sunday morning and as I strolled around the streets, away from the main thoroughfares, I photographed kids having fun in alleyways, old men playing chess on footpaths and captured images of the Pristina's architecture. One particular photo came out really well; I was watching three boys playing football on the edge of a small square, close to a market, with the side of a building acting as the makeshift goal. I pressed the shutter just as one of the boys was celebrating scoring. I didn't notice it until later but the 'goal' was daubed with graffiti, with the ubiquitous slogan '*Jo Negociata!*' It was a warning by Vetevendosje not to enter negotiations with Serbia over Kosovo's sovereignty. I liked the picture so much I emailed it to Alexandra and didn't give it another thought.

Back at KFOR headquarters, it was clear that I needed to play my role with a great deal of care. Officially I sat within a small team called the KIKPC, or the Kosovo Inspectorate of the KPC, consisting of Germans, Swedes, Norwegians and a couple of American officers. There was also a Romanian officer in the team who had been recalled back to Bucharest a few days after I arrived following Kosovo's declaration of independence earlier in the year. In my view, Romania had made the right decision over its role in Kosovo; they disagreed with the declaration of independence and had the political courage to withdraw its military support as a result. That was more than could be said for other nations who had also chosen not to recognise Kosovo's new independent status but kept their troops within KFOR. Spain was a perfect example. Holding down a senior logistics position in the KFOR leadership team, along with a handful of other support staff based in KFOR's headquarters, Spain chose to retain its troops in Kosovo even though it did not recognise the country in which they were based.

The KIKPC had been created to provide an 'independent' audit function of the KPC on behalf of KFOR, through pre-arranged and unannounced inspections of KPC locations, checking for attendance, counting weapons, assessing security arrangements and reporting on the general state of affairs. Each team member had specific areas of responsibility within the KPC's six protection zones across the country. On paper I worked for a Swedish officer, Colonel Bengtsson, known as Chief. In reality I spent most of my time away from the KIKPC team. The Chief and I established a good rapport early on which helped me conduct my role. Much of my contact with the team was during a daily morning brief and via longer Saturday morning meetings, which looked back over the previous week's activities. Managing my relationships within the KIKPC was important for me.

As LNO my primary role was to be embedded in the KPC headquarters with the KPC Commander, Lieutenant General Syleman Selimi, and his deputy, Major General Rama. I was seen as a source of information on KFOR decision making, a steadying influence when things were not going well, an advisor and a confidante to the leadership team. I was driven out of Film City every day and headed towards the KPC building, which was an old driving school, 15 minutes away. I had an office on the ground floor with a phone and unrestricted internet. Keeping in touch with my family was never far from my mind and using Skype from the office allowed me to speak to my wife and children very easily, especially at weekends.

My 'routine' was always hit and miss; on a good day as soon as I arrived in the morning I would be brought a cup of sweet tea by one of the civilians who worked in the building. I would then await the arrival of my interpreter, Simi, and check what was going on. I had heard a lot about Simi before I had arrived in Kosovo, through notes and briefings provided by my predecessor, and I was looking forward to getting to know him. Now in his 30s, Simi was a very likeable individual who had a matter-of-fact, no-nonsense approach to his role as the UK's preferred interpreter for the previous 18 LNOs. And his backstory took some beating; it was as intricate and sensational as so much of what was about to happen in Kosovo during my 6-month tour.

Recruited in the late spring of 1999, towards the end of NATO's air war against Serbia, Simi, as he was affectionately known, had seen and done it all. Anybody in Kosovo who mattered knew Simi, and his tireless support to the UK military effort in his role as the UK Liaison Officer's interpreter over the previous 8 years had earned him a deep respect from within the international community and Kosovan society.

Simi's story started in 1998. He wanted to escape Kosovo for a better life and to get away from the oppression meted out by Serbian authorities in the then breakaway region of Kosovo. He was a keen football player and decided that a novel approach was required to escape the country of his birth. He joined a local football team in Pristina and started to make his plans. Together with the other players, they arranged a football tour in Tunisia. With fixtures in the diary and visas all arranged, they booked their flights direct from Belgrade to Tunis on the way out, but via Germany on their return. Once on the ground in Germany they would then claim asylum. On paper the plan looked to be foolproof. However, they did not bank on their route coming under the close scrutiny of immigration officials and before they had even kicked a ball in Tunisia, they were flown back to Belgrade and their dreams of living in the west were prematurely snuffed out.

Simi did not give up though.

Instead of flying he decided on a much more dangerous and uncomfortable route instead. With friends in Germany he felt confident that if he could cross the Serbian border he would be able to make his way into central Europe and from there be smuggled into the UK, as London was his final destination. So, undeterred after his Tunisia experience, Simi embarked on a long and tiring journey across Europe, hidden in the back of a lorry. Via Serbia, Hungary and Austria, Simi made it to his friend's house in Germany after many days travelling. He then finally arrived in London in late 1998 where he quickly found a job as a waiter under a new identify. The Kosovo Albanian Simi had become a Portuguese waiter called Luis.

Notwithstanding the effort he had made to give himself a new start in life, events back in Kosovo were taking a turn for the worse. The Kosovo Liberation Army, the KLA, were recruiting men to fight a guerrilla war against the Serbs, and calls were made in various capitals, with a large Albanian diaspora, for volunteers. Driven by a nationalist pride and sense of duty, Simi registered his name on one of the lists that was being circulated within the Albanian community in London. Working hard to learn English and how to wait tables (which he admitted was a challenge), Simi was now on short notice to return to the country he had only recently left, to join the resistance movement in its fight against the Serbian authorities. The atmosphere within the Albanian community in London during the winter of 1998/99 was tense; each new atrocity that filtered out of Kosovo was met with anger and a determination to act. The international community was also growing increasingly concerned about the worsening situation in the region.

Meanwhile Simi waited for the call.

The tipping point for a coordinated international response was the Račak massacre in January 1999, where 45 Kosovo Albanians were found dead in a ditch, allegedly killed by Serb forces. This did much to galvanise the international community into responding to the developing crisis militarily. It also expedited Simi's return back to the

Balkans; he was asked to report to a certain location in London where he had been allocated a seat on a coach. The journey took him overland back to Albania, where he would soon come face to face with the war he thought he had left behind. Without a second thought Simi left his Portuguese *alter ego* behind and headed back to Tirana. His short time in London was over.

When he arrived in Albania he was transported close to the Kosovo border where he was allocated to a logistical unit in which he was expected to carry supplies across the mountains to KLA units operating in the west of Kosovo. With minimal training Simi soon deployed towards the border, in the freezing Albanian winter, on a resupply patrol. What happened next deeply affected him. Within days of boarding a bus in London, starting his long journey back to the Balkans, he was trudging through deep snow, together with others he barely knew, carrying essential supplies bound for the KLA. During that first patrol, and without warning, they came under fire and several members of the patrol were killed. Others ran away, abandoning Simi to his fate. Fortunately he escaped and felt lucky to be alive. He carried on his work supporting the KLA, despite the experience.

Some time later, with British Special Forces operating in Kosovo to coordinate NATO bombing missions, a call went out amongst the KLA support teams for someone to act as an interpreter with UK forces. The only mandatory qualification; that the person could speak English. So fresh from London, learning how to take an order for a pizza in an Italian restaurant, Simi found himself living under the threat of attack, in the field alongside some of the fittest men on the planet, as the interpreter for the UK's elite forces deployed behind enemy lines in Kosovo. And when the KPC was set up on 21st September 1999, with a UK liaison officer assigned to the force, it was clear that Simi was ideally suited to continue the role he had performed so successfully during the war, serving the UK military's effort in Kosovo.

Back at the KPC headquarters, once Simi arrived he would quickly nip upstairs to see the outer offices of both the Commander and Deputy Commander, to ascertain what was planned. After finishing my cup of sweet tea, we would head upstairs to see either Selimi or Rama, sometimes both. That was the theory; I never quite knew what the day would bring, so there was always a degree of anticipation as I stepped into the large area at the top of the stairs. With assistants manning the two men's outer offices, situated either side of the first-floor reception space, and with a regular flow of visitors checking in with the KPC's Colonel Xhavit Gashi, the Chef de Cabinet, or Chief of Staff, who was in one of the offices on the Commander's side of the building, it was almost always busy. However, some days I would find the headquarters completely empty of leadership; sometimes I never even made it into the building because I was already on the road heading to a Government Ministry or speeding out of the city, blue lights flashing and siren wailing, on my way to a meeting at one of the 6 protection zones.

As the LNO, I was also invited to attend the KFOR headquarters daily evening briefing. It appeared that everyone in the building, and representatives from external organisations, turned up for this structured, general update session run by KFOR's Chief of Staff, US Marine Corps Brigadier General Berger.

There were around 50 people there most evenings. At least I had my own reserved seat. It had been explained to me that it was a good idea to attend the briefing, mainly for networking reasons. I started to turn up each evening to make sure I met the key people and kept up to date with the wider issues in Kosovo. What I was not prepared for was the monotony and repetition that I experienced, night after night. My impressions of an over-manned organisation, with far too many NATO troops deployed across the country, seemed to be supported by the complete lack of any significant activity from a security perspective. I had been based in Baghdad in 2004 and witnessed what a high tempo of operations looked like. Kosovo was in a different league.

The evening briefing actually became a source of mild amusement as each speaker tried to outdo the previous speaker in terms of drama and impact. This was especially true when liaison officers from KFOR units were leaving; rather than a short sharp briefing they would insert a DVD and show an elaborate film summarising their contingent's tour of duty. When an Austrian liaison officer stood up, he actually referred to the film Groundhog Day when describing his 6 months in Kosovo; General Berger was not amused. The point should have been obvious to anyone watching; there was not enough going on to warrant a daily briefing let alone the high number of troops deployed on the ground.

One evening there was a report that three Molotov cocktails had been thrown into a garden in a town in the east of Kosovo. By KFOR standards it was dramatic, people actually sat up and started to pay attention, listening carefully to what was being said. Then came the punchline; "on closer inspection they turned out to be empty beer bottles". Like the number of bars, restaurants and cafés in the camp, the evening brief was a parody. On another occasion, the Portuguese liaison officer from the departing Parachute Battalion made his way to the lectern to deliver his final goodbye presentation. A combination of him being short, and the lectern being too high, meant he was entirely obscured for the whole briefing. It was beyond bizarre.

Even the regular briefing slots managed to miss the point. The weather report came early in the standing agenda. The 'met man', the resident meteorological expert, rather unnecessarily would spend the first few minutes telling the audience what the weather had been doing in the previous 12 hours. The weather map was also centred on Italy, which was understandable because the Italians were now in charge, but unbelievably it failed to show the borders of Kosovo. Instead it was a map of Serbia with all the place names using Serbian spelling, rather than the Albanian equivalent. It was as if KFOR was in denial that it was in Kosovo at all.

It was yet another indicator that KFOR's stance vis-à-vis Kosovo was overtly politically correct. Despite their representatives in Brussels agreeing that KFOR would work closely with the UN and the Kosovans in de-activating the KPC, and standing up the new Kosovo Security Force, it appeared to have fallen on deaf ears in KFOR headquarters. It was at this point that I began to sense an air of detached indifference towards Kosovo from within KFOR headquarters; it felt as though everyone was just going through the motions.

KFOR's main effort, the focus of their operational and tactical activity, was to ensure a 'Safe and Secure Environment' with 'Freedom of Movement' – SASE/FOM. Sitting in the evening briefing, night after night, I slowly realised that KFOR was only looking at Kosovo through this lens and the fact that there were so few security related incidents was a good thing. In fact, the changes to Kosovo's security institutions – NATO's 'New Tasks' – were the biggest thing to happen in Kosovo's security sector for many years. Yet at the evening briefing the 'New Tasks' were never mentioned and I realised that KFOR had little or no interest in them. To KFOR's command team, it was about maintaining the status quo at all costs. I was to discover this attitude extended towards the

Kosovans time and again during my tour.

It was after the 'Molotov Cocktail' report that I decided that I would no longer regularly attend the evening briefing. I had better things to do with my time. The KPC was soon to be de-activated, a new Kosovo Security Force was about to be established, and both events were happening on my watch. KFOR saw the 'New Tasks' as a distraction, an unnecessary burden, a process to complete, a threat to its comfortable existence. However, it was far from a tick box exercise. Thousands of uniformed Kosovans were about to enter a process that held a great deal of fear for them, with uncertainty at every turn. It was a deeply human process with people's lives affected in a profound way. Sensing a lack of interest from KFOR, I realised that my role was going to become even more important to ensure that the KPC was de-activated with dignity, and the KSF would be able to stand on its own two feet after its establishment.

Walking back to my accommodation that evening, I looked up into the darkening sky. With the sun setting over the distant hills, my attention was drawn to the sound made by the sheer number of birds flying over the camp. There were literally thousands of crows and ravens as far as the eye could see, returning to Film City's trees where they roosted overnight before departing in the morning at sunrise. They put on a breathtaking display of coordinated flying night after night. The sheer scale of the numbers was extraordinary. At times it felt like I was living under a feathered sky. There were plenty of rumours explaining why the birds returned to the KFOR base, including gruesome stories of how they had fed on those killed in a battle which took place in the area, between Serbian and the ultimately victorious Ottoman forces in 1389, and the birds simply never left. However, as with most things in Kosovo, a great deal of caution needed to be attached to what people said.

It was clear that if I was to fulfil my role successfully I would need to make a lot of friends and walk a fine line in order to keep my relationships on an even keel. And I would need to be on my guard; I already sensed that making enemies in Kosovo was unlikely to be good for my health or my future career. Even with these warnings firmly lodged in my mind, I needed to get to know the KPC, and the KPC needed to get to know me, very quickly. I had chosen Kosovo in order to make a difference; I now needed to start to achieve this goal.

CHAPTER FOUR

'Un vieil homme malade'

My impression of the KPC was of an organisation in decline.
Established in the aftermath of a bloody war with Serbia it had, in
most people's eyes, served its purpose. The KPC looked tired and in
need of retirement. Like the stale smoke I encountered lingering in
most of the offices I entered, there was an air of inevitability
hovering over each of the locations I visited in the first few weeks of
being in Kosovo. Whilst some of the commanders were upbeat and
looking forward to the establishment of what the Kosovans hoped
would become their 'army' in the future, many others, especially the
middle ranking officers, were less enthusiastic.

The KPC's rank structure, like most uniformed organisations,
should have reflected a triangle shape with the tip at the top. Instead
the KPC's rank structure triangle was inverted and bulging in the
middle management ranks, reflecting a manipulation of promotions
over time to ensure that people earned a reasonable salary because
there had been barely any wage increases at all during the 9 years of
its existence. The imminent deactivation of the KPC had dominated
conversations for many months before my arrival, and as the KPC
entered its final few months of its existence, it was difficult not to
feel a degree of sympathy with its members.

Meeting a range of KPC characters who had emerged intact from the KLA, it was clear that their days fighting a guerrilla war against Serbian forces had left a deep impression on many of them. Spending hours in their company gave me the opportunity to listen to their stories of survival and success against the Serbs with the help of the NATO bombing campaign; it was difficult not to be a little in awe of what they had achieved against the odds, and in some cases, at great personal cost. However, that was part of the problem; they were still dining out on their accomplishments in the late 1990s rather than facing up to the impending closure of their organisation, bar a small number of seriously impressive characters who were genuinely motivated to achieve a better future for their fledgling country.

With few exceptions, the people I met in the KPC knew what was in store for them and appeared to be prepared for whatever eventuality lay ahead. However I soon discovered that the situation was not helped by two things. The chain of command within the KPC was becoming highly compressed and more ineffective by the day, with mobile phones used extensively to pass messages, issue orders and to share information. The senior leaders were becoming involved in low level issues and the passage of information was no longer efficient. To compound this observation, the complete absence of any recognisable communication campaign, to fill the vacuum that had been created by the ambiguous and unhelpful NATO declarations from Brussels, left the average KPC member adrift of accurate and reliable information.

By the time I arrived the attendance records of many KPC members was sketchy at best. Many members didn't bother to turn up for 6 days and then on the 7th day they signed on at the KPC unit to avoid any disciplinary action against them. In the early years they would have been dealt with appropriately by the KPC chain of command but with less than 4 months remaining of the organisation, discipline had all but broken down.

My main focus within the organisation, the KPC Commander General Selimi, was rarely in work when I arrived. Tall, in his late thirties with a shrewd mind, he was also a heavy smoker and a hard drinker. However, with good connections across the political landscape in the country, Selimi was keen to establish his credentials as the best option for the new role of KSF Commander. He had vision, influence and appeared to have a good relationship with the Prime Minister; on balance he was probably the best suited of all the possible candidates to lead the new force. He was also reasonably broad minded and recognised his weaknesses as much as his strengths. That said, he was not a natural leader and I found that he needed some prompting before deciding to act on certain issues.

It was clear that despite a lack of information to pass on to its membership, I felt that he needed to exert whatever authority he had left within the KPC by going on a road trip. Rather than languishing in his smoke-filled office when he did come into work, I suggested that he headed out to see what was happening across the country, to shake some hands and have his photo taken with people building community projects, instead of taking phone calls and reading occasional reports stuck in central Pristina.

So after being his liaison officer for only a couple of weeks, I suggested to General Selimi that he should start acting as if he was the commander of the KPC, although not in so many words. I felt that he was allowing his organisation to drift and with so much going on, the dangers of losing control were potentially significant. I was relieved when he seemed energised by the idea. A visit programme was organised for the following week, Kosovo style, with plenty of room for last-minute changes of plan. We were all set to head off across the country on a whistle-stop tour that was also to take in meetings with the President of the Kosovo Assembly and Yves de Kermabon, a former KFOR commander and now head of EULEX, the European Union's rule of law mission that was in the early stages of its deployment.

Whilst General Selimi had a more strategic outlook, despite some obvious limitations, General Rama, his deputy, was a soldier's soldier. He was a no-nonsense, bullish individual who knew how to make things work. Tall and strongly built, with close-cropped hair and expressive eyes, Rama was a natural leader who was not to be messed with; charismatic, good company and immensely likeable, he had very quickly worked out that he had a major role to play in achieving a successful deactivation of the KPC. He was the 'go to' man in the KPC when officers from the MCAD team needed something to be done. Inevitably he could get dragged down into the tactical level detail, but he still managed to project his personality to most corners of the KPC deployed across the country. From my arrival, I was completely committed to giving him whatever help he needed. Major General Rama was the only person who seemed to instinctively understand the impact of the deactivation on the KPC personnel; he knew it was a deeply human process. In that sense, the difference between Rama and Selimi could not have been greater.

The missing link in my network was the KFOR Commander. Within a week of arriving in Kosovo, the entire KFOR leadership team had changed over on their annual rotation, a French Lieutenant General handing over to an Italian Lieutenant General, Giuseppe Gay – pronounced 'guy' as we were all quickly advised. With him came a large number of support staff and an Italian Brigadier General who was appointed to oversee the small NATO team, led by Colonel Habel, organising the imminent security sector transition, the 'New

Tasks'. Brigadier Di Luzio was a tall, elegant, self-confident and highly personable individual, with a keen sense of humour who very early on insisted that I should see him not as an officer, but as a friend. This immediately put me on my guard; I was used to a more formal relationship with senior officers and I wasn't about to become buddies with someone who, on paper at least, was going to be playing a crucial role in the 'New Tasks'. It was the first time I had worked for an Italian officer and I was being cautious.

Whilst Di Luzio was not directly responsible for me as a line manager, he had been assigned to oversee the work of the MCAD and, with my pivotal role embedded with the KPC, he wanted to know exactly what was going on with the Kosovans through my weekly reports. I had also been advised that previous LNOs had always enjoyed a very good relationship with the KFOR Commander, and I could see how this connection would be important, but I sensed that Di Luzio would be my focus and I clearly needed to keep him on side.

Getting access to Di Luzio was reasonably straightforward via Eric, his French Military Assistant, but access to the KFOR Commander was a different matter. I needed to meet him but his staff seemed to be reluctant to arrange an office call for me. I found this strange and not in line with my expectations about the normally tight relationship between the LNO and the head of KFOR that I had been briefed on. I eventually secured an appointment in his diary but it clashed with an event I had to attend; the opening ceremony of a medical centre that had been built by the KPC near the Albanian border.

On the morning of the office call with General Gay, I collected General Rama from the KPC headquarters to drive as far west as you could go to witness the opening of the centre, built by the KPC under the command of Colonel Enver Cikaqi, the local protection zone commander. It was my first exposure to some of the community work conducted routinely by the KPC and whilst there I also met the United States' Assistant Defense Attaché, Lieutenant Colonel Terry Anderson. After a few drinks to celebrate the completion of the ceremony with local dignitaries, I accompanied General Rama in convoy on our way back to Pristina. However, what I wasn't expecting was a detour.

We pulled off the main road and called in to Kosovo's best kept secret, the vineyard at Rahovec, owned by wine producers 'Stone Castle'. After introductions with those in charge of the vineyard, who clearly knew Major General Rama and Colonel Cikaqi, we all sat down to an excellent lunch, drinking wine and sampling local produce. I was sitting in the dimly lit caves, surrounded by vats of all sizes, the smell of wine permeating the air I breathed; it was heaven. Around the table with me were Rama, Terry Anderson, Cikaqi and of course Simi. Conscious that I had an important office call with the KFOR Commander, I barely touched my wine beyond a small taste. With time ticking away I reluctantly made my excuses and left them to it. With Kasper at the wheel and Simi in the back, we headed to the capital over an hour away. On the journey I was asked for a biography by Gay's outer office, which I arranged to be sent through. As we approached the outskirts of Pristina, with 10 minutes to go before my appointment, I received a call from his Military Assistant, Major Michele Ionata, to be told that my office call had been cancelled. Obviously disappointed, I was more upset about having to leave lunch at Rahovec.

The following day, with just 10 minutes' notice, I was invited to see General Gay. Fortunately I was in Film City. When I finally sat down in the chair opposite his desk, General Gay seemed ill at ease. It was not an encouraging meeting; he asked me some basic questions about the KPC, answers to which he should have known already. Rhetorically he asked: "Who has the authority to close the KPC?" In the big scheme of things, hearing the KFOR Commander effectively absolve himself of all responsibility for one of the three 'New Tasks' was not a good sign. He did at least ask me what I felt KFOR should be doing, to which I replied 'a lot more!' General Gay had clearly wanted to see me before meeting Selimi the next day for his initial office call – which was routine – but his body language and lack of engagement over the KPC was inauspicious. It reinforced my impression about KFOR in general. It was a disappointing but not altogether surprising conversation; there was little outward sign of any real commitment to the 'New Tasks'. He wasn't even kicking the tyres of the KPC 'vehicle' to check for wear and tear. It was an alarming situation.

The following day General Gay visited the KPC headquarters to meet General Selimi and the senior KPC staff, the first visit since his arrival in Kosovo. We settled into the KPC Commander's extremely comfortable leather chairs and coffees were ordered for everyone. General Selimi's office was generously proportioned so a small group of national media were invited in to record images of the two men meeting, kept a safe distance away by Selimi's staff. With General Gay was his Military Assistant, Major Michele Ionata. I was sitting on a sofa opposite Selimi.

Speaking in English, there was the normal preamble between the men for the benefit of the press who then left the room. After the door closed General Gay began by saying that he wanted to discuss how KFOR could help with the deactivation of the KPC, so that KFOR could 'be part of the solution'. Three months earlier the NATO Secretary General had amended the UN's expectations of NATO's role from exercising *executive authority* to *supervision* of the

'New Tasks'. Now General Gay had dumbed that down even further.

It was extraordinary.

In that comment he nailed his colours to the mast in terms of his degree of commitment to the 'New Tasks'. His position had not changed at all from the previous day. As the conversation proceeded, it was evident that the KPC would not be able to rely on KFOR for the support and leadership we all knew it needed during the challenges ahead. General Gay also said that he wanted to visit a KPC humanitarian project, which I noted would fall to me to organise. During the meeting he reminisced about having left Kosovo the previous year after a 12-month tour in a lower rank as the Deputy Commander. Yet everything I had heard and seen about General Gay gave me the impression that he had no real passion for Kosovo; it was also curious that he had returned so quickly, and on promotion. It seemed to me that General Gay had tired of the place and saw a return to Kosovo as a necessary evil to progress his career. The fact that he had been to Kosovo before suggested he should have known much more about the people and the culture.

As the meeting drew to a close, we all got up and the office door opened again, revealing the media still on duty and clambering for a position as the KFOR Commander made his way out. As he walked past the gathered Kosovan press, General Gay was asked a simple question about the stand down of the KPC. Rather than stop, engage with the journalist and openly answer the question, Gay refused to speak to him and walked out of the building without a further comment. I didn't need my interpreter to understand what had happened. It was quite incredible that the most senior international military officer in Kosovo had ignored the press in such a dismissive way.

The following morning, I was called in to the KFOR media operations office to see Colonel Adriano Graziani, who was in charge of media relations. He invited me to sit down and we exchanged pleasantries; I had not met him before but he appeared to be friendly and welcoming. He showed me the KFOR media digest, a daily summary of all the news stories from the Kosovan media, with one passage highlighted: "Italian General tries to avoid media by all means." It was hardly a devastating statement but it caused the calm waters of KFOR headquarters to ripple. Graziani asked me what had happened. I explained that it was entirely accurate; General Gay had brushed the media aside quite deliberately. It was as if Graziani wanted me to justify the remark. It would not be the last time I sat in his office.

Leaving the General Gay storm in a teacup to one side, I needed to focus on the KPC. After getting Selimi to leave the comfort of his office and hit the road, it gave me my first opportunity to really get under the skin of the wider KPC organisation. Hidden away in Pristina was like being in the Balkan equivalent of the 'Westminster bubble'. Events in the city bore no resemblance to life across the country. Even though Rama had confided in me his reservations for such an undertaking – arguing that by Selimi seeing the KPC personnel without any information was worse than not going at all – I insisted that it was the right thing to do.

So with Kasper and Simi, we accompanied General Selimi, in convoy, often using blue lights and driving way too fast for the environment and road conditions, from one protection zone headquarters to another, always returning to Pristina in the evening. I met the Brigadier Generals who were the protection zone commanders providing the essential leadership to the KPC members, and who delivered a vital link between events in Pristina at the headquarters and within their own areas of responsibility. They varied in quality on first impression, but they were mostly effective leaders and they spoke freely about their concerns over the stand down process that they were about to enforce. I found all of them deeply committed and I was heartened to meet high quality individuals holding down such responsibility. Discipline was ebbing away and the fear within the higher echelons of the KPC, and also in KFOR, was that there would be a complete breakdown of internal order within the organisation.

There were a growing number of examples of ill-disciplined behaviour that should not have been tolerated but little was done to stop it. One example emanated from the KPC officer in charge of the Kosovo Guard, Kosovo's Ceremonial Unit. Brigadier General Nuredin Lushtaku was as intimidating as they came. Whilst undergoing a vetting interview, a prerequisite for senior officers wanting to be considered for the KSF, a process that was ongoing when I arrived, Lushtaku had managed to upset the female interpreter during his interview. This had angered a number of people, not least Dave Finnimore who was in charge of the NATO vetting unit.

Early in my tour I had paid a visit to see Lushtaku with Simi, who had made the arrangements. Wearing his hallmark maroon parachute beret, which he never took off, Lushtaku was the epitome of common sense and reason. He was concerned about the effect on the younger members of the KPC if they were not recruited into the KSF. They were all valid points which he delivered passionately. The reputation that preceded him was not on display. In fact, we got on well and I had a feeling I would be seeing more of him as the weeks and months passed. Lushtaku was a close friend of the Prime Minster, Hashim Thaçi, and his influence extended throughout the upper echelons of Kosovan political life. However, small examples of petulance only added to the impression of an organisation on the brink of collapse. On another occasion Major General Nick Caplin, the UN's KPC Coordinator, and a senior KPC officer, Brigadier General Kastrati, arrived to see the Kosovo Guard. Despite advanced warning, Lushtaku had conspired to make sure nobody was there to host him. Major General Caplin called the visit off.

Elsewhere in the country, Major Rufki Suma, who was in charge of a small unit in the south of the country, had started talking to the media, without any authority, about his own situation and how he was concerned for his men and their collective future. Shortly after arriving in Kosovo the application forms for those who wanted to be considered for the KSF were distributed to KPC units across the country, with everyone encouraged to submit their completed forms. There were only 1,500 places allocated across all ranks, with up to 2,800 current members of the KPC applying for places. Suma had suggested in the media article that he planned to direct his men not apply for the KSF out of protest. Suma was invited into the KPC headquarters to be told by General Rama not to contact the media in future, citing the potential damage that his actions could have on the overall process of standing down the KPC. This would have resulted in disciplinary action in previous years, but everything had changed. And Suma did not listen to the advice.

On the whole, the KPC personnel I met were good to talk to, whether they spoke some English or communicated to me through Simi. Most of the men – as females were in short supply in the KPC – were very concerned about three issues. The first was pension provision. The Government had agreed to pass a pension law for KPC retirees, which would by exception provide an income for life, for those who were eligible, if they were not selected to join the KSF. There were certain criteria, such as a minimum age from which to start receiving a pension and time served in the KPC, which reflected international norms. As with most legislative processes, it was taking its time navigating Kosovo's Parliament. Rumours were constantly circulating around the key issues in Kosovo despite efforts to counter them by the Office of the KPC Coordinator – the OKPCC – the UN body providing the equivalent to Ministerial representation for the KPC in the country. The KPC Coordinator, senior British officer Major General Nick Caplin, was faced with the task of convincing the KPC membership that they were going to be properly looked after.

They were also worried about the resettlement plan, which was being led by the UNDP and a local employment agency, APPK. The International Organisation for Migration, the IOM, had partnered the KPC for many years and in 2007 had conducted a pilot resettlement programme. Although before my time, the result was evidently a disappointment, not only for those who volunteered to retire from the KPC, but for the concept of resettlement as a whole. With the much maligned IOM project held up by KPC personnel as an example of what they could expect, the damage to the reputation of this new resettlement programme had already been done and the narrative was always going to be difficult to counter.

The key issue for KPC personnel though was whether they were going to be wearing KSF uniform in 6 months' time and whether the 'process', as it became known, was going to be fair. Without any coordinated media communications campaign to get the right messages across I could already see that the lack of accurate public information was creating a vacuum that would inevitably cause problems at some point in the future. Different organisations seemed to rely on others to get the message out. The Office of the KPC Coordinator was focused on ensuring the various Government departments and other organisations with a role to play in the KPC's draw down, such as KFOR, were corralled to provide the appropriate support to the KPC members who were not going to be selected for the KSF. It was a herculean task, considering General Caplin's limited influence over these organisations.

Major General Caplin's main effort was cajoling the Government to make sure the pension law was fair and reasonable, and then making sure the resettlement plan, led by retired British Brigadier John Durrance from the UNDP, would be fully understood by the KPC members. A roadshow was planned by Major General Caplin to reach out directly to the KPC on these two vital issues but the wider process remained unmanaged from a media perspective, resulting in an ignorant KPC membership and confused wider public.

The question that had yet to be answered was which organisation should be leading the communications effort to explain what was going on with the KPC and the KSF process. The KPC's media operations unit performed basic functions well, organising press visits, photographing General Selimi and issuing press releases covering the commander's appointments, but they were not empowered or capable of setting the news agenda. And the OKPCC was not resourced for a fully committed strategic communications campaign.

The only organisation with the resources, the expertise and in theory the cultural understanding to shape the news agenda efficiently and professionally over the 'New Tasks', was KFOR.

During my initial meeting with Colonel Graziani, he let it slip that KFOR's media operations team had been directed by Brussels to be reactive rather than proactive towards the media. I pointed out that the decision was clearly an error of judgement. The lack of response to the Kosovan journalist by the KFOR Commander a few days earlier highlighted the dangers of taking that position. Graziani told me that he had not challenged Brussels on the logic of this policy decision. KFOR was beginning to receive negative press coverage – unheard of in Kosovo – and Graziani seemed unable, or unwilling, to do anything about it.

NATO, through KFOR, had firmly placed their collective heads in the sand and appeared happy to let events run untapped in the Kosovan press. By late September the warning signs were there. My brief conversations with the KPC members in Prizren and Mitrovice, in Ferizaj and Skenderaj, all reinforced my view that problems were being stored up and were likely to grow rather than subside as the KPC's de-activation rapidly approached.

My visits to KPC locations, and at events with Selimi and Rama, also highlighted some very odd behaviour by KFOR towards the KPC; at times it was if they had only just started working closely together rather than having spent the previous 9 years in each other company. One morning in late September General Selimi announced that he had to attend a prize-giving ceremony at the Civil Protection Brigade, a large barracks west of Pristina commanded by Colonel Geci. I had briefly met him before with General Rama. Following a period of training for KPC personnel, delivered by the local KFOR multinational task force, the KPC recipients were going to be issued with certificates. It was all pretty routine.

In a large briefing room, filled with desks lined up in neat rows, the KPC personnel sat quietly and attentively. The rest of us, the 'hangers on', were standing around the sides and at the back. There was a photographer to record the event. It was a fairly unremarkable awards ceremony bar one thing. At the front of the room was General Selimi, Colonel Geci, together with the Irish Army KFOR multinational task force deputy commander, Colonel Kilfeather. And standing next to Kilfeather was his armed close protection soldier, fully kitted out and prepared for an imminent attack; wearing dark sunglasses, body armour, combat webbing and with a loaded semi-automatic weapon, his finger extended across the trigger guard. On his hip was a pistol in a holster. He would not have looked out of place in Afghanistan or Iraq. Except this was benign Kosovo. It was the most ridiculous sight I had witnessed since arriving in country. His presence suggested that there was a specific threat from the KPC personnel in the room, the same personnel who had spent hours under training with Colonel Kilfeather's own KFOR troops in the days leading up to the ceremony. It was really poor judgement by Kilfeather and reinforced my view that KFOR still didn't fully trust the very people they had been working with since 1999. Unfortunately I could feel myself becoming immune to KFOR's insensitivity towards Kosovans.

Following the ceremony I was invited back to Colonel Geci's office to sit down with General Selimi, Simi and some of Geci's closest advisors, where the only threat to my life was from whatever I was going to be asked to drink. Colonel Kilfeather was not invited.

The talk was about the usual subjects; de-activation, the impending NATO-led selection process, the pension law, resettlement, politicians and sharing gossip about other members of the KPC. And these men were funny. Through Simi I enjoyed listening to many stories of their lives in the KPC, and with the ubiquitous cigarette smoke the catalyst for every conversation, I found their company enjoyable. Another staple of any visit to a protection zone was being offered a glass of raki, a 40% proof local spirit more akin to paint-stripper than something you would offer to your guests at home. But offer it they did. Always taken with sparkling water I found it surprisingly easy to drink, but the effect on an empty stomach was dramatic. Invited to drink a glass of raki before 10 o'clock in the morning by staff officers in the KPC HQ often resulted in me spending the remainder of the day trying to stay in a safe place, avoiding making decisions or causing harm to myself or anyone else. In Pristina, the KPC's Chef de Cabinet, Colonel Xhavit Ghashi, was a repeat offender and was particularly prone to offering me a glass for no particular reason. More than once during the tour, my life became a series of blurred edges and muffled sounds as the second raki of the morning began to take effect in my bloodstream. Thankfully I had enough sense to refuse these offers far more than I accepted them.

Sitting in Colonel Geci's large office that day, around his conference table, I made a good decision to say no, mainly because even General Rama had refused a glass when we both visited a few weeks earlier. When Geci produced some homemade raki in an old 7-Up bottle from under the table, I knew things had taken a turn for the worse. He poured it into some glasses on his conference table but as he did so he spilt some onto the wooden surface. Rather than getting a cloth to mop it up, he produced his lighter and set fire to the spillage. As everyone laughed I felt a sense of relief that it was burning his varnish rather than my liver.

Even though I refused a glass that day, I knew that I had to join in occasionally. I had to immerse myself in their culture, which meant I had to breathe in their cigarette smoke and drink their wicked brews whilst maintaining a degree of dignity as the Queen's representative in the Kosovo Protection Corps. It was, after all, a rite of passage for the LNO. How I managed to resist the temptation to start smoking cigarettes was a remarkable example of self-control, even though I felt at times that I may as well give in and accept one of the many that were regularly offered to me.

Cigarettes were to become something of an awkward subject in fact. I had been warned that General Rama bought cigarettes from the LNO, who purchased them on his NATO ration card. Clearly this was a practice I did not intend to continue. Within a couple of days of being in the role after my predecessor had flown back to the UK, I was asked, quite subtly by Simi, when I was going to bring General Rama his cigarettes. I ignored him and hoped it would be forgotten; I was not going to compromise myself over something so minor. Yet the issue persisted when General Rama, who spoke little English, even called my phone.

'When will you bring me cigarettes?' he asked.

'I am not going to, General,' I replied.

'I will get a sniper.'

'Then I will wear my body armour.'

Joking aside, the issue was running the risk of becoming a distraction and affecting our relationship. I knew I needed to concede defeat. However I was certainly not going to take his money for myself. The compromise I reached with my conscience was to buy the cigarettes, gift them to him and to put his money in a charity box at work, where we would then find a worthy cause in which to invest. However I wasn't going to accept the situation without at least trying to do something positive about it.

Somewhat radically, I decided that I would attempt to get General Rama to stop smoking entirely by introducing the concept of using nicotine patches to wean him off cigarettes. It was probably a hopeless idea but I was nothing but optimistic. So, after a couple of weeks I visited the British medical centre in Slim Lines and told the doc what I was trying to do. He almost choked with laughter but agreed to help me fill my rucksack with a course of patches that I was going to drip feed to Rama over the next few weeks. As plans go, it wasn't entirely robust but it was worth a try. After all, I had mentioned in passing to Rama that when the KSF was formed he should ban smoking in offices as one of the first rules of the new force, an idea that he initially agreed with. So the next time I saw General Rama I explained that he needed to quit smoking and I had the perfect approach; nicotine patches. The look he gave me said it all, but after a few weeks in his company I knew he was open to try anything. I deposited the box in his office, made sure he understood the instructions on how many to use at any one time, repeated in Albanian by Simi, and then left him to it.

When I returned to his office a few days later Rama immediately rolled up his sleeve and proudly showed me the patches on his forearm, all three of them. I was delighted but realised he had missed the point as he took a long drag on a newly lit cigarette and tapped it against the edge of an already full ash tray. Nobody could accuse me of not trying.

The general content of my reports to the KFOR command team in Pristina and the Deputy NATO Commander in Naples, KFOR's superior authority, was fairly unremarkable in the first few weeks. I got into a habit of writing my report on a Saturday afternoon and sending it to the distribution list I had inherited on the Sunday evening, ready to be put in front of the senior leadership team in KFOR and Naples the following morning. That weekend I commented in my report that I had suggested to General Selimi to get out and about. The next day I went to KFOR HQ for a meeting. After it had broken up, Brigadier Di Luzio pulled me to one side and made the point to me in private that I was a liaison officer, not an advisor. As ever Di Luzio delivered this message with a smile. And he was serious. Di Luzio really did mean that I should just sit in KPC headquarters observing events and not being proactive in any way. He told me I had been wrong to suggest to General Selimi that he should visit all of his troops, to address them face to face, to try to alleviate some of their concerns about the impending de-activation process, to reinforce his leadership of the KPC.

The reality was that KFOR, who had the responsibility for 'supervising' this technically complicated, politically sensitive and interdependent process of de-activating the KPC and standing up the KSF, were hopelessly unprepared and uncommitted to the task. Instead it was left to highly competent military officers and soldiers from the MCAD to make it happen. So I accepted the warning from Di Luzio and decided to be a little more circumspect about how I wrote my reports in future. My approach to the role was never going to change; I knew that the KPC leadership needed all my support and I was willing to do whatever was necessary to ensure they did not receive a raw deal from KFOR's out of touch Italian Command Group. Di Luzio was naïve in the extreme if he thought that I was going to sit in KPC headquarters and allow KFOR's decision-making to undermine the dignity of an organisation that deserved to be treated better. I would not be adding value by following Di Luzio's advice, so I ignored it.

General Selimi didn't always need to go out to meetings as plenty of people wanted to see him in his office. He received regular visitors when in Pristina. I was invited in for all but the most private meetings. On 22nd September, after our country-wide visit programme had ended, and a month after arriving in Kosovo, I was told that Ramush Haradinaj was popping in for a chat later that afternoon. A former KPC commander and leader of his own political party, Haradinaj had also been the Kosovan Prime Minister for 100 days before stepping down from the role to contest charges in the International Criminal Tribunal for the former Yugoslavia in The Hague in 2005. After the collapse of the trial, he was released and returned from the Netherlands to a hero's welcome. I had heard of Haradinaj but did not think too much of it. I certainly did not think I would meet him. I walked up the staircase onto the first floor, which housed both Selimi and Rama's offices, and together with Simi, turned right into Selimi's outer office, waiting for him to arrive.

When Haradinaj walked through the door we exchanged a strong handshake, his physical presence sending a buzz of excitement throughout the KPC headquarters. He was my height, powerfully built, and full of energy. Even General Rama joined the gathering. Everyone sat down and I was invited to sit next to Haradinaj on Selimi's deep, luxurious leather sofa. The conversation began as a serious discussion. Haradinaj was obviously frustrated that he could not have any direct effect on the drawdown of the KPC. He was keen to see the KSF grow much larger than the planned 2,500 cap on troop numbers once fully recruited. He was keen to make sure that he held the Prime Minister to account over the KPC's closure and it was evident that for him, it was a political issue. I took it all in. And then, as if someone had flicked a switch, a bottle of *Chivas Regal* was pulled out and the room erupted into laughter. Fired up by whisky, the discussion became a trip down memory lane and switched easily between Albanian and English, Selimi surprising me with his competent language skills. Simi also joined in the conversation in his own right. It was an extraordinary afternoon; I couldn't remember how many glasses of whisky I drank but it had been great fun. Before Haradinaj left, he asked me to bring him some unclassified maps of Kosovo, which I knew I would be able to source through Slim Lines. I promised I would get them for him. Haradinaj then made his excuses and shook everyone's hand again before disappearing out of the office, down the stairs and into a waiting car outside. I called Kasper to let him know I was ready to leave as well and we were soon driving back to Film City.

During what should have been a fairly routine 15-minute journey, Kasper and I were on the main road that dissected the city, about to cross a bridge in heavy traffic. In failing light, moving slowly, with another road filtering into our lane from the right, I noticed an absolute wreck of a car revving too high and seemingly out of control close to us trying to join the queue. It was if the driver was trying to prevent the car from stopping, moving forward in jolts as the clutch pedal was let out and then depressed again. Almost as soon as it joined the traffic behind us, there was another sound of the engine revving very high, followed this time by an almighty thump to the rear of our Landcruiser. Kasper immediately stopped the vehicle and reached for his pistol. I put my hand on his arm, suggesting it was just an accident, and we both got out. Sure enough, the car, which looked like it was held together with masking tape and had steam rising from his engine compartment, had caused some mild damage. In those few minutes when Kasper was busy trying to write down the driver's details and take photographs for his report of the incident, I decided to assist with traffic control. Standing in the middle of the single-lane highway in rush hour, in fading light, wearing British uniform and after drinking too much whisky with Kosovo's former Prime Minister, was not one of my wisest decisions. It wasn't long before a police vehicle approached and I slipped away unnoticed, back into the security of the Landcruiser. Once cleared to leave, we continued our journey back to Film City, and for me, the safety of my room.

In those first few weeks, during which I was getting to know people and the way things were done, it felt like the calm before the storm. I had encouraged Selimi to get out to meet the KPC personnel, as much for his benefit as for my own, and I had spent many hours with General Rama as he grappled with the subject of the KPC's drawdown. One of the issues that I was surprised had not been put into action already was for the protection zone commanders to compile reports on all of their people, to assist with the NATO-led KSF selection boards later in the year. I discovered that annual reports had been written for a number of years after the KPC's inauguration, but lately the practice had drifted and these appraisal reports were no longer up to date. Still, I felt that the MCAD team should have access to personal reports to provide more background during the selection boards. As things stood, individual attendance and disciplinary records supplied by the KPC HR department, the individual's application form, and the results from a selection test for all personnel below the rank of Colonel, were all that would be available to selection boards. This met what was dubbed 'NATO Standards'.

This initiative, supported by General Rama, was not popular with the head of MCAD. There was a fear that commanders would use the opportunity to purge unpopular individuals from the KPC. Of course this was possible, but it seemed odd that the very people who had known these men and women for many years, were going to be given no say whatsoever on their KPC personnel's individual records. There was an innate lack of trust in the KPC senior officers' judgement. Colonel Karl Habel, an advocate of applying the highly objective NATO's standards approach to the formation of the KSF, opposed the idea. Introducing subjectivity into the process was precisely what Habel wanted to avoid; the 'NATO Standards' mantra was an ideal that sounded good on paper, but which was impractical under the cultural conditions in the KPC at that time. As the organisation leading the planning on behalf of NATO for the de-activation of the KPC and the establishment of the KSF, MCAD was clear on its approach and subjective reporting from the experienced KPC commanders was not a requirement. However, after further lobbying from me on behalf of General Rama, Habel conceded the issue and instructed the KPC to gather the necessary reports together, from a force of 2,800, within a matter of days.

I had a natural connection to Colonel Stuart Roberts, Habel's deputy in the MCAD, as a fellow British officer. Stuart and I were both committed to the process and we realised we would have to work closely together, even if at times we had a different view of the events happening around us. Colonel Habel, who had been leading the planning work for nearly a year, was also a key contact for me, although I was never quite sure what he was thinking because he looked permanently fed up. Colonel Habel was exactly what I expected a German officer to be; intensely logical, focused and serious. However, on occasion his sense of humour broke through, which was just as well dealing with Brigadier Di Luzio.

Undoubtedly a very personable man, Brigadier Di Luzio did not demonstrate much ability to analyse problems fully or make measured decisions. Despite his oversight of the MCAD, he remained located 100m away in the KFOR headquarters building, closer to the coffee shop and the gossip, rather than move into the building housing Colonel Habel's team. Arguably, this was a sign that he didn't wish to understand the detail of the whole process he was responsible for. Or he was worried about his profile dropping off in the HQ. Either way, it created a division between Di Luzio and the rest of the MCAD team.

Of all the people in Kosovo during my tour, I had the most sympathy for the brilliant officers in Colonel Habel's team, who were trying to make the KPC-KSF plan work, in the face of inconsistent, ill-conceived and unhelpful interventions by Di Luzio. I needed all my tact and diplomacy to manage the link between the KPC and the ever growing MCA Division team, where the real horsepower centred on a handful of individuals. And unlike Di Luzio, they saw me as a proactive element in the KPC, as someone who could make things happen. It was a two-way relationship which proved to be crucial. When I needed something to be done, I would deploy my best influence skills to get the MCAD team onside; likewise they relied on me to get certain activities off the ground or to chase up outstanding issues in the KPC.

My relationship with MCA Division was vital. Whilst Di Luzio was, on paper at least, in charge and he did have a decision-making role for the KPC-KSF plan, the real power rested with Colonel Habel and Colonel Stuart Roberts. Fortunately Roberts and I understood each other and were able to work through issues logically and with good humour. He did warn me early on that we had to be careful not to give the impression of a 'British conspiracy', especially with Habel. I heeded his warning and tried to remain at arm's length although with British officers in the key positions within the overall process, it was natural that we would have a large say in how events unfolded.

As the end of September fast approached Simi suggested I should see another former Kosovan Prime Minister. I knew I needed to understand the bigger picture a lot better; I was limiting myself to individuals who were either driving forward the plan, or who were going to be subjected to it. I wanted more of an external view. I said that it would be a good idea and Simi set about making it happen, which he was able to do with a single phone call. Of course, as a KFOR officer, answerable to the KFOR Commander, deliberately going out to meet Kosovan politicians, even though they had strong connections to the KPC, was probably sailing close to the wind in terms of my role as the KPC LNO. I had no doubt that Di Luzio would have objected in the strongest terms. I knew I was going to take some risk but to me it was an important and necessary ingredient in understanding the wider political context. I needed to know the views of those who were on the periphery of the process that I was immersed in, and I hoped to use the knowledge I gained to help me do my job better. Simi came back to me by saying he had arranged for me to see Agim Çeku, who like Haradinaj, had commanded the KPC before entering politics. Of course I also needed to fulfil my promise to Haradinaj by delivering the maps. So the meetings were put in the diary for a couple of weeks' time.

I was always looking for opportunities to improve the information flow between the KPC senior officers and KFOR's command team. I knew that the KFOR Chief of Staff, Brigadier General David Berger, an experienced US Marine Corps officer, needed to have a chat with Major General Rama and I arranged for them to meet for dinner in what was rapidly becoming my favourite Pristina restaurant, Renaissance 2, or R2 as it was known. With the front door always firmly bolted shut and needing to knock to gain entry, it was run by a charming man called Ilhe, who was extremely discreet. His slow-cooked food, always over an open fire, perfectly suited the rustic décor inside his side-street location. My relationship with Brigadier Berger had not developed much beyond a couple of conversations, mainly because the US military tend to be very rank conscious. However, to compound my lack of direct contact with Berger, trying to make my way round his protective military assistant, a US Marine Corps Lieutenant Colonel, was becoming tricky. I needed to draw Berger out of his office to try to break down some of the barriers he naturally had in place, and so I suggested I arrange a dinner between Berger and Rama downtown.

It was reasonably straight forward to organise but I had to agree a few ground rules, such as what we were going to wear and who was going to do the translating. Major General Berger insisted on wearing uniform and bringing his own female KFOR translator. I suggested R2, this was agreed, and the date was set.

The dinner passed off well enough, although trying to get the two men talking was not helped by the translator who evidently thought she was a guest at the dinner rather than working as an interpreter. Both men seemed to be finding it difficult to make conversation, so I made what I hoped would be an amusing comment designed to get Rama involved in the discussion. The interpreter laughed but said nothing in Albanian to Rama; it was infuriating. Things eventually improved and they found some common ground, no doubt aided by the raki that both men started to drink as an aperitif. As the food arrived, accompanied by a lovely bottle of Stone Castle red wine, General Berger continued to drink raki throughout the dinner. It was a rather odd choice but at least it meant that there was more wine for the rest of us.

R2 hosted several high-profile dinners in those first few weeks of the tour, including one with Lieutenant General Peter Wall, who was in charge of overseas commitments in the UK MoD and making a tour of the region. He would later be appointed head of the British Army. After spending some time in Belgrade, General Wall came to Pristina and wanted to know what was going on so he had asked to see the key officers involved in the KPC-KSF plan. Those of us present listened to Lieutenant General Wall hold court during a fascinating two-hour dinner.

The daily routine of not knowing exactly what I was likely to be doing from one day to the next continued. At the end of September I found myself in the same car as Simi and Major General Rama, driving south across the border into Macedonia where Rama had to apply for a visa at the Dutch Embassy in Skopje, ahead of a visit to Holland, as he had been invited to see their training and doctrine centre. It was an unexpected day out of the office and I was not in uniform.

I had been in Kosovo for over a month and was already beginning to get a little worn down; every meeting involved a glass or two of raki, I was inhaling so much secondary smoke I may as well have been smoking myself, I was having too many late nights, and I had not been able to shake off a stomach illness that I had developed in the first couple of weeks. Getting away from Pristina for a day was a welcome change of scene. Once we had arrived in Skopje we found that we had to wait for the Dutch Embassy to open. Inevitably we took refuge in a nearby café. Sitting outside on soft chairs in the morning sun, Rama ordered the usual. The day pretty much followed that pattern; it was just great to be out of Kosovo, to be sitting in a reasonably ordered city. Pristina's chaos had got to me more than I had realised. It was early afternoon when the visa had finally been issued and before driving north back to Kosovo, Rama said that he wanted to go shopping. Fuelled by raki, I was happy to delay our return just a little longer. After entering various shops, Major General Rama finally bought a jacket in a department store, asking us all for our opinions before he paid for it. Back in the vehicle, I reflected on a most bizarre shopping experience as we headed north, refreshed by our day out of Kosovo.

The mechanism for standing down the KPC with dignity whilst at the same time standing up the new KSF was always going to be a very complicated process. Before I arrived in theatre there had been a meeting at R2, attended by all key decision-makers including Colonel Habel's MCA Division team, Major General Caplin's Office of the KPC Coordinator and others from KFOR. The time-honoured way in which decision making within military headquarters is carried out involves staff officers being given some direction by the commander on the issue at hand. The staff officers then conduct an analysis of the problem and arrive at two or three options from which the commander can then choose the preferred way forward. The staff officers then get down to the task of producing a detailed plan. NATO doctrine is clear about this planning cycle and it is tried and tested.

The solution was limited to two realistic options; the first involved a gradual draw down of the KPC whilst at the same time a gradual ramping up of the KSF. The dissolution date for the KPC, 14th June 2009, would therefore be the date at which the KPC would cease to exist and the date which would see the KSF 'live' with all the necessary selections of personnel completed and with people in place.

The second option, identified late in the day, offered a more dramatic scenario; the de-activation of the KPC at midnight on one day, with the KSF activating one minute later, effectively on the next day. The advantages and disadvantages of both options were considered in fine detail and presented to the French Command team in August; this decision would then have been handed over to Lieutenant General Gay and the newly appointed Brigadier Di Luzio. One of Di Luzio's early tasks was to make sure these two courses of action were understood by the new KFOR Commander who would, we hoped, make an informed and early decision.

So when I arrived on 22nd August, this staff work had been completed and the options had been presented to the KFOR Commander. Everyone was simply waiting for the decision on which option to pursue, although the second option had been favoured and contingency planning was being put in place with this in mind. However, I don't think anybody was expecting to have to wait quite so long for the green light. As the weeks passed, the need to know which option we were all going to follow was becoming more and more urgent. The amount of time to complete what was likely to be a complicated and highly emotional journey for members of the KPC was slipping away. I never really understood whether the delay was through indifference by Lieutenant General Gay, and therefore KFOR, towards the 'New Tasks', or whether he was seeking authority from KFOR's immediate higher authority, NATO's Joint Force Command in Naples. Even accepting the fact that he had only arrived in Kosovo a week after me, he should have known enough about the situation to make a swift decision. He had been the KFOR deputy commander for 12 months the year before. So as each week passed by, we all ended up scratching our collective heads trying to second guess the reason for the delay.

The relative calm within my first few weeks reflected this hiatus in decision making. Once the approach was decided, it was likely to change the atmosphere overnight; the magnitude of the tasks facing the KPC, and the enormous challenge facing the MCA Division team to create the KSF, would become a reality for the KPC leadership and Major General Rama in particular. The easy-going daily routine would need to be replaced by much more focus and effectiveness in the KPC's ranks. In other words, the KPC-KSF 'process' would start in earnest.

With the need for a successful KPC de-activation a necessary condition for a successful standing up of the KSF, all eyes would turn to the KPC and its ability to manage the most important and complex task in its 9-year history.

The honeymoon period for me was nearly at an end.

CHAPTER FIVE

'Keep It Simple Stupid'

After a month's delay, General Gay finally made a decision and chose the 'midnight option' as the framework for the de-activation of the KPC and the subsequent establishment of the KSF. However, the delay in the decision did not change the date on which the KSF 'Announcement Day' would take place. In other words the 12th December, identified as the key date when announcements would be made for the new Kosovo Security Force during the planning in August, remained the deadline. In reality this was also the date at which all KPC draw down activity would have to be completed. The time remaining to put everything together and execute the plan was now significantly reduced because of Gay's unexpected month long delay. A hastily arranged meeting was called in the KPC headquarters in order to come up with a plan to stand down the KPC in little over 2 months.

Sitting around a square arrangement of tables in the KPC's large conference room, with a large space in the middle allowing participants to see each other, every seat was taken. More chairs were set out at the back of the room; I had never seen so many people in one place to discuss the KPC-KSF process. Chairing the meeting was Brigadier Di Luzio with General Rama representing the KPC. Also present were members of MCA Division, representatives of the KPC Coordinator, the NATO Advisory Team and many other hangers on. I was sitting on a chair away from the main table, recording the discussion in my notebook. The meeting lasted two hours and by the end there was still an impasse on who should take the lead for the stand down plan. Di Luzio was incapable of keeping the discussion to the main subject, which was to identify a way forward for developing the plan and more importantly to identify who was going to write it. It became evident that he was unwilling to commit the MCA Division to taking the lead – contrary to the UN's 'Ahtisaari Plan' but in line with NATO's direction – which ensured that the meeting drifted, as so many did when he was at the helm. What was indisputable was that KFOR's interpretation of its role towards the 'New Tasks' meant it would barely *supervise* the stand down of the KPC at all. The KFOR Commander had said to General Selimi that he was unsure how to be part of the solution, keeping KFOR at arm's length from the KPC's deactivation seemed to be his answer.

The overall plan, agreed between the United Nations and NATO, had always been for Executive Authority over the KPC to be transferred from the Office of the KPC Coordinator to KFOR by the end of 2008. Even though this activity was in the early stages of negotiation, by the end of September it was self-evident that KFOR would eventually receive this authority and therefore any credible organisation would have had one eye on this future responsibility. My mind drifted back to my initial office call with Gay when he had lamented: "What can we do without executive authority?" There was an absence of pragmatism.

In reality these issues could have been worked around in parallel to the negotiations, but it appeared that a 'can do' attitude by KFOR was missing and common sense was in short supply. A

Supplementary Plan, a NATO document written and issued by KFOR's immediate higher headquarters in Naples, supported by Brussels, was clear that KFOR needed to engage with the 'New Tasks' in every respect, including delivering an information campaign, which would have included a media and communications plan. But the reality was very different in Kosovo; KFOR appeared to have been ignoring the issue for a long time, starting with the previous French leadership of KFOR throughout 2008, and now with the Italians. This reluctance to roll their sleeves up filtered down to every aspect of KFOR's approach. The MCAD team had the responsibility for establishing the KSF, which was predicated on a successful KPC dissolution, but was forced to remain detached from any KPC-related work, with inevitable consequences.

Seeing that the clock was ticking, with Di Luzio unwilling to commit his resources to the task, General Rama, recognising the inevitability of the situation, took the initiative and volunteered to lead on the plan. This was a pragmatic decision from a man who wanted to get on with things. It would also ensure that the solution was locally led and carried out, and it guaranteed a degree of 'buy in' from the KPC membership rather than having a plan forced on the KPC from outside the organisation. Di Luzio was delighted.

The irony was that the Kosovo Protection Corps was about to stand itself down.

As everyone streamed out, Colonel Karl Habel pulled me to one side and told me to ensure that the plan 'would stand up to NATO scrutiny.' In other words, he expected me to play a significant role in its formulation to make sure the plan would 'pass muster', since nobody in the KPC planning team had any NATO planning experience. It was a comment that epitomised the whole bizarre situation; the very organisation that was so unwilling to take the lead for the KPC draw down plan had set the height of the bar above which the KPC would need to jump if the plan was to be accepted. Together with Simi, I joined General Rama in his office after the meeting, where we immediately began to talk about the way forward. I mentioned the Habel comment and it was greeted with one of Rama's trademark shrugs, which said: 'What can we do?'

He ordered more coffee and poured three glasses of raki.

With the deadline for the presentation of the plan only 4 days away there was much to do. It was vital that something credible was devised and the clock was ticking. I arranged to sit down again with General Rama the following afternoon in order to look at timings and at least work our way back from the de-activation of the KPC, which was formally fixed at midnight on 4th January 2009, reflecting the plan to stand up the KSF at one minute past midnight on the 5th January 2009.

With the stand down plan likely to be a complicated and challenging activity for the KPC, I decided that an old British Army planning mantra – 'Keep It Simple Stupid' or 'KISS' – was going to be the order of the day. The KPC-led stand down plan was going to have to be straightforward because there was insufficient time or capacity to do anything else. The KPC's ability to follow a UK or NATO planning cycle was absent so improvisation was called for. The chain of command in the KPC had compressed to the point of fracture, KPC members with the expertise to analyse complex issues did not exist and so the only credible alternative capable of this type of detailed planning was Major General Rama and his cohort of trusted advisors, with me acting as a sense check. This may not have been ideal but the KPC was not looking for a gold-plated plan; it was looking for a simple solution that would work. My role of oversight on behalf of MCA Division was key. There was a good chance that

Colonel Habel's expectation of what he wanted to see, and the reality delivered by the KPC, would diverge significantly. Therefore my role was to close the 'delta', and I had three days to achieve this task. It was a ludicrous situation for an organisation under the 'supervision' of the world's foremost security alliance.

If the KPC stand down plan risked being made unnecessarily complicated, the plan to create the KSF left no room for delay or error. The process was called RSS, the recruiting, screening and selection of personnel, and was split into three phases. The first phase was designed to make sure that all KPC personnel who met the criteria could apply for the new force. MCA Division teams would travel to each KPC location across Kosovo with interpreters to gather all the application forms and answer questions. The next phase was to invite each applicant to attend a 'NATO standards' assessment at a base designated to be a KSF location in Ferizaj, 45 minutes south of Pristina. This consisted of an intelligence test, an interview in the applicant's first language, and physical tests involving press-ups, sit ups and a run. The application forms included the individual's current and preferred area of employment, and their specialised role. The exact nominal roll for the KPC was collected from the KPC's own personnel branch and was used as the basis for the whole process. MCA Division also collated each individual's attendance and disciplinary records, together with the personal appraisals that I had negotiated between the MCA Division and General Rama. The idea of using the term 'NATO standards' was meant to reassure the wider public, and the internal KPC membership, that the whole process would be run objectively and without prejudice.

However, the direction from Colonel Habel to remove subjectivity from the selection process soon led to farce. In Ferizaj, each applicant had an interview with a representative of the NATO training team, perhaps a Corporal or Sergeant in the Italian military. The rules from MCAD were clear; the interview had to be conducted in their own language, i.e. in most cases Albanian. This required an interpreter to translate from Italian into Albanian and back again. Some members of the KPC had spent extended periods of time out of the country on various courses and were proficient in English, a clear asset for the future KSF. In fact their English was probably better than the NATO soldiers conducting the interviews. However these applicants, when they started answering questions in English, were categorically told not to. These English language skills went unrecorded yet they were clearly a significant capability enhancement for the new force. Even if the individual was found to be unsuitable in other ways, it was a factor that should have been taken into account.

In other ways the 'NATO Standards' mantra was being exposed as inconsistent; compromises soon began, as dental records were not included in the assessment and only certain individuals were sent for a medical. As the cost per appointment was €50, it was considered to be prohibitively expensive to send every applicant from the KPC to be assessed, so initially only those individuals who were 'pre-selected' for key roles were sent to the doctor. This included senior officers, logisticians, EOD experts and other individuals with key specialist skills that were to be at the heart of the future force. The 'pre-selection' process took place in MCA Division under Colonel Roberts' stewardship, with representatives from the International Civilian Office always present to ensure fairness and transparency. These individuals had not been fully selected, but they had passed the initial sift and looked odds on to join the KSF. The boards consisted of assigning points to each individual, based on all the objective criteria, so that the formal selection boards later on only dealt with a manageable number of applicants. It was a sensible approach.

The selection plan, which would assign KPC personnel to posts in the KSF, was due to commence with the selection of the KSF Commander on 7th November. Once the KSF Commander had been identified, the nomination would need to be ratified by the Kosovan President, via the Office of the Prime Minister, with the remaining selection boards following in quick succession, using a cascade approach, starting with senior ranks. Firstly the Colonels and above would be selected at the senior officers' selection board, the SOSAB, which was planned for the 24th November. Then Lieutenant Colonels would be appointed, and so on until all available positions had been filled. Reflecting the existing problems with the KPC rank structure, individuals were permitted to drop down a maximum of two ranks in order to fill a slot, if they wished to do so. Nobody would be elevated in rank. The KSF positions had been meticulously planned within the overall structure of the new organisation by the NATO Advisory Team and the staff in MCA Division.

The whole process would culminate in Announcement Day on the 12th December. After selections were completed, over 2,800 envelopes had to be personalised with the exact information for each individual, in a very short timeframe. The envelopes would either contain good news with a role, a location and a time at which to report as a founding member of the KSF, or the envelope would contain very disappointing news, with resettlement information and other pension arrangements, if applicable. The right information needed to be included in each envelope, then put into the right box and taken to one of a number of designated KSF locations around Kosovo. Manned by MCA Division's staff with security provided by KFOR, KPC personnel would report at specific times, by unit, throughout Announcement Day where they would receive their envelopes. Afterwards, KPC personnel would go home for Christmas and return in the New Year to start work in their new role in the KSF on the 5th January 2009. It was a very complex operation and required high levels of attention to detail from the MCAD team. There was little room for error and time was at a premium.

The stand-up of the KSF process was never going to be without criticism and one of the more contentious decisions was to limit the number of medicals for applicants, which was taken for reasons of expediency and cost. Those KPC personnel selected to have a medical would attend a facility in Obilic, close to Pristina, to be examined by a local doctor, and the report would be sent to MCA Division for a KFOR doctor to make an assessment on the individual's suitability to join the KSF. Initially it was difficult to find a doctor who was willing to make the decision based on a third party evaluation, but this problem was quickly resolved. However, the process of inviting pre-selected individuals to Obilic to take a medical, led these KPC personnel to assume they had already been selected into the KSF. This was not true, but the absence of a proactive KFOR media campaign allowed this rumour to become fact.

The plan was tight, leaving a matter of days between the selection boards, which would consist of representatives from the MCA Division, the newly appointed KSF Commander, a representative from the International Civilian Office, members of the Government and senior KFOR personnel. The selection boards would be managed by Colonel Roberts, using the database from which all the information on each individual had been stored. The database was run by a German non-commissioned officer and it was clear that he was the only person who actually understood how to manipulate it. The importance of that database, as a single point of failure, was a metaphor for the fragility of the entire plan. It was hugely ambitious and the month-long delay by the KFOR Commander in making his decision artificially compressed the timeline and conspired to set the MCA Division up for failure.

Knowing how under pressure the MCA Division was at that time, it was clear that General Rama and his team, with my support, were best placed to come up with a plan that worked. I had done some background that week on analysing the problem and had fed this into Rama's own work. The idea to keep things simple had been accepted by Rama and after initially sketching out the plan, I called Colonel Habel and Colonel Roberts to the KPC headquarters to cast their eye over it. It would be pointless proceeding without their initial feedback. They soon arrived at the KPC headquarters, no doubt looking forward to the customary offer of a glass of raki, as well as being given the opportunity to have their say on an issue that they were as much an equal partner as the KPC.

After running through the detail, they were content. So despite religious holidays, unexpected days out of the office and an EU Parliamentary delegation visiting the KPC HQ, Major General Rama completed the work and presented his plan to MCA Division on the 3rd October as directed. There was relief all round when it looked entirely credible and with Rama in charge, the chances of success were high. The plan was signed off by Brigadier Di Luzio and formally issued to all the KPC commanders. There was no stopping it now and like the MCA Division's plan for standing up the KSF, time was short and there was no room for delays or other issues to get in the way.

With a major piece of work out of the way, other smaller but equally important issues still needed to be discussed. The pension law was still making its way through Parliament, the resettlement plan for non-selected KPC personnel was still to be fully announced and another extremely contentious issue was starting to be discussed in KFOR's corridors; that of disarming the KPC officers and removing weapons from every location in advance of Announcement Day. I was getting pressure from the KIKPC Chief, and also from Brigadier Di Luzio, who both wanted to know how this issue was going to be managed. I told them in two words; with difficulty. I mentioned this issue to General Rama and he was ambivalent, mainly because he didn't carry a weapon as it was of less importance to him, but many KPC officers still carried a sidearm and did so with great pride. Carrying arms was almost a constitutional right and suggesting that they had to be handed in to be decommissioned started to become a deeply divisive issue. A large number of weapons were also stored in armouries in KPC locations and all of these needed to be collected by the KIKPC.

At the beginning of October my argument for removing personal sidearms was given a boost when Colonel Zeqiri, the Engineer Battalion Commander, who I had met a few weeks earlier with General Rama in Ferizaj, managed quite literally to shoot himself in the foot. While in his office undergoing a routine weapons inspection by KFOR troops his pistol discharged. Nobody apart from Zeqiri was injured, but it highlighted the dangers of officers carrying weapons without the requisite skills. To my knowledge most of these officers were not highly trained in weapon handling. This incident did not change anything though in the eyes of the KPC Commander, General Selimi, who made it clear that carrying a weapon was something that he would continue to do, regardless of the circumstances. When I raised this with Selimi in his office he immediately became very angry at the idea of giving up his weapon. If Selimi was unwilling to give up his sidearm, and was going to be so animated about the issue, then others would also refuse. I sensed that the challenge of disarming KPC officers would fall to me to unlock over the coming weeks.

With the stand down plan now issued to KPC units across the country, what was being asked of KPC personnel was pretty ambitious. There were risks at every turn and the only way to achieve success was to apply decisiveness and plenty of common sense. The KPC's main challenge involved closing bases in a matter of weeks; the number of bases across the country had to be reduced from 33 down to 7 future KSF locations, with an additional 3 sites in the short term for equipment and vehicle storage. The emotional wrench for those who had worked in these locations for the previous 9 years was not really considered; but it was a necessary activity on the journey towards de-activating the KPC and forming the KSF. Little thought was given to what these individuals would do once their base was closed or indeed how to communicate with them. Frankly, the KPC leadership had other things on their minds, therefore it was up to the protection zone commanders to make sure that their personnel remained in touch with developments. The plan assumed that the KPC was capable of providing this tactical level of leadership and was going to be able to exert sufficient command and control over a nervous and fragmented organisation.

And all this was happening whilst KPC personnel were waiting for information about their pension arrangements, the resettlement plan and trying to maintain discipline with only 8 weeks to go before the KPC was finally de-activated. With a chain of command that was weakening by the day and suggestions of dissent reaching the KPC headquarters, we all crossed our fingers that we would still manage to steer the KPC through the challenge of de-activation with dignity. It was going to be a close run thing.

Then, quite out of the blue, the first major challenge to the KPC stand down plan appeared on everyone's radar. Without warning I was called to the Office of the KPC Coordinator by Lieutenant

Colonel Phil Osment, who was the military assistant to Major General Caplin, at that time away in New York. The Office of the KPCC was on the top floor of an office building that enjoyed a great view looking north across the city of Pristina from Major General Caplin's balcony. I had visited the OKPCC several times, including early in my tour when I initially met Major General Caplin, who had taken the opportunity to set the scene for me in Kosovo. Without a lift installed it was also the only place I always arrived slightly out of breath from climbing the many stairs.

When I arrived in his office I was also introduced to a member of the UNMIK Office of Legal Authority (OLA), and one other, Zarko Milosevic, an UNMIK old hand who had been in Kosovo for many years. I was a bit concerned. UNMIK's role in Kosovo had become increasingly unpopular with Kosovans generally, over the way they had administered the country in the period between 1999 and February 2008 when Kosovo declared independence from Serbia. Resentment was growing towards the UN and their role was beginning to diminish, but they had set up the KPC and retained Executive Authority for now. Although in negotiations with KFOR over this issue, in theory everything the KPC owned belonged to the UN. This included the buildings, the vehicles and the equipment deployed across the country. The OLA representative explained that a proper process of assessing the properties across the country would need to be undertaken and this was likely to take 3 months.

It was not welcome news.

He added that under no circumstances could the KPC's holdings of vehicles and equipment be signed across to the KSF, because UNMIK does not recognise Kosovo and therefore by extension, does not recognise the KSF. It was bureaucratic and diplomatic madness; and I was worried. In a stroke, this issue had the potential to undermine the whole KPC stand down plan without the ink even being fully dry on the document. I knew that some KPC units had already started moving equipment under the direction of the KPC's logistics commander. And I was aware that the first building, in protection zone 3, under the command of Brigadier General Nazmi Brahimaj, was almost ready to hand over. But hand over to whom? The KPC infrastructure disposal plan, which clearly set out the dates and locations when buildings would be handed back to the local Municipality, was a live document. There was no room for delay within the overall process, the consequences of which would be profound. Suddenly Rama's hastily written plan looked like it would not last until the weekend.

Following this unexpected development, I was then called to a related meeting at KFOR headquarters with Di Luzio, Colonel Habel and Colonel Stuart Roberts. Reacting to the news, and with little thought about the implications, Di Luzio insisted that until further notice, when a building has been vacated it must continue to be guarded by KPC personnel. I already knew this decision would go down badly with the KPC, whose livelihoods were under threat and who were being shunted down a path which many of them did not wish to follow. Asking them to continue to turn up to guard an empty building that represented the death of the KPC, was going to be a hard sell under the circumstances. Of course, this subtlety was lost on Di Luzio and KFOR.

I asked Di Luzio why KFOR could not play a role in the protection of these locations to take the heat off the KPC who I knew would find this task very challenging to fulfil. Di Luzio practically shouted that it was "impossible". And why? KFOR did not recognise Kosovo, and KFOR appeared to want as little to do with the KPC stand down as it could get away with. It wasn't as if

KFOR had much to do across the country. With 16,000 troops deployed in Kosovo and barely any security incidents to deal with, it was clear that if KFOR wanted to demonstrate a commitment to the KPC, this was a good opportunity to do so.

I returned to the KPC headquarters downbeat and reported this unwelcome turn of events to the leadership; Selimi was reasonable and thought the guarding issue would not cause too much disruption. Rama on the other hand was not amused. In the whole time I had been in Kosovo I had never seen him get angry, but this news struck a nerve. It also showed the difference between the two in understanding of the KPC's mood. Selimi was probably not quite as sensitive to the implications of this decision as Rama, who saw the issue very much in the same way as I did. So after further discussions with the Office of the KPC Coordinator, I was told that, until Major General Caplin returned from New York, the KPC just had to get on with it.

During this period I had been quite unwell. My defences were weak and I was struggling to complete a whole day without going to my room to rest. The range of sensitive and important issues on my 'to do' list were starting to stack up alarmingly quickly and being sick was the worst handicap of all. My stomach illness had not gone away and it was affecting my energy levels. Being away from the family was part and parcel of military life; at least I had high-speed internet in my office which allowed me to keep in touch via Skype. But being away, in a highly stressful environment and feeling below par, made me miss my family more acutely. The lack of structure to my days did have a knock-on effect because I couldn't call at a pre-arranged time. Often when I got in touch it clashed with the routine at home. Sometimes the children were having dinner or getting ready for bed. Hearing their voices and having a good call was hugely uplifting, but getting my timing wrong had a disproportionately negative impact on my morale. Calls home were entirely focused on what was happening in their lives in England. I found it impossible to explain to my wife what was going on in my world; it was such a different environment I simply avoided the subject. And this started to become a problem.

With strategically important matters dominating most days, my old friend Nuredin Lushtaku reappeared on my radar because he had managed to cause offence again, this time with my colleagues. A KIKPC team had arrived for an unannounced inspection to find him in a particularly belligerent mood. Following a familiar phone call from a KIKPC colleague, explaining their dissatisfaction at their treatment, I said I would find out what was going on. Normal measures would have potentially involved some sort of disciplinary case being initiated, but none of this really worked any more. When I mentioned cases of ill-discipline, Rama would look at me with resignation, the shrug of his shoulders saying it all. Even the KIKPC knew that they were in a losing battle with someone like Lushtaku, who was unlikely to want to continue his uniformed career in the KSF anyway. Widely held suspicions towards the KPC by members of KFOR, resulted in a lack of real understanding of what was going on in the minds of the KPC personnel during this period. For me the KPC personnel's newly found attitude was completely understandable, and frankly, there were bigger fish to fry than worrying about small acts of defiance.

So together with Simi, we headed to Adem Jashari Barracks in Pristina, the home of the Kosovo Guard, to investigate. Parking outside his office building we were met by one of his staff who showed us inside, asked us if we wanted to drink something and took us to Lushtaku's office. As usual he wore his maroon beret throughout our meeting, and as usual, he was pleasant, courteous and entirely reasonable. We drank coffee, we talked about his concerns over those who may not get into the KSF and he complained about the lack of information. His message was nothing unusual and we left the meeting shaking hands and looking forward to our next catch-up. I knew Lushtaku was warming to me. We talked about many different subjects and he valued my visits. It was the way I operated, and one that I had developed during my time as an Army Officer. I always made the effort to meet because it was unlikely that the time would be wasted. And even when others didn't want to have anything to do with people like Lushtaku, it was important to keep a lid on things by reaching out to him. Patience and cultural understanding were central to my approach; but this attitude was lacking in KFOR.

Seeing Lushtaku that day was a good scene setter for the next morning. I accompanied General Selimi to a meeting with the Minister for the KSF, Fehmi Mujota, and immediately afterwards we had an audience with Lushtaku's friend, Hashim Thaçi, the Prime Minister. The meeting with Mujota was formal, we didn't know him well as he was new in post and was getting to grips with his brief. Mujota didn't strike me as an especially purposeful or experienced politician but he was pleasant enough and we got to know each other, in passing, over the next few months.

The real prize was seeing Thaçi. I had assumed there would be a few of his staff sitting in the room with us, but it was the PM, Selimi, me and my ever present friend and interpreter, Simi. It was a private meeting, during which they talked about the draw down process and certain individuals. I was surprised that Major Rufki Suma, our friend down in the south who had been talking to the press again about preventing his men from applying for the KSF, was mentioned by Thaçi. He had evidently been briefed and he was clearly interested in the process as a whole. It was an encouraging sign. The burning question for me though was whether he would support Selimi's likely nomination as the first Commander of the KSF. It wasn't mentioned of course, but it was on everyone's lips as the selection board for the KSF Commander approached. As we were leaving his office, I noticed a framed picture of the art installation, occupying a large amount of pavement space downtown Pristina, bearing the word 'Newborn'. It had been commissioned after the independence announcement earlier in the year, set to rest in a prominent place in the city centre and had been signed by many of Kosovo's great and the good, along with thousands of Kosovan citizens. Having access to senior decision makers gave me a chance to add another layer to my understanding of Kosovo through my expanding network, and in the case of the PM and General Selimi, it was useful to understand their personal dynamics.

With so much going on my appointment to see Ramush Haradinaj at his office came round very quickly and I made sure I had collected the maps from Slim Lines. In fact the meeting with Haradinaj assumed added importance. Like a number of people in the British Embassy, I had been invited to Haradinaj's house two weeks earlier for a leaving party to say goodbye to his old friend, former Military Liaison Officer in the British Embassy, Lieutenant Colonel Mike Clements. Haradinaj was also planning to visit the UK and had applied for a visa. On the day of the party Haradinaj was in Macedonia to obtain a UK visa, but for some inexplicable reason, the British Embassy in Skopje had refused his application. Despite his acquittal of all charges at the International Criminal Tribunal for the former Yugoslavia earlier in 2008, someone had decided that he should not be allowed to travel to London.

No doubt reflecting this decision, Haradinaj had abruptly cancelled the party. I was disappointed but unaware of the reasons until later. Once I discovered the real reason for the party cancellation, I learned that British diplomats in Pristina, together with Mike Clements who was about to leave Kosovo, had tried to recover the situation with Haradinaj through a charm offensive. But he was having none of it and refused to meet any of the Embassy staff. Even Mike's new replacement tried in vain to talk to Haradinaj. For a country that had supported the Kosovans so closely over the years, it was a rather embarrassing gaffe for the UK to have committed. Once I heard the full story I fully expected my imminent meeting with him to be cancelled as well, but far from it; my appointment was on and it appeared that I was the only Brit in Pristina who had access to Ramush Haradinaj at that time.

On the day I was due to meet Haradinaj, armed with the maps, I actually felt slightly nervous. Simi and I drove into the city in a KPC vehicle rather than my KFOR Landcruiser, in order to reduce the profile of my visit. I knew I was going off reservation but I still believed it was important to meet him in his own backyard rather than at the KPC. And by meeting me he then also had an opportunity to convey his views of the impending de-activation process, albeit with a political spin. Walking into his AAK political party offices I was met by an aide who addressed me as Colonel. I was immediately shown into a large reception room, with two identical sofas facing each other and a table between them at one end for drinks and ashtrays. Simi sat next to me and we were joined by a couple of members of his staff.

After waiting a few minutes, drinking a coffee that had been brought out soon after sitting down, Haradinaj swept into the room, full of bonhomie and elegant charm, bringing with him that recognisable buzz from my first meeting at the KPC headquarters. I hoped there was going to be less whisky this time. We talked about his hopes for the future KSF, about my family and what I was doing next. He was intrigued by my background and we talked for about half an hour. Haradinaj had his maps and he now owed me a favour, if ever I needed to cash it in. This medieval honour based system, known as a 'bessa', was something I learned about through Simi and after doing a favour for Haradinaj, I could, apparently, legitimately call it back in at some point in the future.

My time was soon up, we shook hands again – that vice like grip would be difficult to forget – and we headed for the street. As Simi and I left the building and stepped onto the pavement, I checked to see whether there was anyone paying me any attention. Political intrigue was rife in Pristina; intelligence agencies were active in the city and it was highly likely that Haradinaj's political headquarters was under casual surveillance. Whether I was being watched that day I will never know, but I knew I had taken a step into the unknown; I just hoped I had not been compromised. In fact, the next time I entered that building to see Haradinaj would lead to one of the most uncomfortable 30 minutes of my life.

So, after nearly 6 weeks of being away from the UK, and fully immersed in the daily madness which was Kosovo, I needed to do something different. One morning the head of the NATO vetting unit, Dave Finnamore, a jovial and all-knowing former Metropolitan police officer, invited me to join a road trip to the southern ski resort of Brezovica. There was no snow but it seemed like an excellent idea, and I had no other plans for that particular Sunday, as I always wrote my weekly report on a Saturday afternoon. Sunday was truly my day of rest although it often just drifted away aimlessly. The positive side of being the LNO was the fact that I was my own boss; one downside was not really belonging to any team. It could be an isolated and lonely existence as I was beginning to find out. So when Dave asked me to join a couple of members of his team to explore the communist-era ski resort, I jumped at the chance.

I walked across to the 'chicken hut', a small single-storey building that housed the vetting team, and which was surrounded by a chain-link fence. Along with Dean, another former UK police officer who had a sharp wit and a keen sense of humour, I also met Migena, an Albanian American who had moved back to Kosovo a few years previously and was a vetting officer within the NATO team. It was one of those moments when everyone clicked and the banter was excellent; a British Army officer, a couple of cynical ex British policemen and an Albanian-American woman who actually understood the British sense of humour. It was quite a mix. The day turned out to be good for the soul. After winding our way through the Kosovan countryside, we eventually reached the Serbian enclave of Brezovica. It was quite an odd experience to suddenly see road signs in an entirely different language. Feeling as if I was crossing an international border was always guaranteed to generate some excitement in me. We turned off the main road and followed a poorly maintained track that led up, via a series of hairpin bends, to the once thriving ski resort. As we approached the now disused hotel it was as if an eerie silence had descended on this little corner of Kosovo.

I've been to many places in the world that had the potential to be spectacular locations, if only someone was willing to invest a little bit of capital. Brezovica was no different. Under a cloudless October sky, the hotel nestled at the head of a valley, supplied by several rusting chairlifts leading off in several directions. The hotel had been clearly built as a niche skiing location, but the effects of the war and the absence of any sustained investment in its facilities since 1999 had left the building looking and feeling like a deserted film set from the 1960s. Under a bright sun, we walked around the resort, with only a few other people who scratched out a living in nearby houses for company. I was able to walk into the hotel lobby that was entirely empty. I passed the unmanned reception, with phones still sitting on the deserted desk, I walked through wide corridors without a soul around, eventually emerging in what must have been the lounge bar, facing west, where guests could sit comfortably and watch the sun descend behind the nearby hills. Except the huge room was completely deserted and frozen in time; what was left of the furniture was upturned and scattered around the room. It was as if the guests had been given 5 minutes' notice to leave the hotel; it was eerie. I knew I had to return when the snow had arrived and with that promise to myself we all returned to the vehicle and found a local restaurant to have lunch before the 2-hour drive north back to Pristina.

The day out had given me a very important shot in the arm, a morale boost that I clearly needed. For the first time in Kosovo, I had been able to share some of the issues I was grappling with, unburdening myself through the friendships I made that day. Until that afternoon I had not realised how much I was beginning to get run down through the unbelievably unhealthy lifestyle I had adopted since arriving in Kosovo. I was inhaling secondary smoke, I was drinking more than I should have been, I was permanently suffering from an upset stomach and I was not getting enough sleep. In short, I was heading for a crash.

On our return journey, as we headed back through the flat plains of central Kosovo, leaving the towering peaks behind for now, I reflected on how beautiful the country was if you looked beyond the rubbish, and specifically how lucky I was to be there. I had the best of both worlds; I was intimately involved in the security sector transition affecting Kosovo which gave me a very strong sense of purpose, as well as being fortunate enough to be able to escape from the pressure of the job whenever I wanted to. It was certainly a most unusual operational tour of duty.

Just before entering the city limits we stopped for a coffee. We were sitting outside in the setting sun, our fleeces zipped up as the temperature began to drop, enjoying the final exchanges of banter before re-entering the cautious and risk averse world of KFOR in Film City. We laughed a lot that day, and friendships were forged through the simple act of sharing an experience and spending a few hours together on a journey. I had enjoyed being with three people who I had never really got to know until that day. I realised that I missed the company of others and decided that I had to create opportunities to break the routine; to find reasons to go out much more often, even if my body was telling me otherwise.

The following morning General Rama left Kosovo for his visit to Holland, and I had a little housekeeping that needed to be attended to. The KPC Chef de Cabinet, Xhavit Gashi, who had been the source of a lot of background information for me with both Selimi and Rama, had recently disappeared from the scene. It was the second time he had left Kosovo without any mention of his plans to me. Although he was now back in work and appeared to be more efficient than ever, I wanted to know what was going on. He was a key figure for me, even if I thought he worried too much about situations between the KPC Commander and his Deputy. I called Xhavit and asked him to meet me for a drink at the Renaissance 2 restaurant later that day.

Kasper dropped me off and said he would wait around the corner as I knew I wouldn't be long. I walked down the now familiar narrow, uneven footpath that led from the road towards R2, and soon knocked on the heavy wooden door, hoping Ilhe, the owner, was nearby. After a few moments I heard the bolt slide open and I walked into a warm and practically empty restaurant. Xhavit was already sitting at a table next to the open fire. He ordered me a drink to accompany his own and we started to chat. After some probing, he explained his recent absences and apologised. I wasn't really worried about his reasons for being away without explanation, but I did need him to be acting as my go between with Selimi and Rama, and to be more responsible about his role. Xhavit had a supple personality, he knew he had a big part to play in the KPC stand down plan, and over a glass of wine, he seemed to be revitalised and focused as never before. I could never be unhappy with Xhavit for long though, he was that kind of character, and we finished the meeting on good terms. I left the restaurant, the door locked behind me, and walked back up to the road, the street lights now glowing dimly. The nights were becoming noticeably colder and I was glad to get into the car. With Kasper at the wheel for only a few more days before he finished his tour of duty, we headed back to Film City.

After a minute or two, approaching a junction in an empty side street, dusk settling quickly on the city, I heard the unmistakable sound of gunfire ring out very close to our vehicle. I was on the wrong side and had not seen what had happened until the man with a pistol ran towards our car then steered behind it to make his escape. Kasper, who had seen the incident, immediately drew his weapon. In the seconds that followed, rather than get out and pursue the suspect, or even remain behind to see whether anyone needed first aid, Kasper decided to do what he was trained to do, which was remove me from the source of danger. So with our adrenalin pumping, Kasper turned on the siren and blue lights and we accelerated away towards the safety of Film City. As we pulled away, I watched the man in the half-light part stagger, part run away from us across some open ground until he disappeared into the gloom. Once we were in Film City I called Migena, the translator, and asked her to meet me at the main gate to report the incident to the Kosovo Police.

When I eventually got back to my room I found it very difficult to settle down; I knew I was under pressure at work and I had been ill, so my defences were low, but it didn't explain the restlessness I felt. The shooting was just a criminal act; these things happen across the world every day, and there was as much chance of it happening in Kosovo as anywhere else. The shooting was close and although there was no evidence to suggest we were the target it was totally unexpected in what I considered to be a benign environment; it shouldn't have generated the reaction in me that it did. I had experienced close calls in Baghdad so the incident wasn't anything new. But that night I took something to help me sleep, and by the morning the previous evening's events had become a few words on the page of my personal diary.

I needed to be on form the following day; Admiral Fitzgerald, the Commander of Joint Forces Command, Naples, along with his UK Deputy Commander Lieutenant General Pearson, was visiting Kosovo. Admiral Fitzgerald was General Gay's boss, and I have never seen such an effort to make sure the protocol was right. It was as if the Queen was coming to town. Roads were swept, floors polished and the seating arrangements in the conference room were by invitation only. Fortunately I had an invitation because I knew that General Selimi would be expected to speak, and Major General Caplin wanted me to report on how Selimi got on. I had written some lines for Selimi so I was keen to see how the conversation went. We were still in wait and see mode about the appointment of the KSF Commander so Selimi clearly wanted to demonstrate his credentials.

I had met Lieutenant General Pearson in Film City in the first week of my tour in August at the Italian Change of Command ceremony, when General Gay took over KFOR. With General Pearson that day was his military assistant, Lieutenant Colonel Chris Gunning, who mentioned to me that he also wanted to see my weekly reports. The reports at that time were already going to another recipient in Naples through the email distribution list that I had inherited from my predecessor, so adding Chris was no problem. I believed that the more people in the chain of command who knew what was going on in Kosovo, the better.

In my experience, when people do not have enough to do, they lose sight of the bigger picture. This is exactly what happened that morning in KFOR headquarters just before the Admiral's arrival. The protocol had been managed by General Gay's military assistant, Major Michele Ionata. He and I got on well. So when my seat was taken by General Pearson's military assistant, who was not expected and was not on Major Ionata's seating plan but who was going to be seated in the room regardless, I obviously needed another chair. However, when I pointed this out, Major Ionata refused, saying that it was impossible. Not especially impressed with his lack of flexibility, I walked into the next door room and carried a chair back in with me. I was not sitting at the table but on the side which suited me perfectly. While I did this Ionata had been outside with General Gay waiting for the visitors to arrive.

The rest of the attendees were sitting down in their designated places, including General Selimi who was sitting opposite where the Admiral was due to sit. We all stood up when the Admiral entered the room and I caught Ionata's eye as we did so. And he appeared to be very angry indeed. It was a good meeting, I got a mention, Selimi did well and it ended with the customary NATO handshake between everyone, regardless of rank or position. We all left the room. Except Ionata wasn't finished. As I walked away from the headquarters along one of the beautifully manicured paths, Major Ionata caught up with me and said in his wonderful Italian accent, 'Ade, why did you disobey my order not to put a chair in the room?'

Firstly, I pointed out that I outranked him and disobeying his order wasn't the issue. However, it didn't matter how much I tried to explain the importance of listening to Selimi and the wider conversation, Major Ionata was only focused on the protocol and did not understand the context, probably because it did not directly relate to KFOR's main effort; a safe and secure environment and freedom of movement. Major Ionata wasn't listening and refused to laugh it off, despite my attempts to do so. Regrettably the incident soured my relations with him for the remainder of my tour. As the KFOR Commander's gate keeper he was not the ideal person to fall out with, but General Gay's interest in the KPC was so marginal that I calculated it really didn't matter that much.

What was important was the integrity of the stand down plan. Major Suma, the rogue officer in charge of a small unit located in a town close to the Macedonian border, had once again spoken to the media who were beginning to see him as a great source of gossip over events surrounding the KPC. Even though he had been warned in the KPC headquarters weeks before to stop breaking the disciplinary code by talking to the press, he calculated, correctly, that nobody was going to do anything about it. Suma had a problem with the KPC plan and he was going to make sure everyone knew about it. To make matters worse, he had such a grip on the members of his unit, who depended on the KPC for their livelihoods, that Suma had directed his 25 men not to apply for the KSF. This abuse of his leadership was what I found so distasteful about the whole matter. With the cut-off date for all applications fast approaching, and armed with the newspaper headlines in my hand, I spoke to General Selimi and suggested I go down to visit his unit to see if I could make him see sense. So that morning I left early to cover the 90-minute journey south to the Macedonian border town. Simi had made the arrangements and on the journey I considered how a British Army officer, with nothing but his reputation and the uniform he wore, was going to change Suma's mind.

Guarded on two sides by high hills, which dropped sharply into the valley floor, the town's houses were strung out alongside the main Pristina to Skopje road, with what looked like a cement factory dominating its surroundings. Suma's base, a ramshackle collection of low-rise buildings, was a short drive away from the main road up a hill and which gave the impression of an industrial yard that had seen better days. The unit's men were away from the base, hard at work on the side of the dusty main road in town, repairing a stretch pavement underneath the huge conveyor belt that dominated the landscape. I met Suma in his office. He was not a tall man, he was slim and well turned out for the KPC. However, he instantly gave me the impression of being untrustworthy. I often relied on my instinct when I met people and when I shook hands with Suma it set off alarm bells. After an initial exchange I asked to speak to his men alone as I wanted to understand why they were not applying to the KSF. I suspected they were being manipulated by Suma not to do so. He tried to claim that he had not influenced his men at all, but this was not a credible explanation for the wholesale refusal by his small unit of men to apply for the KSF.

Suma agreed to me talking to his men and we drove the short distance down to where they were working in the sunshine. Once out of the vehicle Suma stayed close to me when I met them, which rather defeated the point of my visit. At least I had 30 minutes with them, and they probably appreciated the break from work more than anything. It was clear they were not going to change their minds and the complex interdependent societal and clan networks in these communities meant there was little chance I would really understand why they were so loyal to Suma. Nobody was going to break ranks. It was hopeless, they were not going to speak freely even if they wanted to and so I conceded defeat. I also spoke to Suma about obeying the stand down plan, which was going to see his KPC unit close, like so many. Suma explained that he was refusing to close his camp because there was an illicit trade in fuel from large storage tanks which were located within his unit's perimeter and which he claimed he needed to protect. I couldn't verify anything he said but his reluctance to follow orders, and he penchant for cosying up to the national media, was destabilising an already fragile stand down plan. The whole engagement with Major Suma's unit lasted three hours and was most unsatisfactory.

I was concerned on a number of fronts; despite Suma's assurances to me that he would not go to the press again, his promises were not worth much. His outspoken criticism was already stirring up trouble elsewhere within the KPC, giving succour to others who were also concerned that they would be side-lined in the selection process. General Selimi had already mentioned problems beginning to brew at a base close to Pristina called Vrani Do, where the KPC personnel, led by a cabal of Lieutenant Colonels, were talking about protesting in uniform, just as Suma had been threatening to do. As soon as I had returned to the KPC headquarters, I debriefed Selimi and he decided to go down to visit Suma a few days later. It was only midweek but I was already exhausted. That evening I had my sixth and final Albanian language lesson, which thankfully consisted of the final exam. I scored 69/70, which seemed a much better result than anything I had managed to achieve during my working day.

The next morning was my meeting with Agim Çeku. I had been looking forward to it, fresh from my earlier trip to see Ramush Haradinaj. And Çeku could not have been more different. Simi had arranged for us to go to his party headquarters in Pristina, but there seemed to be much less of the cloak and dagger about this trip. Çeku was charming, possessed good English, and there was none of the underlying caution that I had felt about visiting Haradinaj. As a former KPC commander, former Prime Minister and now party political leader with ambitions to once again achieve high office, Ceku's views were very supportive of the changes happening to the KPC and he was keen to help. Even as a rival to Haradinaj, Agim Çeku was definitely on side and wanted to add some value to the process. I felt that he would be a useful touchstone as things inevitably became difficult in the weeks and months ahead.

One thing that he said to me, which I was concerned about, was his belief that the Prime Minister would not support General Selimi's nomination as KSF Commander. I mentioned the fact that they had been chatting together at the change of command ceremony and that we had visited the Prime Minister for a private meeting the week before. This seemed to reassure him. However he did surprise me in the meeting with what on paper was a simple request; he asked whether I could write a point brief for him so that he could hold a press conference on the subject of the KPC and the KSF. I said I would certainly look into it. It was a very odd thing to ask for from a serving NATO officer and I was mildly amused at the thought of indirectly getting involved in Kosovan politics. Clearly I needed to handle the request with care. Whilst I wanted to cultivate a relationship with Çeku, writing a brief for him was one step too far and quietly, through Simi, I declined the invitation. I hoped it would not affect my ability to reach out to him, but I was sure he was not really expecting me to agree to the idea in the first place.

Finally Alexandra was back in Kosovo after her break and that week I received a message suggesting we meet for a walk in Germia Park on the following Sunday. It turned out to be a busy weekend. I very quickly found that the promise I had made to myself, to get out and try to enjoy myself more, was going to be fulfilled on the Friday night; I had a diary clash! Following the success of the dinner between General Rama and the KFOR Chief of Staff, Brigadier General Berger a couple of weeks earlier, I had arranged another dinner, this time between General Selimi and General Berger, again in Renaissance 2. However Lieutenant Colonel Terry Anderson, the US Assistant Defence Attaché, who was becoming a good friend, had also invited me to join him at the annual Jack Daniels Birthday Party in a nightclub in town on the same evening. I decided to take some civilian clothes with me to Renaissance 2 and explained to Ilhe, the owner of the restaurant, that I would be changing upstairs after we had finished. It was an early dinner, neither men were night owls, and so I would manage to attend both events. In an otherwise unmemorable dinner, Berger gave Selimi some good advice on how to manage everyone's expectations, including his own. I was relieved that General Berger chose not to drink raki with his meal this time.

With the 'duty' part of the evening over, I slipped upstairs, changed out of uniform, then got a lift with Kasper round to the club which was close to the restaurant, leaving my uniform in a bag in the vehicle. With a table reserved for Terry and a couple of his colleagues, I even managed to get Simi and his wife, Valbona, and her brother into the club. It was a great night. In the early hours I stepped onto the street with Terry, a Serbian colleague called Barney and the CIA's station chief. The plan was to go elsewhere and so we walked for a while until we found the station chief's vehicle.

Comically, we squeezed into a tiny Yugo car, an East European classic with only one windscreen wiper on the driver's side and no seat belts, and headed off to 212, a nightclub that most people seemed to end up in at least once a week; it was my first visit. In the club we met some of the members of the NATO Advisory Team, in particular Magnus Bydal and Eliza Elerte, who were the regular party goers. It turned out to be a long night.

After a late start and a trip to Slim Lines for a life-saving full English breakfast, I sat at my desk in the deserted KIKPC office building and for the rest of the afternoon wrote my weekly report while watching a live Premier League football match on the local Kosovan TV channel. As the day disappeared and I struggled with the tiredness that follows a good party, I had another curry supper to attend in the combined Officers' and Sergeants' Mess in Slim Lines. Summoning up the energy with a strong cup of coffee I headed down in the Landcruiser and quickly met up with an old friend from my staff college course who had just arrived for a tour of duty, together with the key British officials working in country. Andy Sparkes the Ambassador, Major General Nick Caplin, former Brigadier John Durrance, who was leading the resettlement programme, and representatives from the various elements of the British Embassy were all there. Being able to let the Ambassador know what was going on, in a relaxed and trusted environment, was useful. It also gave me a chance to discuss one or two more sensitive matters with individuals one to one.

By Sunday morning, after a relatively quiet night and managing to catch up on sleep, I was looking forward to some fresh air. After driving 15 minutes west to the edge of the city, I met Alexandra at the bus stop close to a large children's play area at the bottom of the road that leads to the forest. We were still a short drive away from the main car park so I invited her to hop in while I drove the final few hundred metres to where I planned to leave the car. It hadn't even occurred to me, but she was immediately very unsure about getting into a KFOR vehicle. Once we navigated that issue, we drove for a few minutes up the road into the forested area and turned left towards one of the two cafe restaurants in the park where I stopped the car. We set off walking up a track leading into the woods and the shade of the trees, which were only barely hanging on to their leaves. Alexandra, like her sister, was charming, educated and great company. We talked about family, her recent trip and, whilst we studiously tried to avoid talking about Kosovan politics, it was never far from the surface. However, my association with KFOR remained an issue.

After an hour's walk through the forest, with its clean air and relative tranquillity, I dropped Alexandra off to catch her bus home. I wasn't really sure whether we would see each other again. Reflecting on the escapism I felt by spending time with someone like Alexandra, who was such a contrast to the company I was keeping in Kosovo, I had a feeling that the pressure she felt was likely to get in the way of our friendship. With that depressing thought I headed back into the city and a favourite Pristina café, determined to relax before another week of surprises within the KPC.

Sitting outside the café, on an unusually warm October evening, with a coffee and my notebook, my mind drifted to the situation I was in. It was unusual; I was fully trusted by the KPC officers I was working with so closely, yet I felt I was treated with caution by KFOR, the organisation that I was officially working for. I had reached out to political leaders in the country who were intimately connected to the KPC's closure to improve my broader understanding, and after nearly two months in country I was getting under the skin of Kosovo's political machinations as well as feeling its cultural heartbeat. I could see that the complexity of the stand down plan and the murmurs of dissatisfaction within KPC ranks were going to become louder as we approached its de-activation. The pressure on the plan for standing up the KSF was already mounting, even before it had started, with significant risk associated with the integrity of the data that had been gathered and stored by the MCAD team. But my main worry was the absence of a communications plan by KFOR, to steer the public messaging to cover both major activities. Rumours were rife, the national press were making hay by printing inaccurate and damaging stories almost every day. When I raised these issues I was greeted with Italian reluctance to challenge the wisdom of this direction from Brussels. And to top it all I was about to lose a friend for no better reason that she sat on the opposite side of the ideological divide in a deeply troubled and fragile political environment. So much was happening, my head was spinning.

It was around this point in my tour that I realised one day in Kosovo was like a week anywhere else; and the next week promised to be no different.

Goal! A young boy celebrates scoring in a game of street football in Pristina.

Following a personal visit to the President of the Assembly in central Pristina, Lieutenant General Selimi explains what we are doing next, with Simi, my interpreter.

Standing outside the KPC headquarters, awaiting the arrival of the KFOR Commander, Lieutenant General Gay. The media, ever present, are waiting on the road behind me.

Addressing personnel in Protection Zone 3 in the West of Kosovo, with Brigadier General Brahimaj on his left, Lieutenant General Selimi was in his element talking to the KPC rank and file.

The KIKPC team. My driver bodyguard, Kasper Jernith, second from right.

Without an effective communications plan from KFOR, the media in Kosovo effectively set the agenda during the stand down of the KPC, to the detriment of those it affected.

CHAPTER SIX

'Serb-side'

The spectre of the UN's Office of Legal Affairs in Kosovo – the OLA – effectively forcing the KPC to guard all empty locations, vacated as part of the KPC stand down plan, until the ownership of the buildings had been established, was still hanging over everyone. However, a degree of common sense, so absent from KFOR's approach to the issue, was employed by one of the KPC's senior leaders. Brigadier General Brahimaj, a wily character leading Protection Zone 3 based in the western town of Peja, was a no-nonsense individual who cared more about the future than bureaucratic direction coming out of a discredited organisation like UNMIK. The burden of guarding essentially empty buildings, by KPC personnel unsure of their own futures, was an unpopular order that General Selimi had agreed to implement, while Major General Caplin was out of the country on a visit to the UN in New York. When he arrived back in Kosovo, Caplin's line reflected the legacy of UNMIK's role in sourcing locations for the KPC when it was set up in 1999. The Office of Legal Affairs was absolutely right to point out that buildings that had been, at one time or another, under UNMIK's administrative control needed to be returned appropriately. But it was very late in the day for the OLA to step forward with an objection, particularly since the dissolution of the KPC had been on the cards since February 2008. There was little sympathy for their position from within the KPC. And Brigadier General Brahimaj was having none of it.

I heard through Simi that he was planning to hand the buildings back to the local municipality regardless, so I asked Simi to call him. We had an awkward three-way conversation. When I pointed out that the OLA needed to clarify the legality of ownership of the building in question, Brahimaj replied, with typical clarity, 'The UN didn't build that building, the municipality did, and I am going to hand it back to the municipality.'

And that is precisely what he did. In a stroke, an issue that at first had appeared to be likely to derail the entire stand down plan had been resolved. I am certain the OLA was not at all impressed but the precedent had been established. The example Brahimaj set was replicated throughout the country. The first major obstacle to General Rama's plan had been successfully navigated, albeit rather unusually, and the house of cards, which aptly described it, was still standing.

The week began with a customary visit to the newly appointed Minister for the KSF. This routine meeting allowed me to get to know Minister Fehmi Mujota better and understand the many coordinated activities that were ongoing in preparation for the establishment of the country's new security force. He was always polite but never convinced me that he fully understood the details of his brief. I would sit and listen to the progress of each meeting through Simi's translation, recording in my notebook almost everything I heard. It also allowed me to share and discuss issues of mutual interest with Lieutenant Colonel Terry Anderson, the US Assistant Defence Attaché, who was also playing a major part in supporting the KSF and who also attended these meetings.

When we were leaving the Government building, Selimi explained that we were about to head south to visit our friend Major Rufki Suma in the small town of Hani Elezit. The prospect of spending even more time in Suma's company did not fill me with much joy; I found him to be cynical and manipulative. He was everything the KSF aspired not to be and the sooner he was out of the picture the better. When we arrived in Suma's ramshackle KPC base on the side of the hill, overlooking the cement factory, General Selimi demonstrated all his mastery of how to appeal to members of his organisation during the meeting with Suma and his men. Unlike before, when I saw them at work, everyone was sitting inside the camp's airy conference room and they listened to their Commander with what could be described as respectful silence. Selimi became increasingly energised and he pushed all the right buttons; he appealed to their sense of duty to exercise the rights of freedom they had fought so hard for in the KLA. He passionately believed that every member of the KPC should be included in the process. We left with Suma saying he would reconsider their decision not to apply for the KSF.

A Captain, who I had spoken to during both of my visits, had the courage to speak to me quietly before I left to ask whether they would be disadvantaged for being late. I assured him that would not be the case and at last sensed a breaking of ranks. It was an intelligent question and exposed a lack of unity amongst Suma's men. I assured him the MCAD would be ready to deploy a team at short notice to go through the same process that had occurred across the country. The deadline had passed but it was important to bring Suma and his men into the process. So, after several visits from various people, the likely future commander of the KSF had brought the issue close to a resolution. I was impressed with the way Selimi handled their concerns; he was always good at reaching out to the KPC rank and file. He had a natural affinity with the men. The MCAD team was on standby to deploy by the end of the week. Even with the issue seemingly settled, Suma's behaviour had unsettled the KPC across the country and other protection zones were taking a hard line towards the KPC stand down plan.

That evening I joined General Selimi and General Gay for a dinner at the Renaissance 2 restaurant, which I had arranged through Major Ionata. Sitting with me were Colonel Xhavit Gashi and Simi. My efforts to maintain relations between KFOR and the KPC were on track and any face time between these two men was vitally important. General Gay never seemed to be fully relaxed though and I sensed an innate caution in him. He had established a distance between himself and the KPC, and with me. This was evident from his first few weeks in command of KFOR. He had even moved his office within the KFOR headquarters down the corridor away from his outer office – which housed Major Ionata and his colleagues who ran his life while he was in command – and this alone suggested he wanted to filter who and what he had to deal with. However hard the situation was for me to get close to him, it was clearly advantageous to keep communication channels open, and it wasn't just the military organisations that needed to be brought together.

With so much emphasis on building bridges between the Albanian and Serbian communities more broadly in Kosovo, creating a civilian-led, multi-ethnic KSF was an ideal platform to bring all sides as one. Therefore, it seemed appropriate that General Selimi should also reach out to Serbian Ministers in Thaçi's Government to try to encourage them to influence their communities to volunteer to join the new force. The KSF was open to all ethnic groups and the use of the 'NATO standards' language was designed to reassure applicants that they would be judged on their ability, not on their ethnicity or religion. The idea of appointing a Serb as the KSF Deputy Commander was one particularly good initiative that General Selimi was proposing, and his visits to the Serb members of the Government were important to him. We had two meetings lined up with Serbian Ministers and we couldn't be late.

My Danish driver was away that day, collecting his replacement, confusingly also called Kasper, and so I was left with Simi to lead General Selimi's vehicle to the Government Building in the centre of Pristina. I looked at Simi when we stepped outside the old driving school building which was the KPC's HQ, and threw him the keys. Simi caught them and said, 'Do you want to drive?'

I had been driving the Landcruiser quite a lot up to that point, but only at weekends and normally quite defensively. I had not driven the car in a convoy with either Rama or Selimi's vehicle behind, using blue lights, the siren and driving extremely fast. That had been Kasper's job although I often disagreed with the practice. However, perhaps quite hypocritically, I realised that I would probably not get another clear-cut opportunity to drive in convoy and accepted the challenge; so Simi threw the keys back to me, I got into the driver's seat and put my seatbelt on. I turned on the engine, adjusted the mirrors, and looked in my rear-view mirror to wait for Selimi to emerge from the KPC HQ building. My finger hovered over the button for the blue lights and the siren.

We only waited for a few minutes for General Selimi to exit the building, late as usual, and get into his own car, driven by armed, UK-trained close protection personnel, which was parked behind our vehicle, engine running. When Selimi appeared, Simi said, in his customary way, 'Let's go.'

I am a good driver, but I had never driven so aggressively in traffic before, and with Simi urging me to go faster, driving with blue lights suddenly felt like a quite a dangerous pursuit. I was amazed how people were seemingly oblivious to our siren and continued to cross the road ahead of us, I was willing them to speed up and get out of the way. With Simi saying, 'Drive faster,' and with no thought to the consequences if something had gone wrong, I pressed on, accelerating as I played chicken with oncoming cars that appeared reluctant to pull over as we approached at speed, driving on the wrong side of the road, overtaking static traffic in a busy city centre, the siren echoing off the buildings all around me. I caught myself shouting to the other drivers to clear the way, Simi reassuring me that it would be fine. After what felt like an eternity but in reality was closer to 8 or 9 minutes, we pulled into the Government compound in time for the meeting. I pulled over, jumped out and as we crossed the car park to the main entrance I tossed the keys back to Simi and said, 'You're driving back.'

My heart rate took a while to come down after the journey, but it had been exhilarating. If something had happened it would have been difficult to explain the journey away, but we had arrived in one piece and all was well. With all the serious issues I was dealing with on a day-to-day basis, having fun was not far from my mind, if the opportunity presented itself.

Living away from home though was not easy. I had been calling my family pretty regularly since arriving in Kosovo but my absence was beginning to expose understandable tensions at home. After what had been a very positive day, I received a message from my wife asking me to call. I drove to my office in the KPC HQ that evening where I could use a fast internet connection to call home on Skype. My general fatigue probably didn't help my mood, and after hearing about how my son was making life harder than it needed to me for my wife, I spoke directly to my nearly 7-year-old boy. It didn't take long though for me to get cross with him and to my eternal shame I shouted at him, telling him not to misbehave with Mum. As soon as I had said it I wanted to take the words back. I immediately put my head in my hands as the seconds ticked by, the silence growing more awkward on the line. I felt absolutely terrible. It was completely wrong to have done it and it immediately upset me deeply. It was the worst thing I could have done and resulted in me feeling a profound guilt about my reaction.

The call ended shortly afterwards, unaware of what was really being said, and I was left completely flat. Slumped in my chair, breathing deeply, my mind returned to Kosovo; I had a dinner lined up with the Terry Anderson but I excused myself. Being sociable was the last thing on my mind. Instead I grabbed the keys and drove south of Pristina, out of the city, aimlessly, in need of some space, somewhere to park up and take stock, somewhere to feel upset away from prying eyes. I suddenly felt very depressed. I was missing everyone in England and the reality of how difficult life was back in the family home had finally managed to pierce the carefully constructed bubble that I had created for myself, designed to keep non-Kosovo matters away from the day-to-day challenges I faced. Compartmentalising my thoughts allowed me to focus on my role in Kosovo rather than become distracted by how much I was missing my family. That one phone call, the timing of it, my worsening state of health and the way I had spoken to Seb, my gorgeous son, conspired to affect me deeply. On the edge of the city I pulled in to a petrol station restaurant, parked up, and walked inside. Sitting in my British uniform, I ordered a burger and chips. I knew my presence was incongruous with the surroundings and that I was being noticed. But I didn't care what anyone thought; I just wanted to be away from others. I played the call over and over in my mind. It didn't improve. Eventually, after finishing my food and feeling no better, I drove back to Film City, walked to my room, undressed and went to bed. I soon fell into a drug-induced sleep.

Waking up the next morning, the bitter taste of diazepam in my mouth, I soon remembered the reason for taking the tablets in the first place. However, there was no time to linger on the previous evening's events. If there was one thing that could derail my performance it was allowing thoughts about how much I missed my family to come to the surface; although harsh, I knew I needed to shut out the issue and focus.

With the stand down plan for the KPC now up and running, the reality of the situation started to hit home with many KPC members. Major Rufki Suma, the 'battalion' commander of the small engineer unit near the Macedonia border, who had been talking to the press regularly, seemed to have given KPC members in other protections zones some encouragement to rebel. When General Selimi made his visit to see Suma and his men two days earlier, Selimi had mentioned that there was growing dissent in Protection Zone 5, the central area of the country which included the capital, Pristina. In particular, there was a KPC unit in Vrani Do, just north of Pristina, which had decided not to follow the instructions in the stand down plan to redistribute vehicles and equipment, effectively ignoring a direct order. The KPC commander, the least effective that I had met, could do nothing about it.

It was already a serious situation that needed careful handling. So General Selimi told General Rama to go and find out what the problems were and report back. The stand down plan was the precursor to a number of other vital steps in the KPCs journey towards dissolution. With the selection process effectively now closed to new applicants from the KPC, work was ongoing to prepare for the whole selection process to commence. But with pockets of dissent rapidly turning into tangible disruption, the whole legacy of the KPC, which was supposed to be de-activated with dignity, was at risk. The 'striking' KPC personnel in Vrani Do had forced a small hole in the dam; I needed to make sure that the water trickling out did not become a torrent. I knew there was likely to be some widespread discord, but I really didn't expect the KPC members to ignore direct orders and walk out. But this is exactly what they planned to do.

With so much change in the air, the future for many was unclear. Lieutenant Colonels and Majors were more likely to suffer than most because of the inverse nature of the KPC rank structure compared to the requirements of the KSF. The majority of Lieutenant Colonels and Majors would end up being pensioned off if they qualified for the benefit. And that statistic alone was always at the back of my mind; if there were going to be a lot of unhappy KPC personnel who had failed to get into the KSF, you didn't want them to be Lieutenant Colonels and Majors, who had enjoyed significant kudos over the previous decade. But that was the reality.

I hadn't seen Rama for a week as he had been in Holland, and contrary to many observers in KFOR, the KPC had not collapsed in his absence. Travelling in separate vehicles meant I missed the opportunity to chat things through with him in advance, particularly about the progress we seem to have made with Suma in the south. And knowing Rama, he was unlikely to take kindly to a group of KPC officers threatening to go out on strike. The meeting had been arranged at short notice, but the KPC personnel from the Vrani Do unit were already inside the secure camp in large numbers. After a relatively short journey from Pristina, when we arrived it felt a little like driving through a picket line, with the vehicle surrounded by a large number of men as we made our way to the car park. Not that there was any overtly violent or menacing intent by their actions, but it set the tone for the morning.

It was 22nd October and there were 7 weeks to go before the KPC was going to be stood down.

The room that we were led to was relatively small, with a long table across the end by the entrance, which reminded me of the painting of the last supper. I hoped it was not a portent for what was to come. We took our places behind that table, with the Protection Zone Commander, General Rama, me and Simi and one or two others sitting behind the security of the wooden trestle table. In front of us were around 100 very angry KPC personnel, sitting on chairs, each other's laps and on the floor. It was an intimidating atmosphere. They were crammed in, town hall style and there was a feeling of confrontation in the air. Over the next 90 minutes General Rama variously listened, addressed their issues, challenged their assumptions and, from time to time, raised his voice. The atmosphere remained charged throughout, with the ringleader, Lieutenant Colonel Potera, passionately arguing his case on behalf of the others in the room.

I was busy recording everything in my notebook, with Simi quietly translating for me, and I could sense Rama becoming more and more frustrated. Their arguments focused entirely on the pension law and the lack of benefits for them as veterans should they be unsuccessful getting into the KSF. They cited examples in other Balkan countries where many positive benefits from the various Government ministries had been offered to those who had served their country, such as free bus passes, medical benefits and improved pension conditions. These matters were missing under the pension law, they argued. Lieutenant Colonel Potera, Major Jakupi and Captain Balaj challenged the pension law making its way through Parliament and questioned General Rama's position, arguing that as the Deputy Commander of the KPC he should not be defending it.

The climax of the discussion, which was on the whole pretty bad tempered, saw Lieutenant Colonel Maloku walk to the front of the room, cheered on by his colleagues, and wave the draft pension law document in our faces. He was describing its contents in derogatory terms, the crowd baying for more. Maloku had clearly decided that he was going to finish his soliloquy with an act of pre-planned defiance by ripping up the law in front of us. He had obviously calculated that it would be a highly symbolic gesture. However, he hadn't taken into account the thickness of it, so when he tried to tear it in half he failed miserably. Try as he might, changing hands and grunting as he struggled with the paper, the pension law document had defeated him. After an awkward few moments he eventually threw it on the floor instead to the sounds of cheers. It was comical but the situation was still tense and I had to contain my amusement by concentrating on my notebook more deeply than usual. Rama's sense of timing was perfect and we immediately took a break. Within seconds the tension was lifted as everyone went outside for a cigarette and another coffee. Those of us sitting at the top table joined the KPC personnel outside, away from the building, continuing the conversation in a less formal environment.

After a 20-minute break, we made our way back into the room. I assumed that we were all pretty much done for the day, but Rama had other ideas. As we were taking our seats, he asked me to address the room. I had no idea Rama was going to tee me up like this and I had seconds to consider what I was going to say. It felt like Mitrovice all over again. But I was pleased to finally have an opportunity to have my views heard. I smiled to myself when I thought that this was definitely not what Di Luzio had in mind. Until that point I had always been a passive observer to every meeting I attended, either with Selimi or Rama; now I had a chance to speak directly to the people who were so affected by the changes taking place. And I grabbed the opportunity with both hands.

Speaking through Simi, you could have heard a pin drop. Picking up some of the themes used by Selimi earlier in the week while addressing Suma's men, I described what they had achieved and how they were risking their legacy amongst the population and the international community. I urged them to make the right choices going forward. The responsibility was not lost on me. I had travelled to Kosovo intent on making a difference, and in that moment, I was speaking directly to the people who were under so much pressure that they were willing to sacrifice their legacy. It was both humbling and a privilege to have addressed them. I only spoke for about 10 minutes but hoped I had injected a different dimension to the debate in their minds. With my speech completed, Rama wrapped up the meeting promising to send General Selimi to Vrani Do as soon as he could. And in a deliberate act of concession he also promised to pass on their concerns over the content of the pension law but asked them not to talk to the media again. Rama asked them to continue with the KPC stand down plan but made no further concessions and on his return to the KPC HQ considered the meeting to have been a success.

However, Lieutenant Colonel Potera ignored what General Rama has asked and was back on TV that evening, again making his case for a reformed pension law.

Within a week I was back at Vrani Do with General Selimi, but this time the atmosphere was very different. We were sitting in the same room, behind the same trestle table by the door, with the KPC members packed in on chairs, laps and the floor. Selimi's tone was far more conciliatory and he listened to their demands. Like Major Suma's visit, Selimi appealed to their emotions, to recall the sacrifice that their colleagues had made in the KLA and how they must not undermine this legacy. The men in that room must have been having a sense of *déjà vu*, as they'd heard pretty much the same message from me only days earlier. There was no shouting and no trying to rip up the pension law. He agreed with their issues and promised to take up their case with the President and the Prime Minister. He said that the pension law had to change and he said he would take it to the Government. In a stroke, by being seen to side with the protesters, Selimi had pacified their anger and agreed to meet their demands, with promises that he fully intended to keep. I was not asked to speak, I left the camp with Simi and on our way back to the capital I ran through the implications of his approach. Selimi was playing a dangerous game and he was acting in the best interests of the KPC personnel, even though they were by now openly defying their chain of command in Vrani Do. It was a most unorthodox situation but it led to a very positive reaction from within the Government of Kosovo's corridors.

The operational tour was proving to be quite intense and so I took any opportunity to let my hair down. For a couple of weeks I had been trying to arrange a flight in a helicopter, not so much because I wanted to fly low level and enjoy an adrenalin rush, something I had done many times before, but because I was keen to see the country from the air. When I first arrived in Kosovo I shared a room for a couple of nights with an American pilot who worked in the HQ and we had kept in touch; he had said that he could fix a flight for me in a French Puma helicopter. As a photographer I knew there would be some great shots waiting for me. I had been warned that I might be on a flight on the Saturday so I planned to have a quiet Friday night in. Last thing on the Friday afternoon though I learned the flight had been postponed.

So I was suddenly at a loose end and I could now afford to go out without worrying about the flight the next morning. I had already arranged to have dinner with my KIKPC team, and while I was sitting with my colleagues in the restaurant I received a text from Terry Anderson:

'Hey Ade, how do you fancy clubbing in Gračanica tonight?'

Leaning back in my chair, in case I was overlooked, I tapped out my reply:

'Terry, that's a Serbian town which is completely out of bounds to me.'

Even as I was sending the message I knew I would go. After dinner I headed into town to meet Terry, his Serbian colleague Barney, our good friend Magnus Brydal from the NATO Advisory Team and another member of the NAT, a Swedish Naval officer called Anders. Anders was always a bit of a handful once he had drunk a couple of beers and going into a Serb enclave with him was probably not the best thing to do.

We drove east out of Pristina in Terry's diplomatic SUV for about 30 minutes, eventually parking up just off the road, on some open ground close to the bar. I had decided that I would play the US diplomat card if anyone asked, I just needed to remember to speak with an American accent if challenged. We got out of the car, a sense of anticipation shared equally amongst us. If I needed to know how far off reservation I was, as we walked along the road towards the club, an armed Swedish Army foot patrol approached us. I had images flashing across my mind of getting picked up and dumped back in Pristina, with hours to pack my kit and catch the next flight out of the country. Not wanting to draw attention to ourselves, even though we really didn't look like Serbs, we collectively remained silent as they patrolled past us. Even Anders, who was Swedish, kept his mouth shut. It was a surreal moment. It was already late and so we didn't hang around; we walked to the bar, by now full of local Serb partygoers, under the guidance of Barney. With plenty of international goodwill on show throughout the night between our group and the locals, the night turned out to be excellent. We made lots of alcohol-induced friendships, the Serbs we spoke to were amazed but delighted that we were on their patch. There was lots of back-slapping on display. Even though they were surprised to see us there, they seemed to enjoy the fact that we had made the effort. I woke up in the morning, tired and slightly heavy headed, with a pocket full of Serbian Dinars. My experience of being an honorary US diplomat for the evening had passed without incident.

The weekend once again followed a similar routine. My Saturday morning was spent lazily reading day old papers and eating a full English breakfast at the EFI café in Slim Lines, and in the afternoon I sat down at my desk in the KIKPC building, the Premier League football on the TV with the volume turned down, writing my weekly report. I was continuing to draw attention to the developing situation in the KPC and I quickly recognised that through my reports I had a degree of influence over the KFOR leadership. I was also providing a continuous flow of information to KFOR's immediate higher headquarters in Naples.

I had also heard from Alexandra who had suggested I meet her, and some of her colleagues, in 'Traffic', a bar downtown, the following evening. On the Sunday afternoon, after taking longer than normal to complete my report and send it out to my distribution list, I grabbed my coat and drove into town. 'Traffic' was possibly one of the smallest bars I had ever visited. Tucked away off the main street in Pristina, I almost missed it. In an intimate atmosphere, the bar was only large enough for about 15 people squeezed together, standing body to body, with the music booming out of the speakers, controlled by a laptop in the corner of the room. With cigarette smoke thick enough to distort my vision, I met up again with Alexandra and two of her friends; Rob and Elizabeth. I was pleased to be able to meet Alexandra's friends. Rob, a Brit, had been Agim Çeku's policy advisor during his spell as Prime Minister. It was a fun way to end an unusually sociable weekend, but I was relieved to be out of the bar by the end of the evening, to breathe some relatively fresh air and give my eyes a break. The smoking ban had been in force for over a year in the UK and going to bars in Kosovo was still very difficult to get used to.

Finally, the long-planned meeting between Lieutenant General Selimi and the KFOR Commander, Lieutenant General Gay, at a KPC-supported humanitarian project, had arrived. Together with Major Ionata, I had managed to identify a suitable location south of Pristina where the local KPC personnel were building a medical facility. It was a typical example of how the KPC was supporting the local community, supported, as necessary, by KFOR. The location was in open ground just off the main highway, with plenty of room to park General Gay's convoy of vehicles. It was the ideal location for security and the building under construction offered a good photo opportunity for the media who had been informed in advance about the visit. On the morning of the meeting, Simi and I were driven by Kasper to a local café about a kilometre away from the project site so we could meet up in advance with Brigadier Ilazi, the local protection zone commander. General Selimi, was travelling in his vehicle behind us.

After pulling into the dusty car park, we climbed out of our vehicles and entered the café where Ilazi was waiting for us. We all shook hands and the atmosphere was very positive as we sat down, watched closely by a young waiter, clearly nervous at the thought of looking after the KPC Commander. At 10.24am I drank my earliest raki yet. Selimi had two. It was going to be one of those days. We soon headed off to make sure everything was in place.

The aim was to bring the two organisations together, a show of unity, and to give the national press a good news story. Articles about the KPC's striking personnel, the lack of transparency of the KSF recruiting process, and KFOR indifference towards the media, had generated a febrile atmosphere which I was trying to address through a positive news story. Of course, the risk was that Gay would not talk to the media again but I hoped KFOR had learned their lesson from the last time the two men had met at the KPC HQ. At least I knew Selimi would take the opportunity to address the press, who were joined by the US Commander of the local KFOR Multi-National Task Force and a crowd of local children, who were fascinated by the 'circus' that had come to town.

It was a high-profile event and I wanted to make sure it went well. So when Selimi spoke to the assembled media, he forgot what I had suggested he say. It was either the second raki taking effect or he had planned a different speech from the beginning. In fact, General Selimi took the opportunity, in front of the media and with the KFOR Commander looking on, to declare that he would do what he had promised the protesters in Vrani Do by representing their interests with the Government. Speaking directly to the cameras, he announced that he was going to write to the PM and the President to get the pension law changed, explaining the concerns of the KPC. After listening to Simi's translation of Selimi's speech, I wondered how this would go down with Major General Caplin in particular, who had been working extremely hard on behalf of the KPC over the pension law.

Whilst this was great copy for the media, it was likely to confuse an already inaccurate depiction of what was going on within the KPC – KSF process. And where was KFOR's communications team? At least they could not be faulted for their consistency; they were absent and continued to give the impression of wanting as little to do with the 'New Tasks' as possible. Whilst KFOR's reticence to get involved was evident, and its reluctance to design and deliver an effective communications campaign was a symptom of this, I couldn't connect the dots regarding General Gay's motivations for pursuing this path. So I let them drift over me, unsure what was going on but frustrated that KFOR was not putting the Kosovans at the heart of the 'New Tasks' transition.

Driving back to Pristina from the visit I was very satisfied with my organisation of what was an important opportunity to maintain and build stronger relations between two key men, and their organisations. I knew that General Gay saw the 'New Tasks' as an inconvenience and wanted as little to do with them as possible. So under the circumstances, getting them both to meet at an event which offered the national media an opportunity to publish a good news story for a change about the KPC and KFOR was positive, even if Selimi had gone off script. With very different headlines to those I anticipated, at least General Selimi, who had spoken directly to the KPC personnel, had appreciated my efforts and the protestors at Vrani Do would see their commander fighting their corner.

The event had also allowed me to have a 20-minute chat to a Kosovan journalist who had been following the KPC de-activation story closely. Zija Miftari was from the newspaper 'Kohe Ditore' and approached me once the impromptu press conference had finished.

He introduced himself and explained that he was intrigued about my role in what was happening with the KPC. He said that he always saw me at the side of Selimi like some Machiavellian figure, organising and pulling strings behind the scenes. To an extent he was right. I had been sitting alongside Selimi in a number of high-profile meetings that the national press had covered; my appearance on the evening news was becoming a regular occurrence. He revealed that my nickname amongst the journalists was the 'shadow'. Zija was evidently interested in what was happening so I explained some of the key facts about the process, something that no other organisation in Kosovo had done to date. The following day I noted that he had used the material I had passed on to him, so at least there was some truth finally being put out there. I remained frustrated by KFOR's media operations position though, and the lack of an information campaign was reaching crisis point.

Reflecting on the issue on my way back to Pristina, my thoughts were interrupted when I received a phone call from Alexandra. During my walking tour around Pristina with my camera weeks before, I had taken a photograph of a boy playing football in the street with some friends, celebrating scoring a goal against a wall which had the Vetevendosje graffiti scrawled across it. I had sent the picture to Alexandra. It was not only a good image, I knew she would appreciate its significance. There was something quite dramatic about the message the picture conveyed. I had completely forgotten about sending the picture to her, so when I answered the call I was not quite expecting the news that she delivered. Alexandra explained that when she returned from her 6-week break and checked her emails, she had shared the image within the organisation, as I would have expected. However, someone in the organisation's communications team had decided to use the image in Vetevendosje's weekly supplement which always appeared on a Monday in Kosovo's most read daily newspaper. I didn't know what to say; a photograph that had been taken by a British Army Officer, in a NATO role, serving in KFOR, had been published in a national newspaper by an organisation opposed to KFOR's mandate in Kosovo. I was both absolutely flattered to know that it was in print, but also a little worried. I immediately asked her whether the picture was attributed to me; if it had been I may as well have driven directly to the airport.

I wasn't cross with Alexandra at all even though she apologised; there was nothing she or I could do. My only concern had been whether my name was in any way associated with the image. That could have been quite difficult to explain away, as having any contact with someone from within Vetevendosje would have been a serious issue for KFOR's commanders to deal with, god-daughter's aunt or not. To have been promoting Vetevendosje's message, however unintentionally, would have ended my tour pretty quickly. I couldn't help but laugh. To many in the international community, Vetevendosje was a movement that was both unpredictable and to be managed very carefully. Their message was uncompromising, graffiti ubiquitous. And their ability to mobilise anti-establishment crowds thousands strong was well known. So on the phone Alexandra assured me that my name would never be associated with the image and it would remain entirely anonymous.

Once back in Pristina I went straight to the nearest newsagents and bought several copies. And there it was, in full colour. The surreal nature of the incident brought a smile to my face.

As soon as I returned to Film City I knew I needed to arrange a visit to see Major General Caplin, not only to debrief him about Selimi's now very public statement on the pension law, but on an intriguing conversation I had shared with the KFOR Chief of Media

Operations the previous week.

My meetings with Colonel Adriano Graziani were becoming fairly predictable. From my first encounter with him, when he questioned me over the local media reporting of the KFOR Commander's visit to the KPC headquarters and his dismissive attitude to the journalists present, I had been pretty consistent in my position. NATO's direction to be reactive rather than proactively setting the media agenda was starting to seriously undermine the KPC-KSF process. The national Kosovan media were feeding off renegade KPC officers, giving them airtime and notoriety, reporting untruths and false information, and much of it was entirely unnecessary. NATO's direction to KFOR resulted in daily headlines criticising the whole process, and all of the major stakeholders involved, including KFOR. Every time I went to see Colonel Graziani, whom I liked as a fellow officer, I urged him to go back to Brussels to challenge the order and to get on the front foot; to start setting the news agenda. It would have been easy to fix within a few days. But the underlying political sensitivity surrounding the KPC and the KSF prevented a change of policy direction. And it was a mistake.

So when I went to see Colonel Graziani towards the end of October, fresh from meeting Suma on the Macedonian border, and after addressing the packed town hall meeting in Vrani Do with the Protection Zone 5 protestors, I was in no mood to compromise. It was clear to me that we needed to do something, even if it meant circumventing the direction issued by NATO headquarters. The inaccurate and aggressive headlines was clearly having an effect on Graziani. The NATO and KFOR brands were being damaged by half-truths, inconsistency and inaction. This was not only an issue in Pristina, this was an issue in KFOR's higher headquarters in Naples.

Graziani sat in his chair and asked me what we could do about the increasingly difficult situation. I was honest, I told him that we needed to create a backchannel into the media so that we could brief a respected journalist who could then put the truth into the public domain. At least, our version of the truth. He was surprisingly open to my idea and seemed interested. I explained that I knew someone who could do it, and we might also want to consider someone more senior doing something similar. But I also told him that I would not initiate any contact with a journalist until I saw the direction written down in an email from KFOR headquarters. He agreed that he would try to obtain this clearance to brief the media. I left him in his chair and walked out into the cold autumnal evening, knowing that I had initiated a chain of events that would end up going in any number of directions.

Major General Caplin was always open and willing to meet me. I didn't ask him for his time very often but, when he received a message from me, he normally guessed that it was serious enough to clear his diary. I drove over to his apartment and, over a cup of tea, I explained Selimi's statement to the press and my very interesting conversation the week before with Graziani. Caplin was understandably unhappy about Selimi's plea about the pension law, particularly knowing how he had been steering it gently through Kosovo's Parliament. However, with letters already dispatched to the President and Prime Minister, his hands were tied. I then outlined my conversation with Graziani about the potential plan to speak to the media. The idea of establishing a backchannel with a respected journalist certainly piqued his interest. Without a moment's hesitation Caplin agreed to play his part in the initiative, with the likely senior journalist being sourced and verified by Simi before making the connection with Major General Caplin.

I explained to Simi what might be happening and that Major

General Caplin and I needed his help. The risk to both of us was clear if this was to go ahead, so we needed to know that the journalists would be discreet and we trusted Simi's judgment. I already thought I had found a suitable journalist, but we needed someone for Caplin. Of course neither journalist would know about the other but the potential for the whole thing to blow up in our faces was very real. All I had to do was wait for the go-ahead from Colonel Graziani before we initiated the plan.

There was no doubt in my mind that my role in influencing this process had taken a step into the unknown, but something had to be done and I was willing to commit to this venture. Following the set-piece meeting at the humanitarian project between General Selimi and General Gay earlier that week, I was already pretty sure whom I was going to approach, assuming Simi was also in agreement. My time working as a foreign correspondent for Jane's Defence Weekly during a sabbatical had made me realise the value of having officials inside Government organisations who were willing to brief off the record. This situation was no different even if the shoe was on the other foot. The question remained whether KFOR would actually authorise it. And I had my doubts.

Five days after I had written my email to Colonel Graziani, asking for an update and referring to the 'outcome from our meeting' the previous week, I received a reply. Graziani, referring to our 'project', said that we had the go-ahead and he wanted to know who the journalist was and what I planned to say. I outlined my thoughts and he replied with comments and a fresh set of information he wanted to put into the public domain. It seemed an extraordinary way to do business for the world's foremost military alliance.

In the absence of any other solution, I agreed to brief a journalist on NATO's plan for the stand down of the KPC, and the creation of the KSF, all executed under KFOR's 'supervision'. I had no idea who Graziani had cleared this unusual course of action with in KFOR HQ and I did not care; I had an email from him giving me the green light. Caplin was keen to be involved as he also saw the strategic value in getting some balance to the media's reporting. With authority from Graziani, confirmation of the two journalists to be approached via Simi, the stage was set and the backchannel was established. Finally, in the absence of anything formal from KFOR, the opportunity to bring some accurate reporting was in reach.

Leaving aside the backchannel arrangements, General Selimi's conscious decision to side with the KPC personnel, who were publicly citing their concerns over their future conditions, was setting hares running. However, the pension law was not a veteran's benefits law and Selimi's bold statement to KPC personnel to get it changed was not grounded in reality. The pension law was enjoying support from the wider International Community and trying to introduce additional concessions at such a late stage was unlikely to be successful. Major General Caplin and the United Nations Development Programme representative, John Durrance, charged with overseeing the resettlement campaign for KPC personnel with representatives from a local employment agency APPK, had initiated a series of country-wide briefings for the KPC personnel. The briefings explained in clear terms what was on offer and what their options would be under a range of different circumstances. Even though Caplin had explained this to Selimi during one of their recent weekly meetings, Selimi's decision to stand with the KPC members was high risk. He had already initiated a series of meetings with Government Ministers to discuss improving the conditions for KPC personnel not selected for the KSF. He was driving this agenda forward and was receiving a positive response from the country's politicians.

At the end of an extraordinary week, we were called to a meeting in the Prime Minister's office to discuss this and other KPC stand down issues. Lieutenant General Selimi, Major General Nick Caplin and the Minister for the KSF, Fehmi Mujota, were present. I sat quietly with Simi at my side. With much of the meeting in English, Hashim Thaçi explained that the overall process would be a success, but Minister Mujota was worried that someone political was pushing people 'in the direction of trouble'. Caplin spoke about the resettlement efforts that were in train and the subject of a final KPC parade was raised, a subject that had been discussed several times in the KPC HQ in the days leading up to this meeting. Selimi was becoming less enthusiastic with the idea of marching through the city when so many KPC personnel were likely to be losing their livelihoods. A scaled down parade was suggested but the PM was adamant; there would be no parade.

The conversation then returned to the subject of the protestors and their call for better benefits. Selimi was true to his word and raised the issue with Thaçi. He explained that each ministry should look at what could be offered to KPC personnel and Mujota was given the action to organise an inter-ministerial meeting where these issues would be discussed. Thaçi also said that he would make a statement, supporting the initiative, when there was something to say. Knowing how Lieutenant Colonel Potera in Protection Zone 5 had pressed General Rama and later General Selimi to seek concessions, in such a disrespectful and belligerent manner, it was all credit to Selimi that he had managed to get the issue raised at the highest level within a few days. And after talking to Selimi, Caplin was satisfied that the pension law and the additional benefits being called for by the protestors were complimentary issues.

With only days to go before the first ever commander of the KSF was due to be formally announced by the Prime Minister, with the process needing a rubber stamp endorsement from the President, it was a two-horse race. Even though General Rama also qualified to be considered for the position, he would be much more effective as the new Land Forces Commander, a hands-on operational role. In my mind, Selimi's position appeared to be strong through his obviously close working relationship with the country's Prime Minister.

As we were getting up and saying our goodbyes, I asked the Prime Minster about the framed picture of the 'Newborn' statue on the wall of his office. Surprised to have been asked, he explained that it had been signed by the people involved in its design and construction. It felt entirely normal to be speaking to him and the image gave me an idea for my own leaving gift at the end of my tour.

As we walked out of the Parliament Building, we were all conscious that the decision to appoint the new Commander of the KSF was imminent.

CHAPTER SEVEN

'Backchannels'

After a few months in the country I had managed to establish contact with a broad range of actors, all of whom had a stake in the future shape of Kosovo's security institutions. Former political leaders and ex-members of the KPC were particularly passionate about the stand down of the KPC, an organisation feted by Kosovo's ethnic Albanian population. That the KPC's dignified closure should now be put at risk by the very people who had earned its reputation, was a clear sign of the emotions running through its personnel. The KPC was soon going to be confined to the history books and the Balkans' newest security organisation was about to be born, all under the watchful but not entirely helpful eye of KFOR. The lack of leadership by KFOR's commanders, the actions of KPC personnel who were feeling abandoned, and the media's portrayal of a chaotic transition between the KPC and the KSF, with daily inaccurate and unhelpful reporting, had created a toxic atmosphere which needed a response; but it was going to be an unorthodox one.

I had proposed to KFOR's Media Operations Chief that I should create a backchannel into the media. I had also suggested that Major General Nick Caplin, the UN's most senior military representative, create a similar relationship, by engaging with a senior and respected journalist in parallel with my efforts to get the media's reporting more balanced. Life had become interesting.

However it was the actions of the Protection Zone 5 protestors that I was very concerned about. Their lack of support for the stand down plan, an order drafted by General Rama and endorsed by KFOR, was unhelpful. Kosovo's political elite had also made their positions clear to me over what should happen to the KSF. Agim Çeku wanted to see the KSF join NATO and become a net contributor of security rather than a net consumer. He had asked me to write some notes for him so that he could brief the media on the whole process from an informed position. Ramush Haradinaj, who had entertained me with brandy and cigars in his office had forcibly expressed his views about the future shape and size of the KSF. I was building a broad picture of opinions which enabled me to see the looming crisis from a different perspective.

When I heard whispers that the Protection Zone 5 protestors were acting on the orders of a political figure, using the crisis to discredit the Government, I knew I needed to have a private meeting with a former Prime Minister of Kosovo, a man whose physical presence was enough to make most people feel intimidated. I didn't dare believe the rumour to be true.

It was suggested to me that Ramush Haradinaj was somehow getting involved in the KPC stand down protests in order to score political points. I had come to this conclusion based on what was being fed back to me by Simi, who in turn had heard rumours about political involvement behind the scenes. With an unshakeable faith in Simi's role as my confidante, and with complete trust in his judgment, I knew had to act.

Fresh from the Protection Zone 5 meeting with General Selimi, I asked Simi to make the arrangements for me to see Haradinaj at his political party offices in Pristina where I had met him a few weeks earlier. He was a busy politician and the first time I met him I had waited a couple of weeks before time was found in his diary for an office call. It was different this time. Within the hour Simi told me that Ramush Haradinaj would see us later that morning. I was very surprised to say the least; the speed of the arrangements suggested to me that he also wanted to give me his view of the deteriorating situation. He must also have realised that I also had something to say to him. The scene was set for the most uncomfortable 30 minutes of my life.

As we pulled up, I jumped down from the vehicle and crossed the pavement. I was greeted by one of Haradinaj's aides waiting at the entrance of the building. With Simi by my side, I walked up the wide stairs and entered the AAK's party offices. I was led along the corridor and shown into the familiar reception room, with sofas along both sides and an ornate fireplace on the wall at the end acting as a centre piece. Once more I was offered a cigar, a strong drink and some water. This visit felt different though; I knew I was going to be raising some uncomfortable issues about the tense situation across the country, in particular about Lieutenant Colonel Potera and his crowd in Protection Zone 5. It didn't feel right to me for politicians to be indulging in scoring points, if that was happening, when the fate of the KPC's legacy was at stake. I didn't know whether my hunch was correct, but seeing Haradinaj face to face seemed as good a way as any to find out. Simi remained sitting next to me on the sofa, even though this conversation was going to be in English. I sat quietly, all small talk extinguished, running through my mind what I was going to say. I wanted to get across to Haradinaj that the dignity of the KPC was under threat; that public opinion was changing; that the organisation was being seen in a different light by the international community; and the need to address this behaviour was crucial if the security transition between the KPC and the KSF was going to be completed under the right circumstances. In short, I needed Haradinaj's help in getting the process back on track. What I didn't need were KPC personnel going on strike and appearing on TV every night.

I didn't have to wait long before Ramush Haradinaj swept into the room. He was as ebullient as ever, walking straight over to me, pumping my hand when we greeted each other, looking me in the eye as if trying to second guess what I was going to say, and welcoming Simi like a long lost friend. I liked Ramush Haradinaj very much, he was a strong character and he remained extremely important to the future of Kosovo. But I was convinced he could stop some of the shenanigans that were undermining the KPC stand down plan, and I wanted him to exert his influence to that effect. Now wasn't the time for accusations; now was the time for cooperation.

He quickly asked me why I wanted to see him, explaining that he had sympathy with the KPC, declaring that the KSF, rather than being capped at 2,500 members, should be much larger. I had heard it all before but he was on a roll; he was not listening and he wanted to make his point, to be sure I was completely clear about his priorities. We were only a few feet apart but at that moment it felt like we were discussing different events. Even though he was on home ground, reassured by the familiarity of his surroundings, I was not going to sit quietly. I spoke about my concerns but was soon interrupted by Haradinaj. I re-entered the conversation, interrupting my way back into his flow, the volume increasing as we sparred over a whole range of related issues. We had initially been sitting down to discuss these issues but without any understanding how it happened, we were standing together, face to face, chin to chin, talking over each other, making our points heard. It was an extremely uncomfortable exchange, with no quarter offered or given from either side. Simi was also energised, joining the debate on certain issues. It felt as if I was fighting the whole of Kosovo at times, but Haradinaj was soon done, he had delivered his message, he had listened at times to what I had said, and there was nothing more to add. As quickly as the heat had left the conversation, the smile returned to his face, the charm re-engaged, his tone philosophical and measured. We both relaxed, we laughed and once more we shook hands, the other hand gripping the opposite shoulder as a sign of camaraderie; it felt as if a tenuous bond had been established between us. Haradinaj left the room and his lieutenant re-appeared to show us out and back down to the street. I looked around but to be honest, I didn't care who saw me. I had taken a risk and I felt that it had been worth it. My mind was racing as I opened my door. Simi slipped into the driving seat and we edged our way back into Pristina's thick traffic. I reflected on the meeting as we weaved our way through the city. It had been one of the most challenging face-to-face meetings I had ever experienced, but I was glad that I had taken the initiative to see him, to put my argument across, albeit without much sense that Haradinaj had heard me.

The green light from Colonel Graziani to establish a backchannel to a couple of newspaper reporters was a significant undeclared shift in policy for KFOR. It had been arranged for me to see Zija Miftari from 'Koha Ditore', and for Major General Caplin to meet Ali Cenaj from 'Zeri'. Caplin, who was imminently heading out of office to hold a series of roadshows across the country for KPC personnel, wasted no time in setting up a meeting. I sent Simi to join him so that the discussion would flow; Major General Caplin had total trust in

Simi, as I did. Via Simi we also contacted Zija Miftari and suggested we meet as soon as possible. He lived in Mitrovice and therefore was not always in Pristina, so my meeting with him was not going to be immediate. Zija seemed genuinely surprised at the approach.

The work behind the scenes to keep the KPC–KSF process on track was not simply a UK effort. I had grown close to the US Assistant Defence Attaché, Lieutenant Colonel Terry Anderson. The US had a major stake in the establishment of the KSF and they were significant financial donors to two Trust Funds established by NATO to assist with both the stand down of the KPC and the stand up of the KSF. The two funds were designed to allow the international community to make a material difference to Kosovo's fortunes and to allow the dignified closure of the KPC happen with sufficient support in place for those who were unsuccessful, funded by international donations. Whilst the KPC fund was very quickly over-subscribed, the same could not be said for the KSF trust fund, which suffered a political backlash from countries that did not recognise the newly independent sovereign state.

The US had made many pledges of support and wanted to see the inter-dependent processes go as smoothly as possible. As usual, the US were pragmatic and very much focused on ensuring they achieved their desired outcome. Terry and I had become friends, we had shared some enjoyable evenings out together with others and we both wanted to make sure the Kosovans with whom we worked were treated with respect. Terry's visits to the KPC headquarters were regular and we spoke often, avoiding any misunderstandings about motives and priorities. And it was true to say that my access into the heart of the KPC, and my ability to influence behaviours, was an envied position by those in country who also wanted to see success. However, there were NATO members who appeared to be actively obstructing the dignified closure of Kosovo's civil emergency organisation in favour of their own national priorities. The politically correct nature of KFOR was influenced by the non-recognising countries serving in Kosovo, which only harmed the Kosovans and those of us who were fully committed to the 'New Tasks', although we were in the minority. I hadn't seen or heard anything to dispel the feeling that some representatives were actively slowing down KSF related business in KFOR HQ. And the behaviour of KFOR's leadership, consistently making life as difficult as possible for the Kosovans, remained a mystery, as did their motivations.

It was during a discussion one evening that Terry suggested that he and I go to Protection Zone 5 to talk to the personnel there, to try to make them see things without their chain of command present. We didn't hold out much hope of getting an instant response, but we felt that we had to do something and Terry was probably under a degree of pressure from within his embassy team to make it clear to those KPC members refusing to work that the US was watching carefully. We talked through our approach and I cleared it with the KPC leadership. We made the arrangements through Simi and drove in convoy to the location, armed only with our goodwill and collective experience. Driving to Vrani Do with Kasper, my new driver, I felt confident that we would be able to set out the wider implications of their actions in an objective way. We were greeted at the entrance and invited into a small office rather than the larger conference room. There were only a handful of the KPC personnel who had joined the meeting. The room wasn't large enough for everyone, and with all the chairs taken, others stood leaning against the walls listening to what we had to say. At least nobody lit a cigarette. Terry was keen to demonstrate his solidarity with the KPC and we were listened to politely and with respect. We explained the efforts going into making things better for the KPC through the initiative to bring ministries together. We talked about the pension law and its adherence to international norms. And we covered the impact of their actions and the damage to their reputation. After an hour or so we were invited by Lieutenant Colonel Potera into his office for a coffee, on his own, where we moved away from the core purpose of our visit, speaking about less contentious issues in general. We were all Lieutenant Colonels after all. We eventually headed for the exit and left them to their own thoughts. I had a feeling our words had fallen on deaf ears.

The inter-ministerial meeting on the KPC, directed to be set up by the Prime Minister during our last visit to his office, and convened by the Minister for the KSF, had finally been held. It had brought together all the ministries to discuss additional concessions and benefits for KPC personnel who were unsuccessful in joining the KSF. With every key ministry represented, albeit many turned up late, the stage was set to explore the options. The issue of improved benefits for KPC personnel who were not selected for the KSF was now finally moving forward. The meeting was followed by a press conference by Caplin, Selimi and Mujota. The need to investigate better conditions for KPC personnel was delicately de-linked from the demands of the protestors by Caplin. I even had a sense that the threat of further disruption by the Protection Zone 5 personnel was waning and my visit to Ramush Haradinaj had achieved the desired effect. I could not have been more wrong.

With the announcement of the new Commander of the KSF due in only a few days' time on Friday 7th November, the key stakeholders met for what became known as the first Renaissance 2 dinner. General Selimi had already dined with General Gay in Film City earlier in the week, a dinner also attended by Agim Çeku, the former

PM whom I had met a couple of weeks earlier. These long days were tiring for General Selimi but getting the key decision makers together was vital for a shared understanding and awareness of the most important issues facing the KPC and KSF. So General Selimi was once again out in the evening, this time with Major General Caplin, Brigadier Di Luzio, General Rama, Colonel Stuart Roberts, Dr Syla, the Acting Private Secretary to the Minister for the KSF, Lieutenant Colonel Mark Wentworth from Caplin's office, along with Simi and I. We were squeezed around a large table tucked away towards the back of the restaurant that was beginning to play such an important part in Kosovo's security sector transition agenda. It was always good to get the key players looking each other in the eye in a more relaxed environment.

The agenda included the plan for the sequence of events during the period in December when the KPC would essentially be sent home pending their return to work in the New Year, some as members of the new Kosovo Security Force. The imminent selection of the KSF commander was also discussed, along with a contentious decision to force the KPC's Colonels and above to attend a 5-day training course that week, delivered by Italian KFOR troops, in the KPC's Training and Doctrine Command building in Pristina.

With such high levels of discontent in each of the protection zones across the country, the idea of decapitating the KPC, even for a week, and bringing senior leaders together in one place was considered unwise by the protection zone commanders in particular. Leaving the KPC members to the mercy of individuals who wanted to cause problems was a recipe for disaster, and this point had been made to KFOR. The protection zone commanders had been forced to leave their commands at exactly the time when they were needed most. It had been decided that the training must go ahead even though the timeframe to complete every aspect of closing the KPC and standing up the KSF was extremely tight. It was an ill-advised forced absence that the KPC's commanders could have done without.

As if to reinforce the folly of this decision, midway through the meal General Rama received a phone call from General Halimi, the commander of Protection Zone 4, located at the heart of the divided town of Mitrovice. After the day's training he had returned to his unit in the north. Separated by the River Ibar, with mainly ethnic Serbs living to the north and ethnic Albanians to the south, the city had seen many serious flashpoints over the years. The river had at times become a *de facto* internal border between the Belgrade-facing Serbs in the north and the rest of Kosovo. Rama was told that the KPC members were about to walk out, in a similar fashion to those at Vrani Do. He leaned across to me and said in his best English, 'Tomorrow we go to Mitrovice.'

The next morning Kasper picked me up, we collected Simi and then met up with General Rama on the road to the north of Pristina. In two cars we headed off to Mitrovice, still unsure exactly what we were going to find. I had been to Mitrovice early in my tour with General Rama, when we had relayed a message to a member of the KPC whose son was suspected of plotting a sectarian attack. That attack never took place and I was hoping that the KPC personnel, who were gathering in the KPC's building in the centre of Mitrovice as we were driving, were also open to listening. I had a sense of *déjà vu* following my repeated engagements with the Protection Zone 5 personnel and Major Rufki Suma in the south. The arguments were likely to be very similar so, to an extent, we had rehearsed the lines we needed to take. General Rama was also now used to this level of dissatisfaction.

Tensions were always going to run hot in Mitrovice and it

appeared that it was reaching boiling point. After the edgy confrontation with Lieutenant Colonel Potera and his men at Vrani Do, I was ready for anything. I was keen to see the actual levels of discord that existed in the KPC's northern protection zone. If serious trouble broke out in Mitrovice, the potential for it to become complicated and to escalate rapidly into an inter-ethnic issue, was never far away. Serbia had clearly stated its opposition to the formation of the KSF; I sensed that any break down of discipline in Mitrovice could be exploited by Belgrade-supporting local Serbs.

Pulling into the carpark just across the road from the relatively narrow River Ibar, I walked up the steps into the KPC building, opening the glass doors into an atmosphere full of tension. We walked straight through the entrance hall, saying good morning in Albanian to those KPC members hanging around, and entered a large hall with a high ceiling, darkened by thick curtains drawn across sash windows that lined the walls and stretched up to the ceiling. The air was thick with suspicion, mistrust and cigarette smoke. General Rama made his way through the lines of KPC personnel, his footsteps echoing off the wooden floor, as the room became quiet. There must have been between 100 and 150 KPC personnel, all packed together in a horse-shoe shape waiting for Rama. General Rama was a respected leader and as he walked through the lines to reach the centre, he was quietly greeted by many of the men with a handshake here and personal comment there. General Rama addressed the men and started talking about their concerns as he saw them. I took up post behind him, next to Simi, looking around the room watching people's facial reactions to what was being said. Rama spoke at length.

There was some ignorance in the hall from some of the members; ignorance that was a direct result of a lack of a proactive information campaign by KFOR. The wider KPC membership had, at various times, all been invited to Ferizaj to undergo an assessment which included an interview, an intelligence test, a rudimentary medical and some basic physical assessments. There was a sense that even this activity, this hoop that the KPC personnel who had applied to the KSF were expected to jump through, was not being managed well. They had a point; the intelligence test that had been used as part of the selection process had already been used in earlier training courses provided by KFOR for the KPC. Whilst this was spotted early on by an honest KPC attendee, and the material was changed, the damage was already done. The integrity of the whole process was under enormous scrutiny and any slip or perceived error was seized upon by the KPC rank and file as another example of poor organisation. Credibility was everything in the Balkans, and KFOR was struggling to achieve even a minimum acceptable level of respect over the whole process.

Throughout General Rama's speech Simi was by my side, steering me through the conversation. After about 30 minutes the room seemed to go quiet. I was concentrating on what Simi was saying to me. I looked up and noticed that Rama had stopped talking and was looking at me. Simi then quietly explained that Rama wanted me to step in. Rama was inviting me to address his men. His arm gesture seemed to be saying: go ahead, Ade, I am done here, please, take the floor, have a talk with them and try to get them to see sense.

Everyone's eyes were on me. Feeling those familiar butterflies awake in my stomach, I stepped forward through the crowd into the eye of the storm, turning to look at everyone assembled in front of me. Many of the men had never met me before but knew the British LNO and our shared history. I took a deep breath and started talking. What I said, translated through Simi, seemed to make perfect sense to me. The men had an institutional respect for the LNO and I hoped they would at least accept some of my arguments. However there was an unsettling lack of reaction; perhaps they were internalising what I was saying, perhaps they entirely disagreed with my points, perhaps they were just so tired of being talked at over this issue that they couldn't wait to get out of the building. Whatever their thoughts they were impeccably polite with me and listened to every word in silence. By now my argument was as much about protecting the reputation of the KPC as anything else, and trying to deal with some of the ignorance that was present in the room over the technicalities of the whole process.

When I had said my bit, I turned to Rama who was ready to re-engage. He finished the meeting reminding the men about their status in society, about their behaviour and about their need to accept what was happening, emphasising that fighting it would bring no benefit to anyone. As the meeting broke up, there was a little more back slapping and talk between the men, but it was not enthusiastic and looked more like the last vestiges of energy for the fight had dissipated; it looked to me like they were resigned to their fate.

It must have been a strange situation for some of the men, seeing a British Officer stand in front of them to offer an opinion on a situation that had completely enveloped their lives. It was difficult not to be sympathetic. They were entering a very uncertain period. They had families, children, houses to pay for and they did not know whether they would be wearing the uniform of the KSF or queueing up to find out whether their skills would help them get a job as a civilian. They lived in a country that was not renowned for its job opportunities. The odds were stacked against them and they were worried. I made sure I kept this at the forefront of my mind at every turn. The 'New Tasks' were an inherently human process. This was lost on so many in KFOR. With many international military personnel ready to treat the KPC with a lack of respect; I was certainly not going to be one of them.

After we wrapped up the meeting, I made a few phone calls and was then invited to join Rama and Halimi for lunch to discuss events. The fact that Halimi had been ordered to attend the senior officer training was in his view the reason this incident had occurred. The rigid adherence to the plan by the Italian-led NATO Training Team belied a broader misunderstanding of the human impact that the winding down of the KPC was having amongst the 2,800 members on its books. As it turned out, the men from Protection Zone 4 in Mitrovice followed our advice that morning and didn't step out of line throughout the whole process.

The battle rhythm of life in Kosovo never stopped though and I was soon heading south to Pristina to attend another meeting with General Rama, along with Colonel Stuart Roberts, Brigadier Di Luzio and a British RAF officer, Wing Commander Kim Galway from the MCAD, to discuss sequencing. With Announcement Day still fixed for 12th December, the de-activation of the KPC set for the 4th January 2009 and the establishment of the new force the next day at one minute past midnight, the period when the KPC would effectively be sent home prior to this date needed careful planning. This period, from the 10th December to 4th January, was going to be hugely sensitive because KPC personnel would find out on the 12th December whether they were going to join the KSF, whilst others would be faced with resettlement and searching for a job in a country with 40% unemployment. The ongoing stand down plan, essentially written and implemented by the KPC, was stuttering due to the protests and a growing resentment about the future. The aim of drawing all KPC vehicles and equipment into 10 centralised locations across the country, 7 of which would be used exclusively by the KSF going forward, remained the immediate priority. With vehicles and equipment centrally stored, the task of handing back KPC buildings to the local municipality was also on track and the aim was for these tasks to be completed by the 10th December, to clear the way for the Announcement Day activity on the 12th. There was no room for delay.

The interdependent nature of the stand down of the KPC and the stand up of the KSF meant success in one was predicated on success in the other. With the KPC's members preoccupied with the stand down plan, a series of KSF-related deadlines was also now looming fast. The selection of the KSF Commander in early November (the 7th) was key so that he could then sit on all subsequent selection boards scheduled in the following weeks, including the important Senior Officer Selection and Appointment Board – known as the SOSAB – on the 24th November. The remaining positions for Lieutenant Colonels and below were then going to be selected in a cascade fashion on subsequent boards. The selection boards were made up of senior KFOR officers, representatives from the International Civilian Office (ICO) and the Kosovan Government, with the boards managed by Colonel Stuart Roberts. The selection of senior appointments was also subject to confirmation from NATO's vetting team, led by the indomitable figure of Dave Finnamore, an ex-Metropolitan Policeman who had quite literally seen and done it all during his career in uniform. Dave had been leading a team of investigators who had been interviewing KPC senior officers ever since I had arrived in the country, building up a profile of each one keen to join the new force. They had pulled together information from a wide range of sources, and had made their recommendations about who was fit for employment in the KSF, and those who were not. This list was highly confidential and only a few were entitled to see it.

The stand down plan dictated that all KPC personnel would be sent home after the 10th December, therefore leading to the need for a solution to guard the vehicles and equipment being brought together from across the country into a number of centralised locations. The potential for criminal activity was evident, so a security solution needed to be found. It was clear to most of us that this duty should fall to KFOR and a single vehicle parked in front of a barracks would be sufficient deterrent against criminal activity. NATO was held in high esteem by the Kosovan population and to most observers this was a natural role for KFOR's 16,000 strong military force. KFOR were soon to have executive authority for the KPC and were meant to be supervising the KPC-KSF process. Supporting the KPC over this sensitive period was a perfect example of how they could step up to the plate and add value. However, even this task was too much for them.

I was becoming increasingly frustrated with KFOR's attitude towards the KPC. It wasn't simply the bigger issues that KFOR would routinely avoid taking a position on, but even the comparatively inconsequential details were challenged. I had organised the dinner earlier in the week on behalf of MCAD, which had brought together the key stakeholders including Brigadier Di Luzio. Everything had to be accounted for and charged to someone so I had written Di Luzio's name down as the most senior host for the meal. It would have been inappropriate to charge either Major General Caplin or Major General Rama, as they had been invited guests, and Colonel Habel was junior in rank terms to Brigadier Di Luzio.

A few days after the dinner I was called into Di Luzio's office to be told that he objected to being named as the host for the dinner. I didn't know what to say. I had to laugh; with such major issues to grapple with, Di Luzio's determination to keep any sense of responsibility for the KPC-KSF process at arm's length even extended to his expense account. This behaviour, together with a growing weariness brought on by my declining health, led me to feel more anxious than usual. I knew I had to do something to up the ante. I had to start to write much more blunt assessments for the KFOR senior leadership through my weekly reports and Major General Caplin was encouraging me to be more direct in my reporting over certain issues. Staff officers in KFOR headquarters received my reports, including the Commander and the Deputy Commander. And a copy went to several desks in KFOR's higher headquarters in Naples. When I wrote my reports I was extremely careful to retain a degree of objectivity and balance. I stated the facts and included 'comments', an interpretation on events from my own view point. On the whole this was working well. However, the question of guarding KPC locations over the period between standing down on 10th December and starting work as the KSF on 5th January was now reaching a point where KFOR had to be spurred into action.

I was also beginning to feel nerves in my stomach. It was a strange sensation and clearly reflected the fact that I was beginning to walk a very fine line between getting things done and overstepping the mark. The feeling was a physical reminder of what I had said to myself at the beginning of my tour; I needed to watch my back and make sure I covered my tracks.

However there was no way of disguising the fact that I had finally managed to meet up with the journalist following the go ahead by Colonel Graziani. We met one evening in my office at the KPC headquarters well after everyone had left for the day. The KPC HQ was often deserted by 5pm. Zija Miftari wrote for the newspaper 'Koha Ditore' and we had spoken a couple of weeks earlier when General Gay and General Selimi had met at a KPC humanitarian project. Zija was cautious but sensed that he was about to be taken into my confidence and I made it clear to him that I expected this relationship to remain discreet and below the radar. We spoke for over an hour on the lines that Colonel Graziani had agreed with me, as well as providing much more context that he hadn't. I wanted Zija to write an accurate article, I needed the truth to be put out into the public domain. With Major General Nick Caplin having discussed matters with Ali Cenaj, a senior journalist from a rival newspaper a few days earlier, I was confident that we would at least start to provide some balance to the media's reporting.

Being more direct over the issue of guarding KPC equipment and vehicles, my report had immediately caught the attention of the French KFOR Deputy Commander, General Stolz, who was pragmatic and supportive but who was very clearly not in charge. His Military Assistant, Eric, had been to Kosovo before and he soon became a friend. He knew what my role entailed and he often smiled at me as I metaphorically navigated the corridors of the KFOR headquarters building. General Stolz asked to see me on the Monday morning, and in that meeting he agreed that KFOR should provide the security for the KPC locations during the period in question. It was a relief that someone had finally demonstrated some pragmatism. I was pleased. I knew that Major General Nick Caplin had written to the KFOR Chief of Staff, Brigadier General Berger, to make the case for KFOR to be involved in guarding the locations, so my report had struck a chord more broadly within KFOR's leadership at just the right time. I also felt that Lieutenant General Selimi, as the head of the KPC, should express his view on the matter and had suggested to him that he wrote to Lieutenant General Gay, the KFOR Commander, to express his concern that the barrack locations would be vulnerable over this crucial period after Announcement Day. Selimi had agreed and asked me to draft some words. I had given him the essence of the letter which he then finished off. It was important to make sure that despite my input, the letter still needed to be written in a way to suggest it had been Selimi's own effort. I didn't want Di Luzio thinking I was doing anything but sitting quietly in the corner of the KPC HQ, mutely watching events take shape.

I had a regular meeting with Di Luzio in his role as the Deputy Chief of Staff leading the MCAD. They were often fairly harmless exchanges, mainly because I never really got the impression that he knew what I was doing. He seemed focused on avoiding all personal responsibility for anything to do with the KPC and KSF. This particular meeting did not follow the normal pattern and when he produced a copy of my report, he insisted that KFOR would not provide any security of the KPC barracks over the Christmas period, which coincided with the stand down of the KPC personnel. It was not what I expected him to say and it was at odds with General Stolz's position. Di Luzio insinuated that only the NATO Commander in Naples could order that to happen; it appeared to be another example of Di Luzio doing his best to avoid making a difficult decision. In fact, I learned that the instigator of KFOR's new position was the Chief of Staff, General Berger. He had interpreted an order from Joint Forces Command in Naples, commanded by Admiral Fitzgerald, as the justification for KFOR's position over guarding.

The order that had come out of Naples was to 'unfix' KFOR's Multi National Task Forces that were variously located around the country, broadly in the same areas as the KPC's protection zones. The intent to 'unfix' KFOR's 16,000 forces related to their fairly static role patrolling their areas of responsibility, perhaps with half an eye on drawing down the numbers deployed across the country. However, General Berger applied his higher commander's intent in the most literal way possible. He justified the reversal of General Stoltz's position by arguing that parking a static KFOR vehicle in front of KPC locations whilst they had stood down, to act as a deterrent against potential theft of equipment and vehicles, was in direct conflict with the 'unfix' intent coming out of Naples. KFOR also insisted they were the third responders behind the Kosovo Police and the UN. Without KFOR there was no clear alternative solution.

Not for the first time, I found myself bewildered by KFOR's reticence to contribute to the security transition that was happening under their noses and questioning whose side they were actually on. I was beginning to feel the pressure but, as ever, an opportunity to let off steam was never too far away. I met up with Terry Anderson to have dinner at an excellent restaurant in Pristina called 'Rrons', after which we headed to 'Sokoli e Mirusha', a jazz bar owned by Adrian Koci, someone I had met during our Halloween celebrations a few weeks earlier. Getting together with friends was the only escape I had from the madness that I faced on a daily basis from KFOR.

My own sense of self-preservation remained strong though and by widening my network I was hopefully strengthening my influence at the heart of the KPC's drawdown. It was at this time that I was also asked to brief the UK's Ambassador, Andy Sparkes. He was not at all surprised by what I told him and he requested more regular briefings from me in the future.

The noise being made by Potera and his fellow agitators in Vrani Do had not died down, despite Selimi's intervention on their behalf. Rama was again dispatched with me to speak to them, to personally relay the level of commitment being shown by the Government to find ways to increase the benefits for those unsuccessful KPC personnel. By now I was thoroughly fed up of their moaning. The Government was acting; Potera and his fellow protestors had been granted a personal meeting with the Minister for the KSF without

Selimi or Rama's knowledge. And, with so little time before the KPC was de-activated, there really wasn't anything else that anyone could do about their blatant undermining of the KPC Commander's authority. I had lost count of how many times I had walked through the doors of their KPC building in the last few weeks. This time Rama and I were sitting in a smaller office, again full of rancid smoke. It was uncomfortable and actually difficult to breathe. I knew I had another meeting to attend in KFOR headquarters so, after showing my face, I soon excused myself and left.

I was glad to have had an excuse to get out of that room; I left Rama to exercise restraint and manage their delicate egos. Putting aside his own disappointment with Minister Mujota for even seeing Potera, Rama set another deadline for the stand down plan to be re-started. This was the second deadline placed on the Protection Zone 5 protestors; this time it had to be followed in order to keep the plan on track but I remained privately unsure whether Rama would manage to bring them into line.

There were a number of further distractions to content with. I received another email from Agim Çeku asking me to provide him with briefing material before a planned press conference that he was holding in the coming days. Whilst my initial instinct was to refuse, I wanted to keep him on side and I was also keen to make sure that someone was actually explaining to the media what was going on in the absence of KFOR taking any interest in driving the news agenda. I needed to seek advice and again found myself sitting with Major General Nick Caplin in his flat. I explained that I had seen Haradinaj, I mentioned Çeku's request for support, and I told him about KFOR's reticence to act over guarding the barracks, despite Stoltz's initial position and Selimi's letter to Gay.

Sipping tea in the calm of his large living room in his flat close to

Film City, the events in KFOR a million miles away, Major General Caplin counselled me to be wary over my contacts with Ramush Haradinaj and Agim Çeku going forward. He explained that the Prime Minister was becoming increasingly uncomfortable over the UK's diplomatic relationship with his political rivals and it was obviously going to be misconstrued if I was seen going in and out of their offices. I realised I needed to be more prudent and to avoid any chance of being compromised in the future. I also decided that I would meet Çeku's request, but only by providing information that was already in the public domain. I was meeting my obligation to him, but still managing to maintain sufficient distance from his political agenda.

Life was certainly not dull.

In amongst the political comings and goings, normal life somehow seemed to trundle along in the KPC. Even with weeks to go until the organisation was being stood down I was invited to attend a demonstration of the KPC's Urban Search and Rescue capability, in conjunction with a UK Fire Service initiative called Operation Florian. I had been so engrossed in the day-to-day life as a liaison officer that I hadn't really seen that much of what the KPC actually did. The unit in question had proved their worth many times over both inside Kosovo and in neighbouring Albania during times of crisis, whether in response to landslips or other natural disasters. In Albania they had assisted in the aftermath of an explosion at an ammunition factory, receiving plaudits for their tenacity and expertise. They were internationally qualified to conduct missions overseas. To many, this unit would become the first element of the KSF that could potentially take part in international missions, possibly as part of a NATO deployment. It was an excellent demonstration of what they were capable of doing and having a break from the routine was just what I needed.

Rama was also trying to set aside time to think about the future. I suggested to him that we should have an away day with a handpicked group of thoughtful KPC officers who were more than likely going to be accepted into the KSF. The idea would be to discuss the broader issues of what the new force should stand for, what traditions it ought to retain and create, how it wanted to be seen by external military organisations and how it was going to be different from the KPC. Sitting in his office, discussing this idea, I sensed a very strong determination in Rama to make the KSF a completely different type of organisation to the one he had invested so much of his life in. We talked about the potential for the KSF to one day join a NATO mission, and even join NATO. It was good to have these aspirations. On a practical level I threw into the conversation that he should ban smoking in all KSF buildings. I said it as much as a joke as any serious proposal. After all, it was Rama who had received my package of nicotine patches and the instructions on how to use them a few weeks earlier when I suggested he should give up smoking, only to find him proudly showing me his arm covered in patches and an ash tray full of recently smoked cigarettes. As it turned out, Rama was rather keen on the idea. Although in the big scheme of things it was a small gesture, establishing a smoking ban on members of the KSF in the workplace would be a serious statement of intent. That said, I didn't hold out much hope of it actually happening. The pressure of starting a new security force would soon envelope those who were going to change their grey KPC uniforms for the new military pattern fatigues that were being supplied by the United States.

These discussions with General Rama were rare, such was the level of responsibility that he was carrying with the stand down plan. However he was always open to suggestions and new ideas; he was an intelligent and highly motivated man and I was reassured that things would turn out well if he remained involved in the KSF.

The likelihood that General Rama would play a major role in shaping the future force was high. Nobody expected him to be selected as the first Commander of the KSF and rumours were already on the streets that General Selimi had been selected, his name passed to the Prime Minister's office. But there had been no immediate endorsement by the PM and subsequent ratification by the President. As each day passed we would look at each other and ask what was going on. My new journalist friend, Zija, had written a very balanced and informed article about the interconnected KPC and KSF processes, mainly based on the briefing I had supplied a few days earlier. I mentioned it in my weekly KFOR report to provide some good news to the KFOR leadership, even if they were unaware of the provenance of the information. There had been suggestions in the press that Selimi's name was indeed sitting in the PM's in tray but the lack of action by Thaçi was becoming a very real problem, and one that would have profound implications for the KPC, the KSF and Kosovo as a whole.

It had been another week that felt like a lifetime in Kosovo. I was sitting with colleagues from the KIKPC, the organisation I was notionally a part of, enjoying pizza and catching up with Major Frank McCormick and Major Lance McCoy, both of whom were US reservists, in one of the many restaurants within Film City. They were very focused on doing their job as well as possible and getting home to their families after their 12-month tour. Frank was the lead for managing weapons within the KPC and we both knew that this subject was still unresolved as we approached the KPC draw down; it was my job to unlock the issue of the KPC officers' sidearms. Going out was something that we hadn't done much of and I was enjoying their company. Midway through the meal I received a text. There had been an incident downtown, an explosion. I apologised to the guys and excused myself from the table, then walked over to the Joint Intelligence and Operations Centre where I had been before meeting up with Frank and Lance. They were aware of something having happened, so I suggested I head over to find out a little more.

I called Kasper and told him we had to blue light to an incident in Pristina. We met quickly and drove at speed to the location of the blast, which turned out to be the headquarters of the International Civilian Office (ICO), known as the 'Blue Building'. It was not very far away from the KFOR headquarters so we were soon on the scene. Parking a safe distance away, inside the initial cordon, Kasper and I walked up to the building and from a reasonable distance looked at what had happened. Nobody had been injured and it looked very much like a random bomb attack against infrastructure rather than against any individuals. The building was glass fronted and quite a lot of it had been smashed by the shockwave, leaving it strewn across the forecourt. Anyone within a few metres would have been lacerated, but it appeared that those responsible were either lucky or had deliberately avoided civilian casualties by leaving the attack until a Friday evening. I had already warned off the KPC's specialist explosive ordnance team in case they were needed, however it was clear there was not much I could do and we left just as an 8-wheeler KFOR armoured explosive ordnance specialist vehicle manoeuvred itself into position.

When I eventually got back to Film City, Frank and Lance had left the pizza restaurant so I retired to the sanctity of the 'British' room to have a drink and to relax. My mind was racing about who may have been responsible for the attack. My initial thoughts led me to think that Vetevendosje may have been behind the bomb; it seemed a bit extreme and there were few other contenders. But it didn't really fit with their normal methods of operation. And I was tired. My brain needed a break and thinking about who may be responsible wasn't helping.

Within days, three German secret service agents had been arrested on suspicion of being behind the bombing, only to be released and returned to Germany a few weeks later after significant diplomatic pressure was applied on Kosovan authorities. With hundreds of German troops in Kosovo and promises of financial support through the trust funds from the Government in Berlin, it wasn't in Kosovo's interests to hold on to the men, regardless of their role in events.

It was a most bizarre incident.

CHAPTER EIGHT

'Political Interference'

The rumours surrounding a delay in the Prime Minister confirming General Selimi's appointment as the first Commander of the KSF began to drown out the crows that roosted noisily each night in Film City. I had heard directly from previous commanders of the KPC that Thaçi had a problem with Selimi. Selimi had confessed to me that Thaçi would not want him to be the new head of the KSF because "he would not be able to control me." The fears shared with me by Agim Çeku were coming true; my observations during the two meetings I had attended with Selimi in the Prime Minister's office, that the two men had been business-like and had got on well, appeared to be naïve and way off the mark.

A week after the expected announcement, Colonel Xhavit Gashi, General Selimi's Chief of Staff, telephoned the President's office to find out what the timescale was likely to be. He received the news nobody wanted to hear. They had not received the nomination from the PM's office so there was nothing they could do. It was obvious to me that something was very seriously wrong and the implications were clear for the taut timelines that had been imposed on everyone because of General Gay's delay in making a decision about the drawdown of the KPC and standing up the KSF. I talked at length to

UK officials to explore what leverage could be applied to Thaçi. Terry Anderson and I also discussed what the US could do to encourage him to make the decision. We were 2 weeks away from the senior officers' selection board – the SOSAB – and Selimi really needed to be in place by then to be a member of that board, to offer an informed view as someone who knew the KPC officers well.

I also decided that I would try to see General Gay to explain to him the implications of a delay, a brief conversation that would probably take no more than 10 minutes out of his day. I was not sure that Di Luzio had the courage to address difficult issues with his Italian boss and I calculated I could use my position legitimately to raise this point; I had nothing to lose. In essence, the whole process needed the KFOR Commander to reach out to the PM in order to encourage him to act; every day that passed without a decision by the PM magnified the risk to the entire process. I went to General Gay's outer office to arrange the meeting. My predecessor and others before him had always had a direct line to the KFOR Commander, such was the importance of the KPC to him over the years. It was clear that I had been unlucky with the current Italian leadership but I needed to at least try.

General Gay was not a very personable man, he was rarely seen around Film City, and when he was spotted walking between his office and his vehicle or accommodation, he was always surrounded by his close protection officers. It was an incongruous sight and unrecognisable to any British officer. When out of the office I would always stop and talk to soldiers if I had the chance, especially when I was in command appointments. Meeting soldiers built trust, made you more human to those under your command and soldiers appreciated the opportunity to have a brief conversation with the 'boss'. It was a key element to commanding soldiers that was drummed into us during our training at The Royal Military Academy, Sandhurst.

General Gay clearly felt uncomfortable amongst troops, and this may have shaped his thinking towards the KPC. He had moved his office away from his personal staff, creating a physical barrier between the sanctity of his own office and those who ran his life in command. This alone was an unusual thing to do, building a buffer from the outside world. I stood in Gay's outer office ready to ask Major Ionata, his Military Assistant, for a slot in the diary. Ionata and I had fallen out over my decision to introduce another chair into a briefing room during a visit from the NATO Commander in Naples. It was a storm in a teacup but one that had not been resolved, despite my efforts to do so. As a result, our relationship was strained. I was told that Gay didn't want to hear directly from me, he wanted me to go through the chain of command. This meant raising the issue with Brigadier Di Luzio, which was pointless; I suspected that he did not take these difficult issues to Gay. These two officers were the most important people to me within KFOR yet they were both variously disengaged.

Feeling like I was banging my head against a brick wall, I used my weekly report to raise serious concerns regarding Selimi's nomination instead. I even managed to get a reaction out of Di Luzio. In the report I had suggested it was in KFOR's interest to lobby the PM over the nomination for the appointment of the KSF Commander. Di Luzio's response was entirely predictable:

'It's a political issue,' he said.

As the International Military Presence in Kosovo, mandated by the UN, KFOR was able to do 'everything necessary' to ensure that NATO's 'New Tasks' were fully implemented. It was obvious that KFOR had a role to play. General Gay's role was a military appointment and he had the responsibility to engage at the political level. It appeared that NATO's orders were being interpreted very differently in Pristina.

With an unsatisfactory reaction from KFOR, I set about coordinating a response from every other source I could think of who had a stake in making the KSF process go well. I spoke to Terry Anderson and asked whether he would mobilise the US Ambassador to raise the issue with the PM; he agreed. There was an opportunity coming up because the Kosovan President was about to make a formal visit to the UK. Our Ambassador, Andy Sparkes, was going to accompany him and agreed to bring this subject up while they were both travelling. I arranged a call with Frank Niesse from the International Civilian Office, the organisation mandated to provide a range of support to the Kosovan Government and a key member of the selection process for the KSF. I had never met Frank but he had asked me for help over security arrangements in the immediate aftermath of the bomb attack against the ICO building. He volunteered to do whatever he could to help unblock the impasse. Lobbying through whatever channels left open to me was the only way to get the Prime Minister to sign off the nomination.

Rumours were rife though, both amongst KPC members and in the media, over the reasons for the unexpected delay. Some stories centred on the honour system and suggested that Hashim Thaçi had an obligation to someone, a "bessa", and was duty bound to appoint him instead of the official nominee. However this person was only a Lieutenant Colonel in the KPC, and not only was he not senior enough for the role, he had not even applied to join the KSF. This reinforced my view that Thaçi simply didn't understand his role in the KFOR-led process. There was even word that Thaçi had asked whether he has to appoint Selimi at all. The absence of any effective and proactive leadership from Lieutenant General Gay, the KFOR Commander, by failing to reach out to the Prime Minister, was directly impacting the process at the heart of the 'New Tasks'. Without the KFOR Commander explaining the process to him, or even reaching out to him, Thaçi had no context. This was the conclusion I came to. Instead, the PM was being lobbied by the international community, who he may well have suspected were trying to push other agendas. With the delay by the PM threatening the overall timelines of the process, there were other ongoing issues that were starting to focus people's minds in KFOR and the MCAD.

An essential part of the stand down of the KPC was the very sensitive issue of weapons, specifically personal sidearms, which a number of KPC officers regularly carried, with ammunition, throughout their normal working day. Following the example of Colonel Zeqiri who had literally shot himself in the foot when KFOR troops turned up for an unannounced inspection, I knew this was going to be both a difficult subject to manage and also a dangerous one to execute. I had initially spoken to the Swedish Air Force Colonel in charge of the KIKPC, Colonel Bengtsson. The Chief, as he was known, was supportive and understood these issues. He was also worried about how to raise the issue with the leadership of the KPC. KIKPC was in the lead to collect all KPC weapons and ammunition. They needed to take control of both long barrelled weapons – mainly AK47s – from KPC buildings around the country as well as the personal weapons carried by the KPC officers. The long-barrelled weapons were relatively uncontentious; the personal weapons, issued to officers with a Weapons Authorisation Card or WAC, were a very different proposition.

After seeing Bengtsson, I talked to Rama. He was quite relaxed about collecting in the officers' weapons and WACs before the last day of work for the KPC, currently planned for the 10th December. He understood the need for KFOR to take charge of these weapons and he advised me to get it cleared with General Selimi. General Rama never carried a weapon so he was relaxed about the issue. General Selimi was likely to have a very different view. After making an appointment, I went to see him in his large, high-ceilinged office. Inside, the dark curtains were constantly drawn, keeping the impending Balkan Winter at bay, but with inadequate lighting, the atmosphere always felt claustrophobic and intimidating. Even though both Rama and Selimi's offices were only separated by a central reception area in the KPC headquarters, I never felt able to relax with Selimi as I could with Rama. Selimi always carried a sidearm and saw it as his unalienable right to do so; this was not a conversation I was looking forward to. And a lot of people were relying on me to win this argument.

The first discussion did not go well. Selimi all but threw me out of his office for even suggesting that the weapons had to be put into storage and looked after until sometime in the future, when the KPC officers could apply to have them returned, albeit in an inert state. He refused to give any order directing the WAC holders in the KPC to hand over their prized possessions. After an unpleasant and bruising few minutes I left his office wondering how we were going to convince him to change his mind.

I knew I needed to make progress so I spoke to Rama again. Even though Rama would often avoid taking on Selimi if he knew they had a difference of opinion, he did promise to discuss this with him. When I heard he had received an agreement that Selimi would give the order at the next Protection Zone Commanders' Conference I was relieved more than anything. This was the monthly forum during which the KPC's senior commanders would gather and discuss the issues of the day. I had only attended a couple of these events and it was always fascinating to watch the interaction between the various characters.

This was no different, tagged on the back of the senior officer training that had been so unpopular with the KPC commanders. The meeting, likely to be the last, began with the leader of Protection Zone 1, Brigadier General Jashari, accusing General Selimi of being soft with the protestors at Protection Zone 5, even though the news had come through that the protestors had finally met Rama's deadline and the stand down plan was back on track. Stung by the direct criticism and perhaps choosing to have a smooth ride for the remainder of the meeting, Selimi turned to the issue of weapons. He immediately announced that KPC officers would not have to hand their weapons in until the New Year at the earliest. It was not what Rama had agreed and it was clearly disappointing to hear; I glanced at Rama across the room with an enquiring look. He just shrugged his shoulders, tilting his head and raising his eyebrows in his customary way. I heard his words in my head: "What can we do?"

That afternoon, back in the safety of his office, a strong coffee on his desk, alongside a glass of raki and a cigarette smouldering in the ash tray, I had another go with Selimi, setting out my arguments more clearly. I played his words that he used with the protestors back to him, connecting the issue of dignity and doing things properly for the sake of the KPC's legacy and the future of the KSF. As with most things in Kosovo, it ended with a compromise. He said he would pass on the order as long as the letter came from KFOR. I was delighted that the issue had finally been unblocked, but sceptical that KFOR would want to have anything to do with a letter of this kind. Nonetheless I very quickly drew up a plan and proposed a three-day period in December when we would bring every owner of a WAC into the KPC HQ to hand in their weapon, magazines and ammunition, each carefully documented. These would then be taken to a safe place and secured under Frank McCormick's watchful eye.

Selimi was clearly still unhappy about the weapons issue and I needed to arrange a meeting between him and General Gay. I spoke to his military assistant, Major Ionata, and explained that General Selimi wanted to talk to him urgently. The response that there was a slot in a week's time did not cut it. After insisting he look again, he managed to find time in Gay's diary for later that day, at 6pm. I assumed Di Luzio was also going to be there. I drove General Selimi into the KFOR headquarters for the meeting along with Colonel Xhavit Gashi, who was also with us. I normally had to accompany them through security at Film City and we slowly made our way around the camp to the KFOR headquarters. As normal I walked in with them and led them up to the meeting room, however when I arrived I was asked by Di Luzio to leave. A little confused, Simi and I headed back downstairs to wait in the empty coffee shop. When the meeting eventually broke up I asked how it had gone. Selimi was not particularly forthcoming, but nothing had been said that was ground-breaking, or at least that was my impression.

The following morning I had an unusual task to complete. The long-barrelled weapon collection process was mainly carried out by others in KIKPC. It was simply a case of driving to a remote location, signing for the weapons and returning them to Pristina and placing them into secure storage. On this occasion, reflecting a lack of available staff, I was asked by KIKPC colleagues to drive over to Klina, the hometown of General Selimi, to collect a couple of AK47s used by the guards, together with magazines and ammunition. The weather was not great, with winter's icy grip freezing the roads and making driving hazardous, but any excuse to leave Pristina was grabbed with both hands. I needed to be back in the capital for a meeting in Film City in the afternoon so we could not hang around. When we arrived, the one thing that struck me about the KPC building, and the KPC personnel based there, was their sense of resignation. They knew they were going to be moving out within a matter of days and their expressions gave away this sense of loss. Simi had not travelled with us so I had to rely on my limited Albanian to talk with the more senior KPC member on duty. It was a stark reminder of the human side of this security sector transition. These men's futures were very uncertain. What they would do afterwards was anyone's guess if they were not accepted into the KSF. I felt a degree of pity for them but with a Planning Hub meeting looming back in Pristina we couldn't hang around. I thanked him for his service and once the weapons were wrapped up and secure in the Landcruiser, we headed off.

As soon as we hit the main road I said to Kasper to use the blue lights. Kasper flicked the switch and started driving 20mph faster than we had been; it was as if the blue lights were the catalyst for our driving to be that much more dangerous, overtaking vehicles and putting ourselves at risk on slippy roads in wintery conditions. After a while I told him to turn off the blue lights and we immediately slowed down. I didn't mind if we were going to be late, I just wanted to arrive in one piece. If anyone was planning to pull us over and steal the weapons, good luck to them.

I got back in time to hand the ammunition, magazines and weapons over to Major McCormick and walked across the camp to the 'Planning Hub', a regular meeting which monitored the implementation of the 'New Tasks'. It was the forum to discuss issues like the stand down plan, who would do what, when and so on. It was reasonably useful even though it never included the KPC; I was effectively their representative at the meeting. Di Luzio was in full stride and took great pleasure in explaining that the KPC leadership, essentially General Selimi, had agreed to sign the letters that were going to be hand delivered to those members of the KPC who were either being invited to join the KSF or who were going to be told that they had been unsuccessful and would be entering the resettlement programme. I was writing a record of the meeting in my notebook and physically stopped when he made this announcement.

The penny dropped why I had been excluded from the meeting the evening before.

It was clear that Gay and Di Luzio had created an opportunity to railroad Selimi into agreeing to something that he was not entirely aware of. General Selimi was not dealing with the detail of the KPC stand down or the establishment of the KSF. He was not aware of the nuances and the bigger picture; that is where I stepped in to provide advice. Colonel Xhavit Gashi, who would have been translating, was also ignorant of the detail. General Rama was the only one in KPC HQ who knew what was going on. I am sure that once Selimi had spoken about the weapons issue the evening before, Di Luzio had seized his chance. If Selimi had understood the implications of what Di Luzio had asked him, I did not believe for a minute that Selimi would have signed up to it.

The entire selection process was being driven forward by MCA Division, NATO's team sitting inside Film City, ostensibly under command of Brigadier Di Luzio, the Deputy Chief of Staff, who in turn worked for the Commander of KFOR, NATO's International Military Presence in Kosovo. NATO's 'New Tasks' were explicit about KFOR's supervisory role. The team were driving forward the recruiting, screening and selection of Kosovo Protection Corps personnel who wanted to join the new Kosovo Security Force. It was MCA Division who had invited the KPC personnel to apply, which included Selimi.

I could hardly believe what I was hearing when Brigadier Di Luzio effectively passed the responsibility for signing the letters, informing successful candidates that they had been accepted into the Kosovo Security Force, to the Commander of the KPC, who himself was subject to the selection process.

It made me chuckle; it was another challenge to the KPC, another unnecessary issue to navigate, thrown into the road by Di Luzio, who was obsessed with keeping a distance between KFOR and the 'New Tasks'. It felt like every week I was given another pointless challenge to overcome on behalf of the KPC; the KPC did not deserve to be kicked as often as they were. And the Italian leadership underestimated the UK's commitment to the Kosovans and the KPC in particular. This was an organisation set up by General Sir Mike Jackson after the war against Serbia; I had a duty to retain its dignity and to help until the last minute. I was certainly not going to allow the KPC to be walked all over by the Italians, at least not on my watch.

I was going to enjoy managing this one.

I returned to the KPC and informed Selimi what had been said; he was unhappy that Di Luzio had misinterpreted what had been discussed in the meeting the evening before. It was clear to me that Di Luzio had excluded me from that meeting to try to get Selimi to agree to something that clearly wasn't in his interest. It was schoolboy politics by Gay and Di Luzio and was never going to be accepted by the KPC leadership once they were given the appropriate advice from me and from Major General Nick Caplin. I then called Colonel Xhavit Gashi and asked to meet him down town again. He agreed and we met in the evening, sitting close to where we had met on our previous visit to the Renaissance 2 restaurant. Over a glass of wine, I decided to share with him the repeated attempts by Di Luzio and the KFOR command team to undermine the KPC at every turn. I provided examples, including this latest effort. I wanted Colonel Gashi to understand what was happening, what could almost be described as a concerted campaign to undermine the KPC, and for him to be better able to see the warning signs if he ended up with Selimi being cornered by Gay or Di Luzio in future. My exclusion had been a change in tactics by Di Luzio and one I needed to work around.

I played the issue with a straight bat back in KFOR HQ. I informed Di Luzio that Selimi was surprised to have been misquoted and suggested that a second meeting to establish the facts was the best way forward. Another meeting was then hurriedly arranged for the Friday afternoon. With the appropriate level of attendance, which included Major General Nick Caplin, Major General Rama, Colonel Karl Habel and Brigadier Di Luzio, we were now able to clarify what went on. I was again taking notes.

Throughout the KPC-KSF process, some issues escalated very quickly and became so important that they warranted immediate attention from people who, frankly, had far more important things to be worrying about. This was one such occasion. The 'New Tasks' was not a normal security sector transition though, and KFOR was not behaving as most would have expected it to. It was as if KFOR had organised a coach trip; without a driver, lacking fuel, and with most of the seats missing.

The meeting went as I had planned. The KPC leadership stuck to their guns by saying it was not appropriate for them to sign any letters. Major General Caplin was having none of it and Colonel Habel was a pragmatist who just wanted a workable solution against which to plan. My notes from the meeting highlighted Di Luzio's reticence to be involved in what was essentially his own process:

General Selimi: "The logisticians will open up each of the barracks [on the day] and support the process."

Brigadier Di Luzio: "So the KPC Commander and his chain of command will deliver the letters?"

Selimi: "No. They will prepare the conditions but they will not deliver the letters. That's MCA Division. MCA Division must give these letters, not KPC."

Di Luzio: "We have to discuss this like military men. So, there will be 200 personnel in front of KFOR persons. For example KPC persons will not want to receive a letter from a KFOR person because the KFOR person is not in the chain of command."

Major General Caplin: "This will not be a problem."

Di Luzio: "No, it is the KPC's responsibility to do this."

Caplin: "KFOR invited KPC to apply and it is their duty. It cannot be a KPC responsibility."

Di Luzio: "It is easy for KFOR to organise this. In my perception we are reducing the leadership of the KPC. Who prepared the stand down plan?"

Di Luzio's final comment was a cheap shot; he was right that the stand down plan was written by the KPC leadership but that was because he refused point blank to have anything to do with it, apart from getting Colonel Habel in MCA Division to set the standards to which it had to adhere. Di Luzio's team were also organising the selection process so they were responsible for managing it. Di Luzio, realising that his little game had been exposed, suggested that Major General Caplin should sign the unsuccessful letters instead. Caplin agreed and the Minister for the KSF, Fehmi Mujota, was volunteered to sign the successful letters that would be distributed on the 12th December. It was great to watch Di Luzio dodge and weave every attempt to pin the issue of signing the letters on KFOR or the

MCAD. Whilst this still needed final approval, the issue appeared to be was settled. The resulting compromise suited everyone; Di Luzio was happy that he had again avoided any responsibility for the issue and Selimi had maintained his insistence that it was not his job to sign off KFORs labours.

With the senior officers selection board – the SOSAB – set for the following Monday, the KSF Commander designate required a 90-minute briefing before he attended the selection board and, as usual in Kosovo, everything seemed to be going down to the wire. To deliver this briefing, Colonel Stuart Roberts planned to drive down to the KPC HQ to speak with Selimi. Word had reached me that the PM was going to announce Selimi's name on the same day as the selection board. The long wait for the Prime Minister to finally confirm General Selimi as the Commander of the KSF appeared to be reaching a conclusion just in the nick of time. By now everyone connected with the KPC-KSF process was clinging on to any positive rumour, hoping it was true.

Finally I heard the news that KFOR's Information Campaign had started, through radio adverts, to inform the public about the 'New Tasks'. Except the adverts were exclusively focused on the formation of the KSF, without mention of the interconnected nature of the KPC's stand down. I learned that neither the KPC nor the Office of the KPC Coordinator had been consulted over content. Why would they be? KFOR had entirely cut the KPC out of the campaign, reflecting their stance throughout the previous few months. With the crisis over the stand down plan in the KPC seemingly averted, and KFOR's information campaign starting too late to make a difference anyway, I had given up worrying at this point.

Graziani and I had put a plan in place and I fully intended to maintain my contact with Zija whenever I could.

2008. Zija Miftari recording the moment Selimi, standing beside Lieutenant General Gay, announces his intention to take the protestors' demands to the Government, much to everyone's surprise.

In conversation with a US colleague and the local KPC Protection Zone 6 Commander, Brigadier General Ilazi, just before Selimi's unplanned press conference.

*Standing on the side of the dusty highway running through the border town of Hani
Elezit, with Major Rufki Suma, who became something of a bête noire
for me during my tour.*

'Away Day' in Vushtri - discussing the future of the KSF with General Rama and his trusted advisors. Simi, as ever, is never far away.

Standing amongst the members of PZ4 in Mitrovice, Kosovo's most divided town, listening intently to the words of Major General Rama. Moments later, I was called forward to address the KPC personnel myself.

Sitting in Renaissance 2, the Pristina restaurant that hosted many key meetings which shaped the future of the KSF. General Caplin, hands clasped, with Brigadier General Di Luzio on his left.

CHAPTER NINE

'The Doldrums'

On the morning of Monday 24th November my phone never left my ear as I made last-minute calls to the military liaison officer in the UK Embassy, to Terry Anderson in the US Embassy and with Frank Neisse from the International Civilian Office. I needed to chase up whether the UK Ambassador had any feedback after spending time with the Kosovan President on his visit to the UK. I wanted to ask Terry whether his Ambassador had any final tricks up his sleeve, and Frank Neisse had volunteered to get the Deputy International Civilian Representative to call the Prime Minister's office. Despite these and other calls with certain key KPC individuals and with others elsewhere, there seemed to be nothing to suggest we were going to see an announcement before the senior officers' selection board scheduled for later in the day.

It also became clear that the KFOR Commander, Lieutenant General Gay, had finally woken up to the implications of the delay and had started, belatedly, trying to influence Hashim Thaçi to make a decision. I had heard in one of my phone calls that he had requested a meeting with Thaçi; but it was too little, too late. The Prime Minister had to make a decision in the morning; the implications of not doing so were clear to everyone. A postponement of the senior officers' board, together with the subsequent impact on the cascade system that had been put in place to select the remaining positions in the KSF, would push the whole process to the right. The KPC was already close to ineffectiveness as bases were being closed on a near daily basis. With less and less to occupy the KPC and no bases for them to go to, a delay would create a vacuum which would be a worst case scenario for everybody.

Despite the signs looking ominous for the whole process, Colonel Stuart Roberts briefed both General Selimi and General Rama on the conduct of the SOSAB; Rama was still a nominee for the position but nobody considered him a front runner. It was classic British contingency planning but it looked like being a complete waste of time. By mid-morning General Selimi received a call from the President who confirmed his support for his nomination but he added what we had all suspected; he had not heard anything from the PM's office. By lunchtime the decision was taken within KFOR headquarters to postpone the SOSAB. Nobody involved with the process was happy, including the Minister for the KSF, who probably had as much influence over the PM as anyone.

Later in the day Selimi again spoke to the President who reported that the PM had said to him that approving the nomination was a matter for the Government and not the PM. The PM even explained to the President that there was no rush. This was constitutionally untrue and if further evidence was needed that the PM was ignorant of what his role in the process was, this was it, with the fault lying firmly at the door of the KFOR Commander.

It was a setback with repercussions that needed to be quantified, but life carried on and I had received a text from my journalist friend Zija, asking to meet me later on. I also received a message from Simi who had been contacted by Ali Cenaj, the Zeri journalist, to ask

Major General Caplin for a meeting. Before he left for the day, I managed to catch General Rama to confirm some of the details that I had managed to put in place for our 'away day' brainstorming session in a hotel in Vushtri the following day, an activity I was pleased he had set time aside for.

I drove back up the hill to Film City, changed out of my uniform, and asked Kasper to drive me into Pristina for two important meetings. The first meeting was with Veton Elshani, the Kosovo Police spokesman, whom I had met at an earlier event and who had suddenly become an important contact for me. Since the KFOR Chief of Staff had refused to endorse KFOR troops acting as a deterrent against criminal activity at several KPC locations, when KPC personnel were to be sent home on the 10th December, I needed an alternative plan. Veton struck me as a pragmatic and reliable public servant who I immediately warmed to and felt I could trust. As the spokesman for the Kosovo Police he could see the potential for trouble and during our meeting over a coffee downtown, I appealed to him for his support, explaining the brick wall I had come up against with KFOR. He agreed that something would be put in place. As an unofficial meeting, to explain some of the context, it went well and I was assured that we would be able to come up with a plan. The formal task of requesting this support from General Selimi still needed to be submitted to the Minister for Internal Affairs.

I then met up with Zija Miftari. We met in the Bamboo Café, sufficiently off the beaten track and away from prying eyes. Graziani had given me a few pointers on what to cover after I told him I was meeting Zija later on, but unusually there was little to add. Zija was confused and wanted to know why there was a delay. I told him he wasn't alone. I simply explained that the decision was out of our hands and the PM alone knew why he had sat on the appointment of Selimi with the inevitable implications for the whole process. I did explain that I believed the fault lay with several people, including the KFOR Commander, for his lack of proactive engagement with the Prime Minister. Zija was baffled by the whole thing.

The following day I was called in to the KFOR headquarters before leaving for General Rama's brainstorming session in Vushtri. Over the previous weekend I had written in my weekly report that I had never seen Selimi and Rama quite so vexed as they were after hearing about Di Luzio's misrepresentation of the facts. The report had contained a blow by blow account of the 'did he, didn't he' situation regarding who was going to sign off the selection letters. It had understandably upset Di Luzio. I had described the exchange as objectively as I could on paper, even though I had been instrumental in undermining Di Luzio's rather amateur efforts to get the KPC leadership to roll over. So after the drama of the SOSAB postponement, Di Luzio called me into his office on the Tuesday morning and we had a very frank exchange over my use of the word 'vexed'. He completely failed to see the issue from the KPC's perspective. He had suggested in the second meeting that there had been a misunderstanding in English over what was and wasn't agreed. Unsurprisingly Di Luzio went through the report, line by line, criticising me for what I had written. He repeated his advice that I should be a passive observer, someone simply sitting on the side lines, quietly in the corner of the room, recording everything that was said around me. He had no idea.

My report was my only weapon to raise the profile of important issues. With a KFOR leadership who appeared unwilling to address the 'New Tasks' with any common sense, my ability to be heard through my report was a vital tool in protecting the KPC and ensuring the process was conducted with dignity. The distribution list I had inherited was quite unwieldly, especially in the higher headquarters in Naples, so over the previous weeks I had been slimming it down. I had written to everyone in Naples on the list asking whether they wished to keep seeing the report. After a few weeks I was happy that the smaller distribution list in Naples were the people who had a desire to know what was going on in Kosovo; I imagine they saw my report as instrumental to their intelligence feed. During the October visit to Pristina by the Naples Joint Forces Commander, Admiral Fitzgerald and his Deputy Commander, Lieutenant General Pearson from the UK, Lieutenant Colonel Chris Gunning, Pearson's Military Assistant, had specifically asked me to send him a copy of the report – even more tailored with UK specific comments.

So after having to defend my report over the letters issue, Di Luzio turned to the report's distribution list and questioned why I was sending it to Naples. He could clearly see who was receiving it, I wasn't hiding anything. I explained the provenance of the distribution list but he dismissed my explanation. He made it clear that I was no longer to send the report to Naples and the distribution list had to be internal to Kosovo only.

There was no logic to his decision other than to prevent Naples from knowing what was actually going on. I assumed that my reporting was beginning to trigger a flow of awkward questions from Naples to the KFOR command group in Pristina about the effectiveness of the 'New Tasks'.

As if to reinforce this point, a few weeks earlier, I had received an email from Naples which appeared to sum up the military relationship between KFOR and its higher headquarters perfectly. In response to one of my earlier reports, explaining that the lack of an information or communications campaign was having a negative effect on the stand down process for the KPC, I received an interesting email. Major Roderick Capili, a US Marine Corps officer in the Information Operations Division in Naples, wrote an internal email, blind copied to me, explaining that he was being told by the KFOR headquarters that the information campaign was ongoing. However, through several sources, including my reports and emails from Andy Lennard, the British civil servant inside MCA Division, it was clear that there was no campaign of any kind. He was rightly confused and worried about the impact that the lack of a campaign had been having on the KFOR brand. It was evident that he was beginning to realise the full extent of the damage the current command team in Pristina was doing to KFOR's reputation.

After my meeting with Di Luzio I had no choice but to stop sending the report to Naples, even if I suspected that what was coming out of KFOR was not entirely truthful. However I would continue to send my UK version of the report to Chris Gunning. He would always be able to brief the Deputy Commander, who in turn could choose what to share with the Joint Forces Commander, Admiral Fitzgerald.

I left his office knowing that I was always going to lose out if KFOR decided that they no longer wanted me in my role as the KPC's liaison officer, although removing me would have been very difficult as my position was a UK sponsored post. And I enjoyed full UK support for my role. Nonetheless, through my conversation with Di Luzio, a warning shot had been fired across my bow. Whatever the truth of it, I was certain that Brigadier Di Luzio never expected so much resistance from the KPC. As an individual Di Luzio was a likeable man, but he appeared unsuitable to be leading NATO's 'New Tasks', which were highly complex and involved a high degree of cultural understanding and collaboration. It must have been clear to the KFOR command group that the KPC's response to their frequent ill-thought-out initiatives were being strongly supported by me, and on occasion, by Major General Caplin.

While General Caplin remained in country though I knew my back was covered.

Once I left Film City with Kasper we set out for the hotel with Rama, Lieutenant Colonel Fahri Sadriaj and Major Agron Bajrami travelling separately. Simi was also with us. Leaving the city behind was such a relief after my tense meeting with Di Luzio. The idea for the day was to look forward, to make some concrete plans and to give everyone a chance to think openly without the pressure of Pristina and the delay imposed by the PM. The few hours we spent in a room, set aside for us by the owner of the hotel, was important for the opportunity to reflect on what the future may look like once the immediate issues were navigated. In a relaxed and cordial atmosphere, we discussed commemorative dates, starting new traditions, the conduct of the new force, even the issue of smoking was raised, although the irony of doing so in a room thick with tobacco was lost on everyone else but me. We made progress, we had managed to give a little thought about the future and Rama was fired up to begin a new chapter. I was simply happy we had managed to escape, but the reality was not far away. With the few hours we had set aside already up, and some good ideas noted down for Rama to consider, we returned to the fray.

For me, the week had an added benefit because I had managed to find time for a 96-hour leave pass, to head back to the UK on leave, to see the family and to try to enjoy a break from the pressure of life in Kosovo. I wrote an early report on the Wednesday and headed to the airport. With two children under the age of 8 I knew I needed to see them in person rather than via Skype. The incident when I had shouted at my 7-year-old still haunted me and I wanted to get back and spend some quality time at home with everyone. It was going to be my son's 8th birthday during the short leave and I was keen to make it as special as I could. I was trying to balance the pressure of my role in Kosovo with being a father and husband; at times I very strongly felt that I wasn't getting it right. Any conversations with the kids or my wife that were less positive had an immediate and disproportionate impact on me. I had learned to compartmentalise home life from what I was doing in Kosovo, it was the only way to do my job, but the reality was never far away, knocking on the door, demanding attention. It was wearing me down so, after 9 weeks away from the family, a brief trip to the UK was definitely needed.

Back in the UK, seeing my family, especially being able to hold my kids again, was a very special time. Taking my daughter to the swings, as I had done before deploying back in August, was a joy. Reading bedtime stories once more was priceless. After a frantic few days, including organising an 8-year-old's birthday party which put NATO's 'New Tasks' into context, I was back at the airport and about to board my flight to Pristina; 96 hours had never gone so fast.

All too quickly though the pace of life picked up and as soon as I returned to Kosovo, I needed to understand what the delay was going to mean to a number of issues, not least the fact that the whole of the KPC were planning to go home the following week, just before Announcement Day on the 12th. No selection boards had taken place because the SOSAB had been postponed. The plan to collect the personal sidearms from members of the KPC that had been planned to take place before the 10th was now likely to slip. Quite simply, something had to change. Amongst the key personnel, it was clear that the delay, without explanation from the PM's office, was having a detrimental psychological effect on everyone. Even though I had only been away for a few days, the change was stark.

General Selimi was the focus of newspaper reports suggesting the International Community no longer supported his nomination. General Rama made it clear he was not playing any games and said to Selimi that if he was selected he would not accept the position over Selimi. The International Civilian Representative, Pieter Feith, was also brought into play by Major General Caplin to try to unlock the issue. But still there was nothing coming out of the PM's office.

My main focus was to keep the KPC together. The protection zone commanders were all doing their best but a decision was needed to provide some clarity to the 2,800 members who were waiting for something that had effectively ground to a halt. General Selimi was adamant that he needed to change the plan, to provide new direction over the stand down of the KPC. It was no longer sensible to stick to the original timelines. The way things were looking, the KPC would continue to operate well into the New Year. A meeting was called in the Government Building at short notice between Major General Caplin, Minister Mujota and Lieutenant General Selimi. Seeing everyone's faces said it all to me. There was resignation, yes, but anger as well. It was agreed that the orders for the stand down period, issued by Selimi for the 10th December, needed to be reviewed. The initial direction had to come from KFOR but Caplin then said he would order the KPC to change the plan. Expecting KFOR to make a rapid decision was unlikely; we didn't have time to pander to their games. We needed firm, decisive leadership.

Caplin was very clear what needed to be done; it also looked like Fehmi Mujota was beginning to realise what being the Minister for the KSF was likely to involve. He needed to go to the PM and explain the range of implications from the delay and to impress on him the need for a decision. The selections were going to have to move into January. The weapons collection, due that week, would also need to be put back. Guarding the barrack locations now needed urgent attention. Caplin then raised an interesting point for Mujota to digest; he reminded everyone that Belgrade was watching events unfold in Pristina. The need to start the KSF on the right foot was important for its credibility and for the impression it presented to the world. Delays and half-baked plans were only going to play into Serbia's hands and reinforce their own narrative over the Kosovo Security Force. It was tense; everyone recognised that the stakes were high.

The decision was made to hold another Renaissance 2 dinner that evening to consider the changed situation. Arrangements were hastily made with Ilhe, the restaurant owner, and the key stakeholders again gathered at the table to the rear of the restaurant, away from prying eyes. I knew that Caplin would drive the agenda and make sure Di Luzio did what he was told; the time for KFOR prevaricating was over. When we all gathered it was clear there was a very different mood to the last meal I had attended at R2. The drama of the protestors had passed but now everyone was facing the need to decide on what Major General Caplin had called a 'bold adjustment' earlier in the day with Minister Mujota. The key outcome was for KFOR to give Selimi the direction needed to issue alternative plans for the next 6 weeks' activity. There was no time to lose.

Caplin addressed each issue before then moving swiftly on to the next. It was agreed that if the SOSAB was not conducted by the 10th December then it would have to slip into January. Colonel Stuart Roberts, as secretary to the selection boards, needed to manage the SOSAB. He had the background knowledge and he had designed the process. Caplin was also on standby to add value as required. Everyone, including Di Luzio, agreed that nothing would happen over the Christmas period, mainly reflecting the fact that all the key players – Colonel Roberts, Dave Finnimore the vetting expert, and Major

General Caplin – would be on leave at that time. All the other details were similarly dealt with quickly and without too much argument.

The final issue was raised by General Rama; he explained that all the vehicles and equipment that were stored in the centralised locations really needed to be sorted out. There was a lot that could and should be scrapped, the delay offered an opportunity to conduct an audit of the inventory and, if necessary, get rid of items to prevent them from being taken onto the KSF's books. This sounded like a very sound idea and everyone agreed, including Caplin who said he would give the order. However, there was still one last chance for Di Luzio to raise an objection by asking who owned the equipment. At any other time it may well have been a prudent question to ask. Everyone was sitting around the table acutely aware that we did not have the luxury of time. We needed to act fast and make decisions. We needed a 'can-do' attitude. Yet Di Luzio had again displayed his obstructionist approach, which drew much rolling of eyes from the rest of us around the table. Di Luzio was at least consistent over the 'New Tasks'. Caplin ignored Di Luzio and told Rama to 'get on with it.'

All Di Luzio had to do, on behalf of KFOR, was let Major General Caplin know that he agreed to a delay and Selimi would issue the order. It was finally agreed that unless there was a challenge within KFOR HQ this order would be issued by Selimi at Midday the following day, the 4th December.

The deadline came and went and new orders were issued. Announcement Day, the final KPC parade and the weapons collection activity were pushed back to January. All the subsequent selection boards were also moved to as yet unidentified dates in the New Year. There was bewilderment over the delay in nominating the KSF Commander. I heard that Admiral Fitzgerald was going to fly to Pristina to see the PM to force his hand. I couldn't help wondering why General Gay wasn't able to do this himself, and why he had allowed this process to be hijacked by the PM. There was clearly something going on but it was opaque to me and many other observers.

The stresses of the week resulted in an unexpected plan for the Friday evening; thankfully something a lot more light-hearted. I was invited to join Generals Rama and Selimi, and their immediate inner circle of advisors, to go bowling, along with Terry Anderson the US Assistant Defence Attaché. Everyone needed to let their hair down a little. This was a first for me, and I wasn't completely sure what to expect. Kasper dropped me off, dressed in jeans and a shirt, my North Face puffa jacket insulating me from the freezing temperatures outside. I entered the bowling alley, close to the KPC headquarters. The combined effect of the loud music and the warmth was in such contrast to the silence on the cold street outside. I removed my jacket as I walked through the bar area to where the KPC officers had gathered. I placed my jacket on a seat in one of the two booths that they had taken over. Looking around at the faces of those sitting around the table, I could tell the evening was going to be one to remember; the atmosphere already felt quite intoxicating.

General Selimi wasn't there at first but he soon joined us. There was plenty to celebrate even if things were not looking so good; everyone had been working extremely well together despite the distractions from Film City and elsewhere in the Government. We were all close, we had a healthy respect for each other and it was important to relax from time to time. Drinking Rama's favourite Chivas Regal Whisky, laughing and joking about events, we were all high-fiving after particularly good bowls, including with both the Generals. It was quite surreal. After bowling we moved onto table football. Terry and I challenged Rama and Selimi, with mixed results;

the UK-US team was out to win but Rama and Selimi were good. I don't know why but I was surprised. Everyone was having a good time. It was just what we all needed; we had been working hard and we were playing hard that night.

As we were leaving Terry told me that he could not find his coat. I walked across to where Selimi was sitting to grab my jacket from one of the booths next to the lanes we had used, and I rifled through the coats that had been scattered around. As I moved them to one side I exposed two pistols with magazines fitted, casually lying on the seats. I looked at Selimi who was sitting at the end of the chair smoking a cigarette. He quietly suggested I cover them up again. I wasn't surprised but it was an odd thing to see. Going bowling was never going to be the same again. With both of our jackets back in our possession, Terry and I headed for the bowling alley exit and the freezing Kosovan night.

Even though I had only recently returned from a short break in the UK, things were not going as planned for my posting after Kosovo. I was trying to manage important issues about schooling and housing that were very difficult to do from abroad. My posting required the family to relocate, but there was a lack of understanding about the unusual needs of military personnel and their families in the UK at the time, which made the process of moving house needlessly difficult. The school authority where we were moving to insisted that I needed a home address within the catchment area before I was able to apply for a school place. However I knew that I wouldn't find a house and an address until much later in my tour of duty in Kosovo. This was an added stress that began to creep into my day-to-day thoughts. Over the weekend I then received a call from my wife explaining that our au pair had decided not to return after Christmas. This was both unexpected and unwelcome news; without an au pair she would have to leave her job in Oxford with the obvious impact on her personal morale and our collective financial well-being. That night I didn't sleep.

As ever, I had to put these things out of my mind if I was going to remain on top of my job. Understandably, events at home were always going to be a distraction, but I had to focus on my role in Kosovo. Sleeping badly and allowing negative thoughts to enter my mind only added to the growing weariness I felt. On the Tuesday, after another disrupted night's sleep, I had a meeting planned with Ramush Haradinaj in his office. With the visit following a familiar routine, we discussed KPC and KSF matters over a coffee, cigar and a glass of raki, although this time it was much more light-hearted and friendly. He was very interested to know if one particular individual was going to be selected for the KSF. I told him I would keep an eye out for him, although in reality we both knew I could not affect the selection process in any way. The clan-based nature of life in Kosovo was beginning to come to the surface, and understandably so. An objective 'NATO Standards' process had never been employed in Kosovo before and so looking after fellow clan members was both a natural activity by people but it was also a direct challenge to how the MCA Division wanted the process to be conducted.

Haradinaj explained in detail what he was planning to do during his rearranged visit to the UK in the New Year following the British Embassy in Macedonia's decision to refuse him a visa back in October. It was good to remain on these terms with Ramush Haradinaj, and my earlier concerns about being seen at his offices seemed less important now, over 3 months into my tour. I cared little about what people thought. Despite my increasing levels of fatigue, I felt revived by my meeting with him; as much because of the raki and his enthusiasm for life as anything else. That evening I also saw Zija

Miftari again. Rather than me giving him a briefing, Zija quickly expressed his dissatisfaction with KFOR, at their lack of action over the KPC-KSF process that he now understood so well. There was little I could do to shift his position, and I could hardly argue strongly against it. Even in the eyes of Kosovan journalists, KFOR's impotence was becoming embarrassingly clear when it came to dealing with the Kosovan Prime Minister.

On the Wednesday evening I was invited by the US Defence Attaché for a few drinks. I had collaborated with Colonel McQueen and his assistant, Terry Anderson, on a few issues, so it was good to be spending time with them in a relaxed social atmosphere. With me were Lieutenant Colonel Jules Carmichael, the British Military Liaison Officer based in the British Embassy, and Colonel Xhavit Gashi. I was expecting to hear about the delayed process at some point during the evening, instead we spent a couple of hours making small talk over several glasses of wine. What he did say though was that Admiral Fitzgerald had visited the PM and made it clear that he had to make a decision by the end of the week. Apparently the PM had asked whether he could appoint someone else. Fitzgerald put him straight on the options open to him and Thaçi agreed that he would comply. In the absence of any effective intervention by General Gay, Admiral Fitzgerald had flown into Pristina to see the Prime Minister and urge him to get the process moving again.

I also heard an extraordinary story from Colonel McQueen. He said that Admiral Fitzgerald mentioned that General Gay was becoming frustrated by the Anglo Saxons in his headquarters. And I was mentioned by name. It was an extraordinary statement. I could not really comprehend why General Gay would complain to the NATO Joint Force Commander in Naples about the British in Kosovo and me in particular. Didn't he have better things to be thinking about? From the moment I arrived in Kosovo in the liaison officer role I had quickly realised that the behaviour of certain officers in KFOR was quite shameful. And their treatment towards the KPC and the Kosovans in general was driven by political correctness rather than common sense and cultural understanding. Every week brought another example of stupidity to reinforce this impression. I felt I had a duty to stand up for the KPC and to protect their legacy against the odds. I had been actively undermining the decisions being taken in the KFOR headquarters for months because I knew it was the right thing to do. Whilst I was never going to openly speak out, I had been clear about my role and if this meant challenging what the Italians were trying to achieve, so be it. Major General Caplin had always appeared to be comfortable with what I was doing. In a small way I was proud that I had been mentioned in that conversation; it meant that I had been doing the right thing for the KPC.

The KPC, despite its imminent demise, had earlier in the year dispatched an officer to attend a staff course in Tirana, Albania. With Kosovo's heritage firmly connected to Albania, it was always natural to send an officer there for training. Bringing together different nations through these types of defence education courses was something I knew Rama was looking forward to arranging once the KSF was up and running, however long that would take. So Rama told me that he was going to drive to Tirana for the officer's passing out parade. Always up for a road trip, I immediately informed Kasper and Simi about the plan. Together with Terry Anderson, who was also invited along, we left early on the 10th December. The parade was on the 11th and without a decent road between Kosovo and Tirana, I had been warned that it was likely to be a long drive. They were not kidding. The journey, including a stop for lunch, took 9 hours. After leaving Kosovo via Prizren, its ancient capital, we entered the mountains through which Simi had trekked all those years ago during the war. The road was full of sharp bends, with barely any protective barrier between the road and the bottom of the gorges and ravines hundreds of feet below; the journey was hardly relaxing.

After driving all day, and stiff from being cooped up in the car, we checked into our hotel and soon headed out for dinner. With little else happening in Pristina, Major General Caplin and his military assistant had also travelled to attend the ceremony. It was a marathon trip but it was worth it.

Before the ceremony the following morning, we had some spare time so Terry and I drove into the city centre and briefly walked around Tirana's main square, taking time to see the sights. Wearing British and US uniforms on Albania's streets didn't seem to draw much attention at all and after the obligatory photographs we headed over to the Albanian Defence Academy to watch the closing ceremony. While we were there, Major General Rama and Major General Caplin met the Albanian Defence Minister and spent time talking to various senior Albanian officers including their Chief of the General Staff.

I also noticed a Serbian Colonel in the audience who sat quietly through the ceremony, even though a KPC officer walked onto the platform to be congratulated for passing the course. Serbia bitterly opposed Kosovo's declaration of independence and its plan to establish the KSF, but defence education courses, involving officers from across the world, always found a way of making friends and building bridges.

It was a long way to travel but it was a welcome break to do something different and reinforce General Rama's ties with Albanian colleagues. It also gave everyone some thinking time and an opportunity to draw breath and reflect. The return journey after the ceremony only took 7 hours, following a different route via Macedonia. Despite terrible weather we arrived late on the 12th back in the relative comfort of Pristina.

As a final opportunity to spend time with Terry before the Christmas break, as if 30 hours in each other's company wasn't enough during our road trip to Tirana, we both went out for a quiet drink in Pristina on the Saturday evening. The Sunday was spent getting ready for my R&R in the UK as I was due to fly back on Monday the 15th December, but I still had one last event to attend. The former US Defence Attaché, Lance Dickinson, had invited Selimi, Rama and the usual crowd to his house on the Sunday evening. It was very relaxed and good to discuss some of the issues of the day over a drink. Everybody was pushing in the same direction even if there were occasional disagreements. Everyone wanted to see the KPC stand down with dignity and the KSF start on the right foot. It was notable that Brigadier Di Luzio had not been invited, or, if he had, he did not attend. In many ways it was the perfect way to close out the first four months of my tour before heading back to the UK.

Walking back to my small, sparsely furnished accommodation unit that evening I suddenly felt quite vulnerable. Maybe it was time for me to leave Kosovo for a break; my body was run down and it needed a recharge. I had thrown my heart and soul into the role up to that point. I had made lifelong friendships and I believed I was respected for what I was doing within KPC and international circles. I needed some time with my family, even though I really didn't know how I was going to be able to relax into routine family life after the intensity of the tour in Kosovo so far. The process that had dominated my every waking hour was stalled, the difficulty of balancing day-to-day pressures with my responsibility as a father had been exposed, and I was dog tired.

I had plenty to think about as I walked through the airport's departure lounge and onto my British Airways flight home.

CHAPTER TEN

'Rushed Selections'

I was shopping in Sainsbury's just outside Swindon on the 18th December when I received a phone call from Colonel Xhavit Gashi. It was not quite what I was expecting as we prepared for Christmas back at home. Exactly 41 days after he had received the nomination for the position of Commander designate of the KSF, the Prime Minister had finally forwarded Selimi's name to the President for the official confirmation to take place and for his name to be announced. It was the worst kept secret in Kosovo but it should have been announced within days of the selection board in early November. The PM had been lobbied by the UK, US, the NATO commander in Naples and by the International Civilian Representative in Kosovo. The impact of the delay had pushed the stand down of the KPC and the stand up of the KSF back into January 2009. There was a risk of damage being done to newly independent Kosovo's reputation under the watchful eyes of its opponents in Belgrade and elsewhere. Reputational damage had already undoubtedly been done to KFOR's standing in Kosovo. In the freezer section of the supermarket, with a trolley full of Christmas food shopping, I phoned General Selimi and offered him my congratulations.

On the 20th December, the day Major General Nick Caplin was heading back to the UK on leave, I received another call from Xhavit Gashi explaining that the selection boards were going to go ahead over the Christmas break; this meant that they would proceed without any of the key UK staff officers present. The timing of the announcement with Caplin going on leave, was certainly no coincidence. This was not what had been agreed between Major General Caplin and Brigadier Di Luzio on the 3rd December dinner at Renaissance 2 and the news prompted a flurry of phone calls in the UK and with Pristina. I spoke to Major General Caplin first after he had arrived back in the UK. I then called Colonel Stuart Roberts who was the designated secretary to the SOSAB on leave in Scotland, and to Dave Finnamore also in the UK, who was the vetting expert and knew exactly who should and who shouldn't be a part of the new force.

I called Colonel Xhavit Gashi several times, suggesting that Lieutenant General Selimi should talk to Lieutenant General Gay and point out that the SOSAB should be delayed until the UK officers, so integral to the process, were back in country after the New Year. This scenario had been studied and it was an agreed fall back option. Instead Xhavit Gashi told me that Selimi didn't want to be seen to be holding up the process and had agreed to Commander KFOR's request. Xhavit then left Kosovo and with him went my ability to influence Selimi.

Lieutenant General Gay announced that he would hold the SOSAB, with the officers who were left in Kosovo, on Christmas Eve. I made one final call to Caplin to ask whether he thought there was anything that anyone could do; his answer was short and to the point. We simply had to let events unfold. The 'NATO standards' mantra was beginning to creak as it became clear that the Second XI were going to be running the selection board. The rush to hold the selection board was unclear and the contingency plan to run the board in early January had inexplicably been ignored. General Gay appeared to be making a concerted effort to complete the board without any specialist oversight from the very officers who had driven the process forward. The board was convened without any UK influence around the table at all; it was highly unusual and suspicious. Something wasn't right.

In an effort to spend quality time with my family over Christmas I had decided to extend my stay longer than originally planned. I had been due to fly back and spend the New Year in Kosovo, but I had remained in the UK instead. It had been an error of judgement; I wanted to be with my family, but my mind was elsewhere. I was present at our friends' New Year's Eve party but I wasn't celebrating. I couldn't help it. Knowing what was going on in Pristina served to make me restless for those final few days of my leave. The job had not been finished in Kosovo and with unexpected events happening while I was away, I was keen to get back to Pristina.

When I returned to Kosovo after the Christmas and New Year break, I learned how the SOSAB had been conducted from Colonel von Andrian, a German officer who had replaced Colonel Habel as the leading staff officer in MCAD. With the hastily convened meetings taking place on his watch, he had no choice but to deputise for Colonel Stuart Roberts as the SOSAB secretary in his first couple of weeks in the job. He reported a chaotic and highly unusual process with external interruption and many delays. He explained that the interruptions became so frequent during the first meeting that the board had to be reconvened on the 30th December to complete the process. There were accounts of Minister Mujota taking phone calls from the Prime Minister, who was applying influence to push forward certain names. Unnamed others were calling the Minister's phone and highlighting individuals who should be included in the

KSF. The commander of the Kosovo Guard, Brigadier General Lushtaku, who had resigned from the KPC a few weeks earlier, was the subject of intense debate. There was talk of re-admitting him to the KSF even though he had not shown any interest in joining the new force. This conversation alone had taken an hour.

From Von Adrian's account, the calls from the PM and the Deputy PM to Mujota's phone were incessant. Mujota was directly lobbied, exclusions were questioned, demotions were challenged; the pressure on the Minister for the KSF was intolerable. Even the KFOR representatives sitting on the board produced their own lists of names, lobbying for people in the KPC they felt should be in the KSF. It was clear that the conduct of the meetings entirely discredited the 'NATO Standards' mantra so often cited as the high water mark of transparency and fairness.

I had lobbied for personnel reports to be included in the process so that there was a degree of subjectivity applied to the objectiveness of the various other tests and standards that had been applied to each candidate. After initially losing the argument because it would have been incompatible with KFOR's much cherished 'NATO Standards' mantra, Colonel Habel had agreed to allow them to be a part of the selection boards. I learned from Von Adrian that they had been entirely ignored.

By the time I returned to Kosovo after my break, the final list had been drawn up after the two part SOSAB. If what had been relayed to me was right, the integrity of the selection process had been severely compromised; and it had been orchestrated by a 3* NATO General. To those inside MCAD who knew how the process should have been conducted, it became clear that certain members of the KPC had been selected for the KSF who would not have been recommended if the original members of the selection boards had been present. One of those original members was Dave Finnimore, the head of the NATO vetting unit, who had prepared detailed reports on all the candidates describing their suitability for service in the KSF. Going ahead without the vetting officer present appeared, at first glance, to have been reckless. General Gay had received a brief from Colonel Roberts, he was a senior officer in the Italian Army and should have understood the implications of selecting people who were unsuitable for vetting reasons. The motive behind actively selecting individuals who were below the line was extremely worrying.

One individual in particular had been very quickly flagged up during the vetting process as being unfit for the new force. Dave Finnamore, the head of the vetting unit, was incensed that his team's hard work over the previous 5 months had been ignored; he was adamant that a change needed to be made. I spoke to Dave and volunteered to discuss it with General Selimi, who was unsighted on the names included on the vetting list, but Dave sensibly advised me to keep my neutrality and to not get involved. Colonel Stuart Roberts had specifically mentioned this individual when briefing the KFOR Commander, making it clear he should not be selected for the KSF. Instead, General Gay had not only selected him, he had approved his appointment to a critical role in the new organisation. Roberts, who had been instrumental in setting up a fair and transparent 'NATO Standards' process of selection, was lost for words. Dave Finnimore said to me that he had never come across such crass behaviour from a senior NATO officer. Nobody in the International Community who witnessed this process was impressed. It was all deeply unsatisfactory. In the days that followed, the individual in question was quietly moved out of one position and into another. But he remained on the list of people who would be receiving an envelope inviting him to join the KSF a few weeks later.

The delay of the whole programme into January created unintended resource issues for the MCA Division team. Many of the staff officers who had been driving the selection process forward over the previous 4 months, had already left Kosovo to be with their families over Christmas. Their end-of-tour dates had been arranged to coincide with the initial December date for Announcement Day. New staff officers who were arriving over the Christmas and New Year period were oblivious to the context and the implications of the delay. Some had no handover and there was precious little time for the remaining staff to brief them.

One of those key people was the German Non-Commissioned Officer who had built the Excel spreadsheet containing the details of the 2,788 KPC personnel hoping to join the KSF. His knowledge of how the database was designed and constructed was crucial to its successful implementation. However, he had already left Kosovo at the end of his tour before Christmas, and with him the in-depth understanding of how to manipulate the complicated datasets held within it. The collective experience that had been lost across so many functions in MCA Division over the Christmas and New Year period could not be replaced quickly. The delay created by the Prime Minister, aided and abetted by poor leadership in KFOR, had generated almost untenable levels of risk in the plan. The febrile atmosphere within the KPC in its final few weeks, together with its personnel who were already sceptical about the whole KPC-KSF process, was a toxic combination.

CHAPTER ELEVEN

'The Home Straight'

After arriving back in Pristina immediately after the New Year, one of the first meetings I arranged was with General Rama in his local café on the Sunday evening. His message to me was clear; following the delay, we have to confirm the programme of events leading up to and following Announcement Day.

It was with this backdrop that Major General Rama, Brigadier Di Luzio, Major General Nick Caplin, Andy Leonard, Colonel Stuart Roberts and I met to bash out the arrangements for the stand down of the KPC and the establishment of the KSF. Several options were discussed; these included having a longer period between Announcement Day, when the KPC were due to receive their letters informing them about whether they had been selected for the KSF, and the time at which those selected need to report for duty. The issue of guarding the barracks full of equipment and vehicles remained contentious though, with KFOR unwilling to commit resources, leaving the KPC to resolve the problem itself. It was clear that the time when the barracks were going to be empty needed to as short as possible. There was a growing consensus that a two-day period should be adopted; so the 19th January was agreed as the day when the KPC stood down, Announcement Day would be the 20th and the Kosovo

Security Force would be formally established the next day.

There were other matters to address; uniforms donated by the United States and delivered to a secure KPC location before Christmas had subsequently been moved to a US base shortly afterwards, much to the KPC leadership's bemusement. The message from KFOR was clear; we don't trust you. Finding agreement over when the uniforms would be moved back to Adem Jashari Barracks was important. The uniforms needed to be in place with enough time to distribute them before the 21st. However, the issue remained unresolved by the end of the meeting.

There was also the relatively straight forward issue of signage on KPC locations around the country that were going to undergo a metamorphosis into KSF bases overnight. When it was suggested that signs should be removed on the last day of the KPC, the 19th, Brigadier Di Luzio launched a strong argument saying that this could not happen until the 20th so that people 'didn't get the wrong impression.' As usual with Di Luzio he was lost in the fine detail, unable to climb up high enough to see the bigger picture. Everyone around the table, except for him, knew that people in Kosovo would not care a jot if the signage was removed on the 19th or the 20th.

Finally, Di Luzio once again raised the matter of who would sign the letters given to those people successful in being selected for the KSF. This was a re-run of an issue dealt with before Christmas and I didn't understand why he had brought it up. Colonel Roberts suggested, perhaps mischievously, that the letters could be signed by both KFOR and the Minister for the KSF. The original decision had been for the Minister alone to do it and that had been agreed. Di Luzio fell for it and immediately said that 'we' – KFOR – must avoid difficulties with NATO nations who do not recognise Kosovo. He was adamant that KFOR could not sign the letters. He didn't want

KFOR to be seen to be responsible for the decision of who had been selected, even though everyone in the country knew that KFOR had organised the entire process of KSF selection. Major General Caplin, measured as ever, replied with typical brevity, 'Local resistance in Kosovo from non-recognising countries is irrelevant; the NAC, SACEUR and Naples are crystal clear.' It was a priceless put down from a serious military officer.

Explaining that the North Atlantic Council in Brussels, the Supreme Allied Commander in Europe and KFOR's higher formation, which had issued the orders for the 'New Tasks' and were fully supportive, undid Di Luzio's weak argument. Knowing glances were exchanged across the table at his expense.

Even though the decision to settle on the 19th-21st period had increased the risk to the programme and piled the pressure on the staff in MCA Division in Film City, the scene was set for the formation of the Balkans' newest security organisation at one minute past midnight on the 21st January 2009. Knowing there was a date in the diary was positive for everyone, even if the date was too close for some.

In KPC headquarters, the first few weeks of January promised to be very busy. With General Selimi, now appointed as the KSF's first Commander, spending more time in the Ministry for the KSF, a highly motivated General Rama began aligning dates with the various activities that needed to be completed before the KPC was going to stand down. These activities included a KPC disbandment parade with the President as the guest of honour; the weapons collection process; a medal ceremony for past members of the KPC; and moving the US supplied uniforms back to Adem Jashari Barracks in time to kit out senior officers before the 21st January.

The security plan for guarding the equipment and vehicles in KPC locations over the period between standing down the KPC and launching the KSF now became less of an issue. With only two days to cover, a different plan was proposed. Reflecting KFOR's unwillingness to commit its forces to having any kind of presence at each location, it was decided that around 100 or so logistics personnel, 'pre-selected' for the KSF, would be employed. MCA Division supplied the names of the personnel who were likely to be selected and arrangements were made for them to be brought together and sworn to secrecy just before the stand down of the KPC. The logisticians would then be assigned to guard the ten empty barracks locations for 48 hours. They also needed uniforms and these had to be issued in advance of the 19th.

In MCA Division, the new members of the team were thrown into planning for a rearranged Announcement Day which, combined with the fragile database, was far from ideal. Every staff officer worked diligently to put the pieces of the jigsaw into place in time. The database had become the single point of failure within the entire process and it was being maintained by newly arrived staff officers from across NATO. The highly unusual strikes held by KPC personnel throughout October and November, combined with the lack of a timely and effective KFOR communications campaign, had undermined the KPC's perception of the overall process. As the KFOR Commander headed back to Italy for annual leave on the 9th January, KFOR's preparations were reaching a critical moment. Both Announcement Day and the selection process needed to go without a hitch; KFOR badly needed to repair some of the self-inflicted wounds to its brand that had been exposed through its lack of leadership over NATO's 'New Tasks' up to that point. The international community, which had already lost patience with

General Gay, was watching and waiting.

Following the meeting to agree the programme for Announcement Day and the revised KPC stand down, I was again invited to go bowling with General Selimi, General Rama, their inner circle and Terry Anderson. I went back to Film City as soon as I knew what the plan was going to be and grabbed some food in the dining facility; having experienced a similar evening just before Christmas I knew it was going to be a long one and I didn't want to drink on an empty stomach.

Again, dressed in civilian clothes, wrapped in my North Face puffa jacket to ward off the cold Balkan evening, Kasper picked me up outside my accommodation and we headed into the city, dropping me off outside the bowling alley as before. I walked in, wondering what was going to happen this time. Inside the bar area, with the familiar loud music filling my ears, all sense of being on an operational tour was again forgotten. I found the KPC crowd gathered around a table, a bottle of Chivas Regal in the centre, a half-full glass in front of each person.

Accompanied by the ever present fug of cigarette smoke, the evening took on a very similar shape to the last one. The decision to go out had been spontaneous. Even though there was still much to do, I could sense that the KPC officers were beginning to realise that they wanted to see the KPC off in their own style. I didn't really know or care why we were out mid-week, behaving as if it was a Friday night. The KPC's senior officers were going to celebrate and it was my duty to be with them. However unexpected, spending time in Rama and Selimi's company was always good value and it also gave me a chance to forget about some of the personal issues that were beginning to mount up in my mind. But it came at a price; drinking whisky on a Wednesday evening was not what I had planned and the following day was a struggle. At least the following morning gave me something to smile about.

Nursing a slight hangover, my mood was lifted when I heard, via Di Luzio, that the KFOR Chief of Staff, Brigadier General Berger, wanted the uniforms to be returned to Adem Jashari Barracks on Announcement Day. By making this suggestion, Berger had demonstrated a surprising lack of understanding about the KPC-KSF process by favouring the day when the entire KPC membership would be receiving news about their futures, then going back to their families to share the news. To conduct a routine transfer of over a thousand uniforms, at the last safe moment as far as KFOR was concerned, on one of the busiest and most emotive days in the KPC's history, was laughable. Who would do the work? Where would the resources come from? It felt like KFOR's lack of respect for the KPC was complete. And it fitted a pattern within the KFOR leadership: Di Luzio lacked pragmatism; Gay was indifferent; and now Berger had failed to understand the human impact of what was happening. I hastily contacted Major General Rama and Major General Caplin and over a short-notice meeting in Caplin's office with Di Luzio, the matter was resolved. Dealing with these ill thought through edicts from KFOR wasted so many people's time.

With the delayed plan for the collection of the KPC officers' sidearms now taking shape, I spoke to Major Frank McCormick, who was responsible for looking after weapons within the KIKPC organisation. I had asked him where the sidearms would be secured once they had been handed in. Frank was a US Reserve Officer serving in Kosovo for a one year tour of duty. He offered to take me to the ISO container where he had dozens of AK 47s and other weapons under lock and key, collected over the years and safely stored since the disarmament of the KLA in 1999.

The weather had turned seriously cold in those early days of January. I drove down with Frank and my driver, Kasper, taking care to stay on the road. Newly fallen snow was now freezing on top of layers of existing hard packed ice, creating a permafrost effect. There was little wind, sounds were muffled, and everyone's breath sent clouds of condensation into the still, biting air. It was no time to be hanging around in unheated ISO containers but I wanted to know where the KPC's weapons would be stored so that I could give a plausible answer to reassure anxious KPC officers. I had spent plenty of time in armouries so the sight of row upon row of weapons didn't really impress me, however it was the provenance of the AK47s that was interesting. These semi-automatic rifles and pistols had been used in the guerrilla war against the Serbs; in my mind that was quite significant. After a few minutes I let Frank re-secure the weapons, locked up in a freezing metal container, a tangible reminder of Kosovo's historic fight for independence years earlier.

Settling back into life in Pristina after Christmas leave was more difficult than I had expected. The extended period of leave at home in England had provided me with precious time with my family but it had come at a price. I was feeling guilty that I had not returned to Kosovo on the original date. On my return I had the sense that I had missed out on events that I really should have been attending. During the last few days in the UK my mind had been elsewhere; I was with my family but I wasn't present. The saving grace was that my children were too young to notice. These thoughts weighed heavily on my mind and I was not yet in the swing of things. Putting aside my personal conflict and emotions, I was trying to get on top of the crucial tasks that needed to be completed by Announcement Day. Everyone was still trying to work out the impact of the rushed selections during the SOSAB over the Christmas and New Year break. It was an unsettling time. And I had also been asked to meet the now retired Brigadier General Nuredin Lushtaku in a café south of the city on the Friday afternoon. I hadn't even been back in Kosovo a week and so much had already happened.

When Simi and I arrived, we were initially met with a bizarre and upsetting scene. Close to the car park was a cage with a small bear inside, exposed to the snow, clearly unhappy and looking for a way to escape. It could have been a metaphor for those in the KPC desperate to start a new life in the KSF. We stayed long enough to take a photo then entered the warmth of the café. We approached Lushtaku's table where we shook hands. After sitting down he said he wanted to know about his own weapon but was more interested in what he had been hearing about selections. Equally, I was keen to know what his intentions were; knowing what key people were thinking and doing on the periphery of the KPC-KSF process was important. I knew that Di Luzio would not have approved of me meeting him which is why, when I mentioned it in my weekly report, I omitted to say that we had met face to face, instead explaining that I had heard the information second hand. Lushtaku explained that if he was asked to work in the Government he would willingly step up if he felt he could add value. He hadn't applied to join the KSF and he was also clear that he was not interested in receiving any severance pay or pension that he was entitled to. It seemed a magnanimous gesture and as Simi and I walked back to our vehicle after the meeting ended, through the deep snow in the car park, I realised why. Lushtaku opened the driver's door to a Porsche Cayenne before driving off into the cold of Kosovo's capital city.

The pace of life was picking up and 'ground rush' – the term used by parachutists who think they have lots of time but suddenly realise that they are seconds from landing – was hitting several people, including Rama. At least the weekend gave everyone a chance to catch their breath. It was my first Saturday morning back in Pristina and Simi had arranged for me to see Agim Çeku again at Pelumbi, a restaurant just outside the capital. I was keen to keep in touch with my network and I was looking forward to seeing him, although I was now wary of whether he was going to ask to provide more information on the KPC-KSF process. In truth, I didn't mind and in a way I was flattered. We discussed life after the formation of the KSF and I offered a few thoughts on how I saw the force developing its capabilities and how those capabilities could enable Kosovo to begin to add value to the international community. The KPC had an excellent search and rescue unit, it also had developed an effective explosive ordnance disposal capability, and these skills would be a valuable asset to any future NATO or international coalition deployment.

The following week's focus was disarming the KPC officers. The plan to receive all the personal sidearms had been agreed and Rama had given the orders to all relevant KPC personnel. Any officer in possession of a Weapons Authorisation Card had to report to the KPC headquarters to hand in their weapons over a 2-day period. What troubled me was the frequency with which KPC officers trained with their personal sidearms. Handling weapons required regular practice and we had seen what happens when this training did not take place. As a result, I decided to take measures to prevent getting caught in any negligent discharge of a weapon by borrowing some discreet body armour from a contact in Slim Lines. I never felt in danger in Kosovo at any stage, but being in close proximity to KPC officers handling weapons under these circumstances was as close to a genuine risk as I could imagine. My kids would not have thanked me had something happened and I not taken the precaution.

The weapons collection was an emotive subject and was not

supported by many of those who turned up to hand over their pistols, including Selimi who remained defiant. The activity was due to take place on the 12th and 13th January and preparations were on track under the technical guidance of Major McCormick.

However, while this key activity was taking place, the pressure to select the right people for the KSF was gaining momentum outside of the formal 'NATO Standards' selection procedure. Under Colonel Stuart Roberts' supervision the selection boards were convening with representatives from various organisations in Kosovo, the wide participation designed to ensure fairness and transparency. However behind the scenes, in the form of scraps of paper, scribbled names were being passed from one officer to another in the KPC, with their ultimate destination the MCA Division. The horse-trading was beginning to take up much of Colonel Von Andrian's time. Faced with a rigid procedure that had already been discredited during the two SOSAB selection boards, Colonel Von Andrian made the pragmatic decision to apply a degree of subjectivity to the remaining selections. Generals Rama and Selimi were invited to share some names whom they believed should be in the KSF and why. Both Selimi and Rama were keen to ensure the right people, in their eyes, were selected for the new force. Colonel Roberts was accommodating in understanding their positions in advance of the key selection boards, but not everyone on their lists was agreed. The system, albeit belatedly, was beginning to right some of the wrongs of the process, even if the method was a little unorthodox.

The pressure was building rapidly on everyone at this time. I was struggling in particular, although I could not put my finger on why I was feeling so out of sorts. Perhaps it was the impact of being back in Kosovo and missing my children; perhaps I was allowing a less than harmonious Christmas break to creep into my mind and unsettle me.

I didn't know; I was not myself that much I was certain of. It was a bad place to be when you had to expect the unexpected at any time. And with the stage set in the KPC conference room for the imminent weapon collection, I wanted Selimi to be the first in line to hand in his weapon. However, before Christmas when I had brought this matter up with him, all I achieved was to generate a very negative reaction. Undeterred I had approached him again a few days later to make some progress and we had eventually settled on a compromise solution to allow him to retain face in the eyes of his officers. In the end, the actual order was written by General Rama and there had been no complaints.

So on the second day, I had asked Simi how he thought I should approach the issue of Selimi's personal weapon, which needed to be handed in. Simi suggested I speak to Rama, which I did. What I hadn't factored in was Colonel Gashi's intervention. Although I was not at all sure what had been said, he came downstairs to the conference room to tell me that Selimi wanted to see me. I left the others to it and walked up to his office on the first floor. Selimi was not happy with me for asking others how to approach him over the issue of his own weapon. It seemed quite petty, the implication was clear though; I should have gone straight to see him myself. With everything else going on, it caught me by surprise.

I was not expecting his reaction, and under the circumstances, I was not really thinking things through clearly either. My overall mood was beginning to cloud my judgement. I excused myself from his office and went back down to the conference room to continue with the job in hand. Up to that point the weapon collection process had gone very well, with everyone's weapons being recorded, including the amount of live rounds handed in with the magazines. Everything was bagged up and stored safely; all weapons had been recovered, a task which had appeared to be almost impossible a few months earlier. Receipts were issued to the KPC officers who had left without comment. It felt very much like the end of an era, even if some in the KPC appeared rooted in the past and unwilling to move on.

Foolishly I allowed myself to run the events of the afternoon over and over in my head. I was very unhappy with what had happened and I felt even more isolated as a result. I didn't need to have a difficult relationship with General Selimi at this stage; always hard to read, we had rubbed along pretty well for my tour up to that point and I didn't want our relationship to turn sour over a relatively small issue. That said, Selimi was under enormous pressure. Somehow a list of names of those selected for the KSF was released in the media. Selimi's phone was bombarded with calls from those whose names did not appear. Where the leak had come from nobody knew, but it was deeply unhelpful and conspired to make the final few days in command for Selimi even harder than they needed to be. With the list now public, those who appeared to have missed the cut started looking for someone to blame. Later that day when I was back in Film City I was taking care of some of the mundane aspects of deploying on operations by collecting my clean washing from the camp laundrette. Regrettably, and for the first time, I allowed my darkening mood to spill over and managed to upset one of the girls who worked so hard at the laundry reception. Like before with my son, I regretted what I had said straight away. I was so ashamed of how I had acted that after dumping my clean uniform on my bed I immediately went back to apologise.

I was not on form and I knew it. When I was back in my accommodation I took a shower and just slipped down the wall, eventually sitting on the floor, with the water cascading over me, feeling ill and totally drained, trying to find a hand hold to pull me back up to where I knew I needed to be. I had to talk to someone, I didn't feel able to talk to my wife, the situation was simply too difficult for her to comprehend over Skype. The pressure was building; I needed a release valve. On the Friday morning I decided to text Migena and ask whether she would meet me later that day. Migena was the interpreter who I had met during my day out at the ski resort in Brezovice in the south of Kosovo. We had got on well enough that day and she agreed that she would meet me later on in a café in Film City.

There was no time to dwell on the last couple of days though. That morning the reception for former commanders in the KPC had been organised although it was something in the diary that I had paid little attention to. I wasn't sure what to expect; I walked downstairs into the conference room which had already begun to fill up. Kasper was with me and Simi was explaining who was who. As it turned out, it was very interesting. I was meeting some new people as well as some old familiar faces. Agim Çeku was there, dressed in his trademark long black winter coat. We shook hands warmly as he moved around the room to catch up with people he hadn't seen in some time. Ramush Haradinaj also arrived and we greeted each other warmly, firmly shaking hands. Good natured bonhomie filled the room, the volume growing louder by the minute; it was friendly and uplifting. Food and drinks were laid out on the tables, probably the last time that the KPC HQ team would need to cater for an event. It was a very special reunion, it was upbeat, signifying the closure of an organisation that had replaced the Kosovo Liberation Army, known to all as the KLA. The KLA had been engaged in a guerrilla war against Serbian paramilitary forces since 1994 but the conflict escalated significantly throughout 1998 and into 1999. The KLA, men and women, numbered many thousands of volunteers, who had either fought against or supported the guerrilla war against the Serbs.

I had a very interesting conversation with Rexhep Selimi, one of the KLA's founding members, who told me he had written a book about his time in the KLA. It was a very distinguished group of individuals who had once been brothers in arms. Also present were Rehmi Mustafa, the Head of the Security Commission who I had met with Selimi all those months ago in September. Daut Haradinaj, Ramush's brother, was also in the room. I had never met him but had heard much about him and, as a founding member of the KLA in 1994, his place in Kosovo's history was assured. In all, the invited guests probably made up at least the top 5 most wanted in Serbia.

Simi knew everyone and everyone knew Simi. The reception was more like a reunion. When General Selimi stood up to welcome his guests he referred to the KPC-KSF process as the hardest thing he had done in his life; it was clear that his behaviour in the last few weeks reflected this state of affairs. Both Ramush Haradinaj and Agim Çeku also gave speeches, medals were handed over to everyone present and the event finished off with the obligatory photographs. It had been an enlightening 90 minutes.

In the afternoon there was another meeting between Colonel Von Andrian and General Rama to discuss KSF appointments. Earlier on, before the commanders' reception, General Selimi had been to see the President at short notice and then travelled into Film City to meet Di Luzio, to talk about personnel and selections. It was messy and the signs were not good. As I began to pick up some of the names of who would be selected, it started to dawn on me that we were going to be creating a real problem for ourselves after the announcements the following week. But time had run out on the process and apart from some obvious errors which had been highlighted in the previous weeks, there was not much more that anyone could do. I steeled myself for a rough ride.

On the Friday afternoon, I drove back to my accommodation with Kasper, ready for a working weekend. Firstly though I had an appointment at a café in Film City. I met Migena over a pot of tea and even though we had only seen each other a few times during my tour, I was able to discuss some of the issues that were troubling me; Migena listened and understood. Having the opportunity to offload what I was dealing with had been very important for the state of my mental health. Even though we only spent an hour together, I felt a lot better for it. That night I slept more deeply than I had done in a while.

The following morning I felt re-energised; it was as if a weight had been lifted from me. It was a working weekend and with only a matter of days to go before the stand down of the KPC, there were activities happening on both Saturday and Sunday. Leaving Kasper to have a weekend off I drove the car down to the KPC headquarters to attend a briefing for the 119 logisticians who had been pre-selected for the KSF and were going to be issued their uniforms under a threadbare cloak of secrecy. Driving down to the headquarters, the scene of so many good and less good times, allowed me to reflect on how far we had come. It also allowed me to put the last 7 days into a broader context.

It had been a bruising week for many, not only me. General Rama had confided in me that he was unhappy with the final list of officers who had been selected via the newly defined 'NATO Standards' approach, adopted by Colonel Von Andrian after the debacle of the SOSAB. He knew that some good men had not been selected but he was unable to negotiate a place for everyone he felt deserved a career in the KSF. The new force was initially smaller than the KPC for a reason; the stand down of the KPC and the formation of the KSF was not intended to be a transformation, i.e. a one-for-one swap. It was a transition. The KPC was being confined to the history books and new, fresh blood was needed to join the KSF and make the organisation what it had been designed to be; a multi-ethnic, civilian-led security organisation which would be attractive for both young men and women, from all quarters of Kosovan society. A great deal of effort was being invested in the recruiting campaign for Kosovo Serbs, which was due to start on the same day as the KSF went live. What better way to start to break down ethnic barriers than having young Kosovo Serbs and Albanians working closely together in uniform.

When I arrived at the KPC and walked through the door, I was met by all the logisticians chatting together loudly in the entrance hall with an understandable air of expectation. I acknowledged their greetings as I walked through the mass of bodies. I immediately had that slight adrenaline rush which always accompanied these moments. I could see they were excited and ready for whatever they were going to be asked to do. In their minds, they had been selected for the KSF and this was the first opportunity for them to demonstrate their worth to the new organisation. To be honest, I was excited for them too. After filing into the conference room and being congratulated by General Selimi, they were then briefed by General Rama on what their task entailed. Following a short Q&A, everyone moved *en masse*, but sworn to secrecy, to Adem Jashari Barracks where the uniforms were now stored after being returned early from the KFOR warehouse. Under the supervision of KFOR, the logisticians were handed their uniform and told to keep them in a bag until midnight on the 21st.

The following day we all assembled in the KPC headquarters again, this time for the senior officers who had been pre-selected. It was clear that command and control was required on the ground from the first moments of the KSF's existence and the senior officers who had been selected needed to be dressed and ready to look the part. In his role as the Land Forces Commander, General Rama briefed the group on the role of the logisticians and what he expected from the first few days. He also explained how he expected the KSF to be different; he mentioned behaviour, professionalism and even the smoking ban. I was delighted that he was taking such a strong line to start the KSF off on the right foot. The senior officers also then moved to the barracks to collect their uniforms. We were getting close.

There were just two final activities for the KPC leadership to organise and attend before the curtain came down on the KPC's nine years in existence. When I had arrived in the August of the previous year there was talk of a parade, marching through Pristina with flags flying and people lining the streets to thank the KPC for what they had done. The parade would usher in the next chapter on the country's journey towards establishing an Army and a degree of regional normalisation. How things had changed. By November, with KPC personnel refusing to obey orders and talking to the media about their demands, effectively going on strike in uniform, the appetite for a very public event to mark the closure of the KPC quickly evaporated. Local ceremonies in the towns and villages around the country did go ahead before Christmas, but a large-scale event in the capital had long been forgotten. Instead, the sloping access road between the small housing estate and the old driving school, which had housed the KPC for nearly a decade, was the chosen location for the final parade. On a cold January morning with a gathering of dignitaries from KFOR, the UN and the international community, the ordinariness of that stretch of tarmac somehow became a fitting metaphor for how the KPC saw itself by the end of its life.

I walked into the KPC headquarters, as I had done countless times over the course of the last 5 months, knowing we had 45 minutes before the President was due to arrive. And, as usual, the preparations were in mid flow. I smiled at the chaos because I had learned over my time with the KPC that everything always came together at the last minute. Chairs were still being lined up outside, place names were being printed inside, and members of the ceremonial Kosovo Guard, the unit formerly commanded by the now retired KPC Brigadier General Nuredin Lushtaku, were doing final checks to each other's uniforms in formation on the side of the road. Even though the President was expected, in the big scheme of things, it was a low-key send-off.

In the few minutes before the start there was a buzz about the place. I stood on a grassy bank, watching the whole show come together on time as KPC officers were dashing about, doing last-minute tasks before the ceremony began. The guests, officers from KFOR and the diplomatic community, were renewing old acquaintances with KPC officers. I seemed to be the only person not moving. I was taking it all in. Many of us knew we were heading out of Pristina to Kosovo's famous Stone Castle vineyard at Rahovec for a celebratory lunch, so there was an end-of-term feeling about the event. Within moments the assembled audience stood up and the Guard came to attention, saluting the President as he walked up the short hill accompanied by General Selimi.

The parade had even enticed General Gay out of his secure bubble in Film City, standing prominently next to the podium, waiting for the President to arrive. When I saw him separated from his close protection team I couldn't help wondering why he hid behind them when he walked around his own camp up at Film City. As I pondered the moment, I remembered what someone had said to me when we had been trying to get the Prime Minister to make a decision on the Commander of the KSF nomination. The 'someone' in question was a diplomat who did not have a high opinion of General Gay. He disclosed that he and his colleagues had decided that whenever the opportunity presented itself they would mention in diplomatic circles that General Gay was ill, in the hope that his reputation would be undermined. In my view he had been doing a pretty good job of that himself.

An hour later, after a simple yet dignified parade, the President took his leave and the Kosovo Guard was dismissed, flags were gathered up and chairs were returned to the KPC building for the last time. The small legacy cell that would remain in existence for a further 6 months to oversee the resettlement of former KPC personnel was all that was left of a once highly regarded uniformed organisation.

That was that; the KPC was officially de-activated after serving the people of Kosovo for 3,408 days.

The celebration at the Stone Castle Vineyard was particularly poignant. It was as if stepping over the threshold into the famous old caves, which had survived the war in 1999, removed a weight from everyone's shoulders. Disagreements and the tension of the last few weeks were all forgotten. General Selimi and all his senior officers hosted the invited guests, including General Caplin, who was clearly relieved that the delivery of KPC's stand down had gone as well as hoped. He was due to leave the country permanently at the end of the month and he was in a mood to celebrate, wrapped up in a thick military down jacket to combat the freezing temperature inside the cave.

There was also no shortage of firepower in the room with several armed close protection teams from the KPC, the UK and Norway lurking in the shadows of the caves, leaning on huge wine casks, chatting quietly amongst themselves.

After lunch Selimi stood up and made his fourth speech in as many days, then invited some of us forward to receive the same medal and certificate that had been given to the former commanders of the KPC at the ceremony the Friday before. It was quite unexpected but all the same it seemed a fitting tribute for those who had worked tirelessly to make the whole process a success. Nobody was thinking of what might happen the following day when over 2,700 KPC personnel would turn up at a designated time and place to learn their fate. That was for the morning. For now it was all about toasting the KPC; and for some it was good to leave it behind.

After the formal lunch, with a plentiful supply of wine to hand, conversations were breaking out across the floor of the cave away from the table. I was standing talking by the huge stack of barrels when, with no warning, the loud chatter was dramatically interrupted by 5 gun shots being fired in rapid succession. The room momentarily went silent as everyone orientated themselves to the source of the shooting. I quickly turned round to see General Rama standing by the table aiming a pistol into the roof of the cave. It was as hilarious as it was unexpected; I could only imagine what the close protection teams were thinking when they heard the first shot. It had been an act of celebratory fire, and everyone soon carried on with their conversations, as if nothing had happened at all. I later picked up one of the empty cases from the floor to keep as a memento. All remnants of the formal luncheon had been overtaken by pure revelry, with the Kosovans singing traditional songs and setting the tone by dancing on the table. In response, the British officers sang traditional rugby songs, also on the table. I was happy to concede that we were out sung and out danced that evening.

Not long afterwards everything wound down. Grateful to the owners at Stone Castle who had been the most welcoming hosts every time I had visited, everyone found their respective drivers and close protection teams, and left the caves, heading back towards their homes in every corner of the country. However the evening had not yet finished for those of us bound for Pristina. Rama had decided to stop on the way back to the capital for a night cap in a roadside restaurant, even though we really didn't need to consume any more. The group consisted of General Rama, Colonel Gashi, Lieutenant Colonel Jeton Dreshaj, together with Colonel Stuart Roberts, Lieutenant Colonel Terry Anderson, a US female civilian called Shana, and of course, Simi. In fact, I think Simi would happily have gone straight back to Pristina; he was as relieved as any to see the KPC finally put to bed and had celebrated hard.

In the course of the next hour someone suggested that General Rama should swap uniforms with Colonel Roberts. It seemed like a good idea at the time and they staggered off to the bathroom to make the swap. They soon emerged and after photographs had captured the moment, the decision was taken to finally call it a night. Everyone was going to be up early the next morning to oversee Announcement Day. Although I had drunk a lot, it had been over a long period of time, so I was feeling fine. Simi though was suffering and Kasper drove quickly but smoothly back to Pristina. I had called Simi's wife, Valbona, to arrange a rendezvous point with her so that I could hand him over into her custody once we were back in the capital. When we met, I told Valbona that Simi didn't need to come into work until later the following day. What I didn't realise until later was the rather awkward situation Colonel Roberts found himself in, trying to navigate his way back into Film City, still wearing the uniform of the Deputy Commander of the KPC.

There was no time to linger on the evening's remarkable celebrations though, I had an important appointment the following morning. I had already collected a box of envelopes and was meeting Kasper for an early breakfast before heading out of camp to deliver the first of them to the logisticians guarding the camp at Ferizaj, south of Pristina. Announcement Day was nearly upon us.

CHAPTER TWELVE

'Announcement Day'

The 20th January 2009 started early. I was sitting in the Dining Facility, a building known as 'Dublin', by 6.30am. In Film City every building had been given a name from an international town or city, so the walk to 'Dublin' from my accommodation block, 'Buenos Aires', was only two minutes away via 'Oslo'. It made navigation simple for everyone and reinforced KFOR's international flavour.

I caught up with Kasper and we sat down to a quick bowl of cereal and a cup of tea whilst I mentally prepared myself for what promised to be an historic day. In fact it proved to be one of the more memorable of my tour. I also bumped into Lieutenant Colonel Peter Bell from the Canadian Army, who worked in MCA Division and was leading the envelope distribution activity in an old Ammunition Factory near Skenderaj in Protection Zone 1, the heartland of the Kosovo Liberation Army back in the day. In Peter's mind it was a potential flash point. We briefly chatted about how he thought things would go.

Peter had been concerned about security at the site and had requested additional support from within KFOR. I had spoken to him about the general mood and my belief that there would be no problems from KPC members. Peter was a level-headed officer who understood risk, but even after reassuring him about the current situation he still felt the need for additional KFOR armed protection during the day. It was a constant factor that I found at times frustrating; there was a sense of suspicion towards the KPC that pervaded KFOR.

On the previous Saturday, 119 logisticians had been called in to the KPC HQ where they had been told about their guarding task and where they would be performing these duties. They naturally took it as good news regarding their selection for the KSF. The logisticians had then moved directly to Adem Jashari Barracks where they had been issued their uniform. This activity had not been advertised and there was a degree of risk by bringing that number of people into a position where they could pretty well work out for themselves that they had been pre-selected for the KSF. The issue was sensitive and we all hoped the logisticians would play their part by respecting the confidentiality of the situation. If the media had discovered what was going on it would have made for interesting headlines. There was nothing we could do about that.

The logisticians, who had been trained by the British Army on a 4-week course the previous autumn, were therefore ideally placed to guard the centrally stored vehicles and equipment at each KPC location. They each deployed to one of 10 former KPC bases across the country. With their KSF uniform safely stowed away in their bags, and sworn to secrecy, the logisticians had set out the previous day to report for duty.

With my tea drunk we prepared to leave Film City for the short 40-minute drive south to Ferizaj, the home of the future KSF training base. I had the envelopes on the back seat and the list of personnel who I needed to see and we set off through the near-deserted streets of Pristina. I was feeling pretty positive about the day ahead. The way the plan for distributing the envelopes had evolved meant that there were two groups of guards who would not be at one of the Announcement Day distribution points. Someone had to take the envelopes to them and I was the obvious choice. In fact I was actually quite pleased to be able to deliver the first envelope of the day.

We headed out on the main dual carriageway south from Pristina on a clear and fresh morning, the sun shining brightly through the car's windscreen. Listening as usual to the breakfast show live from Germany on the British Forces Radio Station – BFBS – I was thinking through the first few hours of the morning. I needed to meet Major General Rama in his café at 8.30am but I also needed to issue envelopes at Ferizaj and the old KPC headquarters. I knew it would be tight but with Kasper at the wheel and the faithful blue light and siren on call, I was sure I would not be late. As usual, when we approached Ferizaj, we lost BFBS and flicked to 103.5FM, a local Pristina-based station that played some excellent, if fairly eclectic, music. I was in a good mood and with the morning traffic hardly causing us any delay we made steady progress. We turned into the town of Ferizaj and made our way past streams of school children. Even at 7.30am school was about to begin.

The camp at Ferizaj was vast; it had been bombed extensively by NATO in the war but had undergone a significant re-building programme. As the future home of all KSF training, much work still needed to be done. As we entered the barracks I asked Kasper to pull over by the guard house where the first envelope was delivered to a bemused and non-English-speaking KPC guard at the gate. I managed to get his signature and handed over his letter. As I was sure that KFOR had only selected logisticians who had been successful, I maintained a positive manner. It was a low-key, matter-of-fact exchange with the first guard; a million miles away from the activity that was to take place elsewhere in the country. The ball was rolling and nobody could stop what was about to unfold over the next 12 hours.

We quickly pointed the Landcruiser north and returned to the capital in preparation for a long and potentially interesting day. As I was on the outskirts of the city I received a call from Lieutenant Colonel Jeton Dreshaj who had not forgotten a promise he had made the evening before at the vineyard. He told me to come to the KPC headquarters to collect the KPC flag from the entrance hall, which he and Colonel Gashi had removed and folded up for me. I arrived at the KPC HQ building and quickly established myself in the ops room where I issued out the envelopes one by one as the guards filed in. Checking their IDs against the master list, everyone was present and correct. I then walked upstairs to Colonel Xhavit Gashi's office, the scene of so many good times, and there in front of me was Lieutenant Colonel Dreshaj, with the flag from the entrance hall. I was absolutely delighted to receive it and the significance was not lost on me. The flag had stood in its place for a long time, a symbol of the KPC's presence and influence in the country. For the flag to be given to the last British Liaison Officer to the KPC somehow seemed appropriate. I was touched and went downstairs to put it safely in my office.

We then drove fairly quickly across town the short distance to Fratelli's café where I met General Rama, Simi and a few other KPC officers. Simi was looking a bit rough but nothing was said. We didn't have time for a coffee and left almost immediately to go to the TRADOC building, as Rama wanted to be one of the first to collect his envelope; a formality but one that everyone had agreed was necessary to try to retain a degree of transparency about the selection process.

TRADOC was in central Pristina and as a result it was inevitably going to be the focus for the national media. As we arrived, the numbers of both KPC members and journalists was already high, as the former hoped for good news and the latter for some unexpected reaction to the process. The guard had been clearly briefed not to allow journalists to enter the location and this was to be strictly enforced. After stepping out of the car, as I stood in the car park outside the building, I noticed Simi run across to the main gate. This in itself was unusual. The plan for the day was clear; each unit or group would be given a specific time in which to arrive at their allocated Announcement Day distribution point and they were then to pick up their envelope and leave. There was little room in the plan for things to go wrong and that was how KFOR wanted it. Instead it already looked like a free-for-all.

When Simi returned he explained that two enterprising journalists had managed to evade detection from the gate guards. To be fair, it would not have been too difficult to do this with the melee of people trying to push their way into the camp. The attentiveness of the KPC guards was not always what was desired. The journalists had been intercepted just short of the room in which the envelopes were being handed out and their intention of getting a picture of the process had been prevented. Why KFOR hadn't allowed a couple of journalists into one location so that a pool photo could be taken of Announcement Day was beyond me; the treatment of the local press by KFOR, and its reluctance to take the initiative over shaping the media narrative had infuriated everyone. KFOR had simply repeated the defensive line that it was a matter for the Institutions of Kosovo to manage rather than KFOR itself.

After watching events for a while and taking a few of my own photographs, I decided to visit the distribution point at Adem Jashari

Barracks 10 minutes away. The morning was bright and reasonably warm in the sunshine. Snow lay on the ground and the chill remained in the shade, but the weather had been kind to the KPC.

However, all was not well.

The conduct of Announcement Day was clearly mixed; TRADOC had been reasonably controlled but the scene at Adem Jashari Barracks was chaotic. The KPC members were so desperate to know what their fate was, they were crammed into a small entrance hall inside the Logistics Building with only a glass partitioned wall and door separating them from the calm of the main auditorium, where the KFOR personnel were manning desks and handing out the envelopes. It was like a scene from a pop concert, with adoring fans pressed up against the window to catch a glimpse of their idol. I suggested that a better system should be employed by the KFOR soldiers who were in charge, but, to be honest, the soldiers controlling the heaving mass of bodies came from a country where chaos and civil unrest were perfectly normal activities, so I left it. It was quite undignified; it wouldn't have happened if the Brits had been in charge.

We soon pulled into the Vrani Do Barracks and stopped in front of a large group of men milling about outside the main building being used for the envelope distribution. When I got out of the Landcruiser I sensed a different atmosphere compared to the other two locations. Walking from the car to the building was only about 30 metres but in that time it was evident that there were some unhappy people outside. The men were all huddled in groups of 5 or 6, discussing their results, smoking and looking furtively at my vehicle. I did not feel in the slightest intimidated, even though I was unarmed and without body armour, unlike some KFOR troops in Kosovo. I had barely been there two minutes when I received a call from General

Rama, via Simi, to go back into Pristina to meet him for a coffee as soon as I could to discuss a major error. After I had entered the building and said hello to the KFOR team who were checking names and handing over envelopes, I walked back to the car with Kasper and headed back to the capital, 20 minutes away.

As we approached Pristina, we drove past the monument erected to commemorate the 600th anniversary of the Serbian defeat at the hands of the Ottomans in 1389 and used by Serbian President Milosevic in 1989 to change the lives of Kosovo Albanians for ever. During the short journey Simi confirmed what I had sensed at Vrani Do; that there was already some dissent over selections. As events unfolded during the afternoon, the reason became very clear why they felt like this. The omens were not good and I braced myself for a busier day than I had hoped for.

The news I had been told earlier via Simi involved a double appointment for the same Battalion Commander position in Gjilane. It seemed inconceivable that it could have happened considering there were only three Battalion Commander appointments in total. I headed over to Fratelli's, Rama's local café near his home, with Simi by my side. It had already been a stressful day but as I saw General Rama sitting at a table smoking a cigarette, I had a feeling it was about to become even worse. He was sitting outside, unhappy to have been disturbed but more concerned about the emerging number of selection errors. There had been some fundamental mistakes in the selection process by MCA Division and stories were beginning to circulate, via text message. One story described a woman with a prosthetic leg, who had somehow avoided the run during the physical selection tests, and had been offered a place in the KSF over an able-bodied woman in the same unit. The Battalion Commander issue was serious though and needed immediate action. General Rama confirmed the problem; two Lieutenant Colonels had been selected to command the same battalion that was about to be formed up at one minute past midnight the following morning.

I tried to get to the bottom of what had happened; it was reported that another Lieutenant Colonel, Bekim Shyti, had received orders to assume the same appointment as Lieutenant Colonel Jeton Dreshaj. I had asked whether anyone had actually seen the letters and it appeared that Dreshaj had been at TRADOC at the same time as Shyti, and they had seen each other's envelopes; Dreshaj verified what it had said. A decision from KFOR was needed as soon as possible on the way forward. Time was of the essence.

After leaving Rama I learned that Shyti's name had been raised a few days before Announcement Day, as someone who was not to be offered a role in the KSF. But something had gone wrong with the subsequent staff action and he had been appointed in error. While waiting for what I thought would be an imminent decision from Colonel von Andrian, I drove to the restaurant Collection to find General Selimi, Colonel Gashi and Lieutenant Colonel Jeton Dreshaj huddled around a table drinking coffee, supping raki and smoking as heavily as usual. Simi and I joined them. Kasper sat with Selimi's close protection team at another table close to the main door.

Collection had become an extension of the KPC headquarters. We had often de-bunked to the restaurant when we needed a change of scene. I had also become friendly with the waiter and he invariably looked after me, making sure I was given my usual snack of toasted bread with olives and yoghurt, along with a macchiato. After only a few minutes though it was clear that nobody was celebrating the successful execution of the Announcement Day activity. General Selimi was particularly concerned and collectively the three of them began giving me names of individuals who should have been selected into the KSF but who had been rejected.

I sat and recorded their concerns and made sure that I was clear about each individual's current status and what Selimi and the others wanted; I doubted I could do much but I took the names nonetheless. The last-minute horse-trading that had been conducted immediately before Announcement Day was beginning to come back to bite everyone. I obviously needed to take Selimi's concerns back to MCA Division. I made my excuses and returned to Film City in order to see Colonel von Andrian, who had executive authority over the process in MCA Division. Seeing Von Andrian was the right call; Brigadier Di Luzio would not have been able to make an informed decision that would have helped the situation. Colonel von Andrian, an HR specialist, was a breath of fresh air and he alone had helped massage the selection and appointment process ahead of Announcement Day. Now though he was responsible for tidying up the mess that a rushed and flawed selection process had created. Shyti needed to be told, and told today. After a delay of 3 hours I was finally given the clearance from Colonel von Andrian to tell Lieutenant Colonel Shyti the bad news. I got in touch with Rama and arranged to see him again back at Fratelli's.

I really didn't think things could get much worse. Allocating two officers of the same rank to one of only three positions of commanding officer within the new force was unbelievable. We had been fighting the issue of credibility throughout the recruiting, screening and selection of KSF candidates over the previous 5 months. The flow of negative stories about the final selection list was doing serious damage to the KSF and KFOR, which had overseen the entire process. I knew how under pressure the NATO team had been, made even more challenging following weeks of delay by the Prime Minister. It was a perfect storm and was only going to get worse.

My mind raced; how were we going to get out of this one? Dealing with someone who had been dishonest to avoid a run was relatively easy to solve. Telling a Lieutenant Colonel, who had no doubt told his family and friends of his appointment, was a whole lot more complicated.

'Someone has to tell him.'

I had said these words to General Selimi and the other officers gathered in Collection an hour earlier. Jeton Dreshaj knew that his own position had been offered to someone else; someone who I knew should not have been a candidate in the first place. Something had to be done and it couldn't wait. I volunteered to make the journey to Mitrovice and deliver the news to Shyti, to explain that there had been an error. I was the NATO liaison officer appointed to the KPC, NATO had screwed up, and none of the staff officers hidden behind the wire in Film City were likely to want to drive an hour north to the troubled town of Mitrovice to tell someone that there had been a cock-up.

Sitting in front of Rama, his determined stare fixed on me, cigarette smoke seeping from between his lips, he made a decision. The General said at last, in his unfamiliar English, 'I will call him.'

I reminded the General to check whether the officer I was going to meet also spoke English. I asked whether he thought the meeting would go well. Rama assured me everything would be fine.

As the coffees arrived, General Rama removed his phone and called Shyti. Rama said that he was to go to the KPC headquarters in Mitrovice, alone, and to be there in an hour and a half. He should be prepared to meet the LNO. Everyone knew me as the LNO. Using my newly acquired Albanian, I guessed enough to know the outline details of the meet and that it would be awkward. Following Rama's advice I also called Shyti and it was obvious that his English was excellent so I decided to leave Simi in Pristina. In many ways, conducting the meeting in English made it a lot easier for me; trying to explain something so serious through an interpreter would have been very difficult. Without much more to say I shook the General's hand and left with my Danish driver body guard.

In the car I told Kasper the basics of what was going to happen. I explained that I had to tell someone who had been selected that in fact there had been an error, and actually he hadn't been selected at all. This was going to happen in Mitrovice at the KPC headquarters and that there was a very small chance it may not go well. We drove north in almost complete silence. I was feeling quite nervous, rehearsing in my mind what I was going to say to him. At one point Kasper tried to start a conversation with me, but it was as if his words lost their way. I was intensely focused on the meeting; my tension must have transferred to Kasper, who also seemed quite preoccupied with what he may have to do within the next hour or so. It was an odd atmosphere for us, we had never been so quiet. There was normally a good feeling in the car, with music or conversation filling the space; but not today.

The miles seemed to pass more slowly as we neared Mitrovice. The feeling in the pit of my stomach grew more acute and I was starting to feel a little nervous. At least I knew I would be on edge and therefore on top of things. However, there was something nagging in the depths of my memory over the officer's name, but I could not quite put the pieces together. I was sure I had seen his name before but I couldn't place him. He was not a well-known individual within the mainstream of the KPC so his appointment must have been a surprise to him at the very least, as it was to the officers I had been with earlier in the day.

As we pulled into the headquarters car park, the last of the afternoon light was fading fast. It was cold and unwelcoming. The street lights were on, barely cutting through the gloom outside, the weather matching my own mood. Inside the entrance of the building the logisticians huddled around a portable heater. With initial greetings out of the way, I was too focused on my forthcoming conversation to ask whether any of them had been successful. I think they sensed that something was not right. Even though my Albanian was poor, we managed to communicate my needs and the senior KPC person led me to a warm office on the ground floor, 20m along the corridor, in which to conduct the interview. The room must have been where the guard had been sitting, keeping warm, before we arrived. I felt no pleasure in having temporarily evicted them.

The room had two chairs, a table and large drapes covering the windows. The walls were decorated with years of KPC paraphernalia and framed photographs. In the corner there were dozens of calendars rolled up on the top of a locker. I took one down to see the geographical image of a Greater Albanian, which included the borders of Kosovo. It was a dream held by many. The room was warm and cosy, with a television rigged up with some fairly dodgy wiring on the sideboard, a table in the middle surrounded by chairs which had seen better days. Newspapers were strewn across the table and a noticeboard on the wall was decorated with KPC instructions and out of date orders. To my surprise the room was not at all smoky – perhaps the intention from General Rama to ban smoking in KSF locations had been adopted early in Mitrovice.

Inside our temporary interview room, Kasper and I hatched our plan. Kasper told me where to sit and we discussed triggers in case the conversation turned nasty. I had no idea whether the individual may have guessed that something was not right and had armed himself. We had to prepare for any eventuality, however unlikely it seemed. I was feeling vulnerable but reassured that Kasper would, quite literally, be watching my back.

However, before the main event I had another task to complete. One KPC member, Emin Musa, had received an envelope telling him that he had not been selected when in fact he had. He had been called earlier and told to meet me so that I could give him the correct information. Colonel Von Andrian had given me the envelope to pass on. The coincidences just seemed to be never ending. The man I gave the envelope to had been the barrack room lawyer when I had visited Mitrovice with Rama to speak to the KPC members about the need to avoid going on strike. In that meeting, standing to the side and surrounded by his colleagues, I considered him to be someone who was unfit for service in the KSF due to his conduct that day. He was ill informed and belligerent. Briefly leaving the warmth of the office, I walked back down the corridor and gave him the correct envelope. He soon left, leaving me to prepare with Kasper for Shyti's arrival.

For the first time during my tour I needed Kasper's close protection skills. He wedged the door open so it wouldn't click shut, allowing him to enter the room immediately. Kasper told me where he would stand; basically about 5 feet behind me and the other side of a 4-inch dividing wall, next to the door. I explained how I wanted him to act by hanging around in the entrance of the headquarters building and then when we were inside the room to follow us up the corridor to take up his position. From there he could hear every word of the conversation and assess the atmosphere. I did another quick check of the room, rearranging the chairs again by a few millimetres and then walked out to the entrance to greet my visitor.

After speaking to Shyti in the afternoon it would have been clear to him that I had something fairly serious to say. Whether anyone from the KPC had pre-warned him I was unaware, but there was a possibility that he could have already been told the reason for my visit; after all he knew about the similar letter addressed to Jeton Dreshaj in the morning. It was perfectly possible that he was only expecting me to tell him that he was in fact heading for another job rather than the Battalion Commander position. He was in for a shock either way.

As he walked into the brightly lit entrance hall from the cold and dark Mitrovice evening, his eyes squinting slightly, I immediately recognised him but again could not remember why I knew his face. Although it didn't wrongfoot me, my brain starting trying to place him even while we were exchanging pleasantries, as was customary in Kosovo. I invited him to follow me and we walked together to the allocated room where he entered first. I asked him to sit in the chair opposite the door. I sat with my back to the exit. This way I would not see Kasper enter the room but he would be able to immediately assess the potential danger to me and to himself. I sat with the table on my right to allow me to use my hands and fingers to touch a surface; this was a subconscious action that I knew I would rely on during the imminent conversation.

I was feeling surprisingly calm considering what I was about to tell him. He was sitting in front of me, wearing jeans and a long black leather jacket. He looked relaxed. I said, 'Sir, there is no easy way of saying this but there has been a mistake and you have not been selected for the KSF. I'm sorry.'

I had been considering how to break the news and I decided that the direct approach was best. The silence that followed seemed to last forever. His face suddenly became distant as he took in my words.

At last he cleared his throat and replied. He was incredulous and refused to accept it. I explained that I was speaking with the authority of NATO and that unfortunately there had been a mistake. He wanted to know why he had been selected in the first place (there had been an error in the staff work) and what he was going to tell his family whom he had arranged to meet to celebrate later that evening (no response). He had told his family and friends about his selection, they were going to have a party, they were ecstatic. I sympathised but maintained my position, despite him becoming quite angry. He explained to me that he could work for his brothers and earn plenty of money but he wanted to wear the uniform of the KSF.

As expected I found myself using my forefinger to emphasise the news by touching the table in a slow and deliberate manner. In a strange way touching the table gave me the ability to focus my emotions whilst returning his stare. His eyes never left mine and I corralled all my concentration on his face. I didn't want the meeting to drag on. In the end he accepted the news with surprising grace. There was nothing I could do and he could see that as well. After 10 minutes or so I wound things up. I thanked him for being so understanding and I wished him luck.

We stood and I asked him to leave the room first. It was only at that second that I remembered Kasper had been outside and I hoped he had enough time to return to the entrance hall. Sure enough, professional as ever, he was nowhere to be seen. We stopped together once more in the entrance where we shook hands a final time before he disappeared into the Kosovan night.

I felt terrible for Shyti, especially when the situation was far from my fault. I also knew that whoever had failed to carry out the staff action in the first place was blissfully unaware of the impact the error had had on him and his family. Whether he should have been in the KSF or not, it was an experience he should not have had to sit through. Personally, I never wanted to repeat it again either.

I returned to the room to rearrange the chairs as I had found them and took a moment to think about the whole unbelievable situation. I exhaled slowly and reflected on the impact these errors would have on the overall selection process for the KSF. I had given Shyti the correct envelope that had been hastily prepared by the staff in MCA Division. Unfortunately he had not brought his original letter that he had been given in TRADOC eight hours earlier, so he ended up with two letters from KFOR, each with a contradictory message.

We headed to the car. We didn't hang around. Mitrovice was not the sort of place you would want to stay in too long and I needed to get back to the relative comfort of Pristina and my room. I was exhausted. Announcement Day had been a partial success. Hundreds of former KPC personnel had been accepted into the KSF. They were all delighted. But many had been on the wrong end of a series of administrative errors which others, like me, were doing their best to untangle.

I called Colonel von Andrian and General Rama to inform them that the deed had been done. On my way back to Film City I reflected on the fact that he could easily go to the press and make some uncomfortable headlines for everyone concerned. I rather hoped he would not choose that path.

The mood in the car was back to normal between Kasper and myself. As we drove slowly through the security gate at Film City, and even more slowly through the roads inside the barracks, I congratulated him on a good day's work. He then dropped me off at the dining facility where we had met 12 hours earlier.

After a quick meal in the salad bar I retired to my room. It was early evening and I was absolutely shattered; I had been feeling jaded after our exploits in Stone Castle the night before. Having had little sleep and an early start, things were beginning to catch up on me. I decided to get my head down, to grab some sleep, before the highly symbolic de-activation of the KPC at midnight and the activation of the KSF one minute later. I called Simi and we arranged to meet in a bar in town at 11pm. Just before I closed my eyes I thought once more about my meeting in Mitrovice with Shyti. When I had met him, I was sure I had seen him somewhere before, but I was unable to connect the dots, and the thought soon evaporated as I fell into a deep, albeit short, sleep.

When I woke up 30 minutes later, the plan had changed. I was to meet General Selimi, General Rama and others in the KPC Commander's office for the last time at 11.15pm, before driving to the TRADOC barracks. I turned up, dressed in civilian clothes, and greeted everyone. The mood was excited.

Towards the end of its life the KPC had created many problems for everyone and its de-activation was an event they had been looking forward to for months. But there was still one more thing to be organised. General Selimi had decided that he wanted to inspect the new KSF guard at 5 minutes past midnight. I was going to suggest that it may not be a terribly wise thing to do but he was already dressed in his KSF uniform so there was little point in raising the issue. I had already lost some ground with General Selimi over his personal weapon; I didn't want to push it.

So without any rehearsal, no 'Lines to Take' for the media and no plan for the conduct of this activity, which was inevitably going to be held in the full glare of the Kosovan media, we headed off to TRADOC.

I had already called the NATO Advisory Team Public Relations expert, Gerdur Kjaernested, and informed her that there was going to be a bit of a media scrum at midnight. She asked me to ensure the word 'transformation' was not raised by anyone talking to the media. No lines were discussed apart from this final piece of advice and with that we all headed out into the freezing cold, under a clear night sky, for the final act of the KPC.

By this stage I was getting pretty tired of the absence of any formal planning for anything connected with the KPC. I was desperate to start afresh with the KSF. The parade two days earlier had only just come together at the last minute. The same thing looked like it was going to happen again at TRADOC when we arrived.

After walking through the main gate, I asked the guard whether he was aware of what was happening in 25 minutes' time; he was not. I then sought out the commander, a Captain, in charge of 6 guards, who also didn't know what was planned. It was at that precise moment that I realised how rooted in the past the KPC was and how the KSF had to be different from day one. The leadership by committee approach by General Selimi's favoured few was incompatible with a modern force and this was something they would have to wean themselves off. There was a Colonel, two Lieutenant Colonels and a Captain trying to organise 5 guards. Rather than get involved I stepped back. I realised that I was not needed there, even though General Selimi had asked me to make sure things went well. It was overkill so instead I watched the preparations take place from the shadows, a safe distance away.

With only 15 minutes to go and with the media arriving outside the barracks *en masse*, the KPC guard were conducting rehearsals in front of the gate. I could not stand by and let this undignified performance go on and suggested they move away from the cameras, just in case anyone was carrying the story live. They listened and finished their rehearsals away from the glare of the media. With 10 minutes to go, an older KPC guard, who had been selected to stand to attention at the main gate, was changed for a younger, smarter version; the other guards disappeared into the building and started getting changed into their new US-supplied KSF uniform. The scene was set for an historic, albeit rather *ad hoc* changeover.

At two minutes to midnight the new KSF guard marched out to meet the KPC guard at the main gate. Predictably they were early but I don't think anyone noticed or was interested. The flash lights lit up the night sky, bringing the ceremony into sharp focus, and the television camera bulbs flooded the main entrance with bright light.

It turned out to be a simple yet highly symbolic event, and the media loved it. It was probably lost on everyone observing the spectacle that the weapon, ceremoniously handed over, was a former Kosovo Liberation Army AK47, now employed as the weapons of choice for the new Kosovo Security Force. At midnight, a solitary KSF guard stood to attention outside the very small guard hut within the secure perimeter of the TRADOC barracks; the KSF era had officially been ushered in.

Without warning, the media decided that they wanted to get a better view of the guard and literally walked into the camp and surrounded him, looking for the perfect image of the new KSF. Neither the guard nor the other KSF soldiers who had returned to the safety of the guard room inside the building had any idea who was entering the barracks during those few minutes. I kept an eye on things but everyone was lost in the moment and the likelihood of anything untoward happening was pretty remote. It was a good job there was little or no external threat against the KSF; in fact the main threat to its success was coming from its security partner.

For several minutes the journalists took photographs of the most famous KSF guard in Kosovo, unaware that the main event was about to happen. At exactly 5 minutes past midnight a Land Rover Discovery, sporting the KSF Commander's new registration plates, approached the TRADOC barracks. I watched with amusement as the media's attention started to turn towards the approaching vehicle, word spreading quickly throughout the group that it was General Selimi. The soldier at the gate finally had a chance to get his night vision back as the media turned 180 degrees and filmed the car entering the camp.

Away from the glare of the cameras, the solitary figure was hurriedly joined by the full complement of guards as General Selimi stepped out of the vehicle, full of pride. Blinded by the flashing lights from the photographers, Selimi slowly marched across to where the new KSF guard had lined up in readiness for his arrival. The media were surprised to find the single KSF guard had become 6. They must have thought the ceremony had been meticulously rehearsed. Selimi received the salute from the guard commander and then inspected the men. Even if it was entirely off the cuff and executed without any real thought, the event looked good.

The whole show was only for the benefit of the press and they got what they wanted. It did feel quite surreal; it was 20 past midnight and we were standing outside the TRADOC building under a freezing cold, moonlit sky in Pristina, watching an impromptu press conference with the leader of the new Kosovo Security Force who had moved away from the guards again to address the media.

When General Selimi had finished he walked back to his car and disappeared into the night. As the media crowd began to break up I spotted Zija from Koha Ditore, who thought it had been a good media opportunity. I was happy that we had achieved something positive out of the day. Even though Colonel Gashi and Jeton Dreshaj were heading off for a coffee, I had had enough. I was exhausted and needed to sleep. It had been a long few months and the pace of life and the pressure on me was beginning to tell. The last 48 hours had also been typical of life in Kosovo; excessive drinking, inhaling too much secondary smoke, too many late nights and lots of stress from all directions. I could sense my defences weakening and I needed to escape.

Kasper took me back to Film City and I headed to my accommodation, exhausted from the intensity of the day. I climbed the metal steps attached to the side of my portable accommodation block, onto the first-floor external landing, and entered the nondescript, silent corridor that led to my room on the right. My door opened easily with my key and I stumbled in, deciding to leave the light off to protect my thoughts from further scrutiny. In the dim light from the outdoor street lamps, I undressed clumsily, kicking off my shoes and leaving my jeans in a pile on the floor. I sat down on my bed, shivering slightly from the cold, and looked around me. The portacabin room was depressingly bare, save for some photographs I had stuck on the walls when I arrived to remind me of the most precious people in my life, my family. I urgently needed to creep under the duvet and close my eyes for the second time that evening.

Announcement Day had finally ended. Exhausted, I slept deeply.

Deep in discussion; I look on as General Caplin discusses pressing issues with the newly appointed Minister for the KSF, Fehmi Mujota.

Disarming the KPC officer corps. One of the most hazardous activities during my tour.

Announcement Day at TRADOC. Members of the KPC queue impatiently as they wait to be called forward to receive an envelope which will tell them whether they are going to join the KSF, or head towards an uncertain future.

Invited guests look on during the KPC's final parade. The snow lying on the ground mirors the sombre nature of the ceremony.

The President of the Republic of Kosovo, Fatmir Sejdiu, inspects the Kosovo Guard, accompanied by Lieutenant General Selimi, on the final day for the KPC before the midnight de-activation.

Stone Castle winery - celebrating the end of the KPC; Major General Caplin (centre) with Major General Rama to his left, both looking reflective.

CHAPTER THIRTEEN

'Blind Faith'

I knew when I woke up, things were going to get worse before they got better. Over the previous 24 hours there were more murmurs about errors having been made. A perceived unfairness about the NATO-led selection process had taken shape throughout the day. While I had been correcting one glaring mistake in Mitrovice, other stories had started to circulate. One thing the members of the KPC were good at was sharing information via mobile phones. All the signs were there, even before Announcement Day's highly synchronised events. The publication in the media the previous week of a list of names, which was at least partially accurate, had kicked things off. As Announcement Day had progressed, these murmurs had become calls for action, with discontented KPC personnel citing examples of poor selections. It was hard not to sympathise with what was being reported.

As I got ready to drive down to the new KSF Land Forces Command, located close to the British military camp, I was nervous about what lay ahead. I stepped out of my room to go to breakfast and bumped into a neighbour from the block I lived in. He was a Greek officer who I had never met before. I struck up a conversation with him. He asked me what I was doing and when I explained about the 'New Tasks' he looked blank; which didn't surprise me. We quickly moved on to NATO deployments in general, in particular the ongoing operation in Afghanistan which NATO was heavily involved in. He confided in me that deploying to Kosovo in a multinational environment was a much safer option for European armies than going to Afghanistan. It was a statement that had some truth in it, but the fact that he admitted it surprised me. We shook hands, a custom in NATO deployments, and I left him to his busy day in the headquarters.

After a 5-minute drive down the hill to Land Forces Command on a grey, overcast day, I arrived to find chaos. Only the senior officers and those manning the guardroom, the logisticians, were in uniform. People in civilian clothes were milling around on the road outside and throughout the building. Nobody appeared to know what they were meant to be doing. Those who had been selected were smiling and joking in small groups while others, who had unwisely been allowed into the camp, were trying to find someone to speak to, to ask why they had not been selected. It was a toxic mix of emotions which was never going to sit well together.

Those who had not been offered a role in the KSF could draw on some very public examples of what they perceived to be an injustice over selections. One case was very personal to me; I had sat in front of Lieutenant Colonel Potera back in Vrani Do three months earlier, appealing to him to stop discussing issues with the media. I had urged him not to organise a strike over the stand down plan, but to no avail. He had been an agitator, he had corralled a number of colleagues to make a very undignified and public display of disobedience in an organisation at the time creaking under pressure from all sides. But Potera had been selected for the KSF.

I disliked what Potera had done and disagreed with what he stood for. I had previously sent an email to Colonel Roberts suggesting that he and his men should be removed from the board, reflecting their persistent breaches of discipline. This was a decision supported by Major General Caplin, although in all the last-minute horse trading it was clear that it had not been acted on. However I wasn't alone in my frustration about Potera; there were members of his unit in Vrani Do who had not gone on strike, who did not agree with his approach and who had followed orders from the KPC HQ in Pristina. They had not been selected and they were not happy. Even the officer who had so dramatically stepped forward and attempted, comically as it turned out, to rip up the pension law document, had been selected.

The woman with the prosthetic limb was an unusual story, but there were others. In another bizarre example, a lorry driver who lived and worked in Germany, and who had once been in the KPC, returned to take the tests and had been selected. This highlighted the lack of accuracy in the KPC's manning records more than anything else, but the stories just kept coming. A Corporal had been selected for the KSF and promoted to Major, a jump of 8 ranks. One story upset me more than most. To my deep shame, even though I was not responsible for the error, one of the 'pre-selected' logisticians, who had guarded the camps and who had been issued with new KSF uniform, had not been selected. It felt dishonest, even though I knew that the explanation was more likely to be a cock-up than a conspiracy. I was genuinely lost for words; I just hoped I would not have to meet him.

Even though the number of errors was relatively small, the integrity and credibility of the process had been fatally damaged, and that was all the unselected personnel needed to rally around.

Mistakes aside, at the end of Announcement Day over a hundred

KPC personnel had not turned up to receive their envelopes, so I took charge of them. As the only member of KFOR on site I was asked to hand over the envelopes as each individual arrived. Throughout the day a steady stream of former KPC personnel were pointed in my direction to sign for an envelope that would change the course of their lives. I knew that within the pile of envelopes were only 17 successful candidates.

I had heard that one young man had been in a car crash the day before and had broken his leg. I was gearing up to make arrangements to send the envelope to his home. Unknown to me, he had convinced the hospital to let him out so that he could make his way to Pristina. I was inside the building when his friend, speaking no English, came to my office and told me that he was here. I checked my list.

'That's great, send him in,' I said.

Instead, using sign language, I was beckoned outside. Intrigued, I walked out and was taken to a car parked on the side of the road. In the back, sprawled across the seat and in obvious pain was the candidate, his newly splinted leg sticking up towards the window. He spoke some English so I handed over the envelope, sat in the front seat, and turned round to watch his face as he opened the letter. I knew he had been selected and when he read the contents he was incredibly happy. We joked about his situation and I wished him well; it was a rare moment of joy in my day.

To his great credit, General Rama, the new Land Forces Commander, was getting a grip. He held his inaugural meeting with his Brigade Commanders and set out what he wanted to see and what needed to be done; making his direction clear to interpret and follow. It was impressive stuff and set the scene well for his tenure, despite some of the negativity that was swirling around. The first day of the

KSF's existence passed quickly and the earlier scenes of chaos were replaced with slightly more order and purpose by the end of the day.

An issue that I had flagged up in KFOR weeks earlier was the absence of a mentoring plan for the newly appointed staff officers in all of the headquarters locations. Some personnel had been selected for the KSF and placed in positions that they had no experience of. They needed guidance, over an extended period of time, to learn what to do and how to do it. They were starting from scratch without any instructions or support to rely on. KFOR had not put these plans in place and it was clear they were playing catch-up on this issue. Retaining a strong link between the KSF and KFOR was key, but as ever, political correctness had won the day in KFOR and there was a reluctance to supply the experienced KFOR personnel to meet this need.

The NATO Trust Fund, established to support the KSF, had been poorly supported from NATO member states. The issue of Kosovo's legitimacy, a political issue, had filtered down to the military level. As some KFOR-contributing nations refused to recognise Kosovo, this issue prevented KFOR's troops from providing the same levels of support that the KPC had enjoyed. Whereas weeks and even days earlier, the KFOR Multinational Task Forces had been routinely supporting the KPC, which was under the authority of the United Nations, the moment the KPC stood down and the KSF was established, there was a change in approach. Certain task forces refused to extend their support as they had done before. It was clearly an unsustainable situation that would need to be resolved by KFOR's leadership.

The main task for Rama was ensuring that his units collected their uniforms so that they could begin to look like a new force. On my way down to Adem Jashari Barracks the next morning I received a phone call from him, telling me that a group of protesters were going to meet at the Government building in central Pristina later that morning. The unselected KPC personnel had started to organise themselves. Rather than carrying on to visit KFOR troops who were on standby to issue the new uniforms, I quickly headed back to my accommodation and changed into civilian clothes, so that I could be dropped off in the city centre by Kasper to watch what happened.

We were entering uncharted waters and nobody really knew what was going to happen next. When I arrived in the centre and walked along Mother Teresa Boulevard, I saw the group outside a hotel. In all there were about 80 of them on the pavement. They then marched together along the wide pedestrianised street, past the prominent statue of Albanian national hero Skenderbej, and on to the tall, sleek Government offices, the weak winter sun reflecting off the upper floors. The Government building was surrounded by a fairly inadequate low fence and relatively unsophisticated entrance gate, guarded by a couple of fairly relaxed-looking Kosovo policemen. The protestors took the police by surprise and simply walked through the gates and onto the lawn which surrounded the building. All the key offices of the Government were located inside, including the Prime Minister. I was not surprised how easily the fence had been breached.

Nothing much took place but the fact that they had come together didn't bode well. I reported what had happened to Rama who told me it would be bigger the following day. It was not a good turn of events for the KSF. Rama and his newly appointed commanders were trying desperately to begin a new era, meanwhile unselected KPC personnel were marching on Parliament to demand their reinstatement. The day drifted by, the actions of the protestors leaving a bitter taste in my mouth. Events were spinning out of control.

The next morning I learned that two hand grenades had been

thrown at the old KPC Protection Zone 3 headquarters in Peja, in the west of the country. The local KFOR Task Force was an Italian Division. I knew the incident would be reported in the KFOR evening briefing and I guessed it would send shockwaves through the KFOR leadership; through this isolated but violent act in Peja, the 'New Tasks' were finally threatening KFOR's precious 'Safe and Secure Environment'. The potential for the situation to get out of hand was looming.

The whole process of selection had not gone anywhere near as well as people had hoped, for a number of reasons, all of which had been predicted and were coming home to roost. General Gay's delay, back in September, in making a decision over which type of approach to take with the 'New Tasks' had initially, and needlessly, impacted the planning time for MCA Division. General Gay lacked a granular level understanding of the KPC-KSF process. His fear of acting outside of his perceived role as impartial actor in Kosovo had resulted in a lack of strategic engagement with the Prime Minister in particular. In terms of the 'New Tasks', the rot had set in almost as soon as Gay had arrived in Kosovo.

Arguably the KFOR Commander had also been poorly served by his Deputy Chief of Staff, responsible for the day-to-day implementation of the entire process. Brigadier Di Luzio, a rank conscious and risk averse Italian, seemed unable to 'speak truth unto power' – to be clear to his supervisor. He did not appear to want to pass on bad news or difficult decisions to General Gay, perhaps to protect his own position, and this undermined everything. It is perfectly possible that Gay had no idea that anything was wrong at all, but that seemed unlikely. Gay's unwillingness to engage with the Prime Minister even when the nomination for the KSF commander was stuck in Hashim Thaçi's in-tray, encapsulated his lack of understanding of the entire process. He had allowed Kosovan politics to highjack a NATO plan. It was a mess.

And the only people who were left to pick up the pieces were the newly installed Kosovo Security Force senior leadership.

Rama's prediction of a larger crowd at the second protest was confirmed when over 300 unselected KPC personnel met outside the Illryia Hotel, a short walk from the main Government building. I wandered towards the group as they set off and followed them at a discreet distance. A few minutes later I could already see that there was a very different reception committee at the Government building. This time the police, larger in number, were not going to let them through the gate and instead Remi Mustafa, the Head of the Security Commission, who was a former KPC commander, walked out to greet the protesters. Mustafa appeared to invite half a dozen of them to go inside with him while the remaining men waited in the cold on the street. One individual dramatically broke through the police lines, but it led to nothing. Everything was reasonably good natured; at one stage General Selimi appeared, walking out of the Government building, turning away from the protestors towards his vehicle. When he noticed the group he looked back and waved as he strolled away; his gesture was met with jeers. The longer the men waited outside the more chance something may happen; more police turned up and at one stage a small fire was started by the protestors, although to be fair to them, it wasn't warm. After 90 minutes the leaders came out and everyone broke up into their protection zone huddles to discuss the outcome of the meeting. I learned later that the Minister for the KSF, Fehmi Mujota, had also joined them.

The crowd quickly dissipated, suggesting they had received some sort of concession. I went back to Land Forces Command, via Film City to change, so that I could brief Rama; that evening he and

General Selimi had a meeting with General Gay and Minister Mujota to discuss developments and I wanted him to be up to speed. It was clear something had to happen, but what was the solution? In the short term there was little I could do. I had talked to Rama and he favoured a more gradual approach to resolving the problem. He wanted to see a reserve list created and individuals removed during training through vetting or performance reasons over a period of months. It was a manageable solution and could have satisfied the protestors; I was certain he was going to explain this to General Gay and convince him of its merits.

That evening I had been invited out to Terry Anderson's flat in Pristina to celebrate Burns' Night. Once again all KSF-related business was forgotten for the evening. I had helped Terry with the planning and had arranged for a haggis to be sent over to Kosovo from the UK, organised by the British head chef in the dining facility in Film City. Terry had an enviable selection of whisky in his flat and we had recruited Shana, the American civilian who had attended the KPC party at Stone Castle, to make the traditional speech on behalf of the ladies. Despite having received the flu jab before Christmas, I was really suffering with a heavy cold and drinking whisky was the last thing on my mind. After working for 12 days straight all I wanted to do was curl up and sleep for the weekend, before the next set of developments on the following Monday. I toasted Burns' memory with a glass of single malt and made my excuses. I had to get my strength up.

Less than a week after Announcement Day, the KPC's unselected personnel had twice taken to the streets of Pristina and both times they had been courted by the media. Each former KPC protection zone throughout Kosovo had elected representatives to sit on an organising committee; they had then selected a spokesman. By the

Monday morning the pressure generated by media coverage over the weekend had created a step change in response by the Government. By the afternoon the KPC organising committee were finally given what they had demanded; an audience with the Prime Minister.

I had learned from Simi that their hastily installed spokesman was called Adrian Mehmeti and I knew that he had requested a meeting with the KPC Coordinator, Major General Nick Caplin. However the KPC had been formally de-activated and Major General Caplin was in his last few days, preparing to leave Kosovo. In one of my last phone calls to Major General Caplin, he agreed that the meeting would not further the protestors' cause and he felt it was no longer appropriate for him to get involved.

Instead of meeting Major General Caplin, Adrian Mehmeti was going to have to make do with me. I asked Simi to make contact and arrange a meeting if he still wanted to go ahead. I waited for his call for the remainder of the day.

When the call came, we arranged to meet at short notice in a fairly quiet bar near the centre of Pristina. Kasper dropped me off by a taxi rank next to the square at the end of the pedestrianised Mother Teresa Boulevard. With dusk falling and the street lights reflecting on the wet paving stones following an afternoon of wintery showers, I walked quickly across to the rendezvous and pushed open the door to the café, the windows fogged up with condensation. I didn't know what Mehmeti looked like but I figured he would spot me. We soon shook hands and I joined him at the bar. I looked forward to being given the inside track on what was happening.

Earlier in the afternoon, the Prime Minister had met the protestors for the first time. Mehmeti said that they had explained to the PM that 'errors' had occurred in the selection process. He then said that

General Selimi had been called to a further meeting with the PM, along with the Minister for the KSF, Fehmi Mujota and the KFOR Commander, General Gay. I knew that this was the pivotal moment.

Unable to follow up with Selimi that evening after his meeting with the PM, I met Mehmeti again the following day after the protestors had seen the PM for a second time in as many days. Sitting in the same bar, with a coffee in front of us, Mehmeti explained that many of the unselected personnel simply wanted to know why they had not been selected. Some had taken medicals and wanted to know if they had a serious health condition unknown to them. I agreed that this was a fair point; MCA Division, which had driven the whole process, had refused to give any reason for their non-selection. There had been no plan to give unselected personnel any feedback, nor any resources in MCA Division to provide this feedback; it just had not been considered. The medical angle was a fair point and I made a note to raise this with Colonel Roberts and Colonel Von Andrian.

However, what Mehmeti said next stunned me and sent a chill down my spine. The Prime Minister had suggested that those unselected personnel, aged between 25 and 40 years old, would be invited back into the KSF training process once all the initially selected KSF personnel had been trained up – an activity already fully resourced over the next 6 months and integral to the establishment of the KSF – adding that they would be independently evaluated for their suitability for the new force.

It was unbelievable.

I soon excused myself from our meeting, thanking him for his insights, and called Kasper. I needed to pass this information on pretty quickly. As I drove through the streets, Pristina's population going about their everyday business at the end of the day, with little care for the extraordinary events unfolding within Kosovo's security sector, my mind was racing to work out the implications of what I had just heard.

There was no way that Hashim Thaçi would have said this unless it had been agreed by the KFOR Commander, General Gay. I knew that MCA Division, the team of staff officers who had driven forward the plan, knew nothing about it. It appeared that the KFOR Commander had made a concession to the Prime Minister without any recourse to his staff or any understanding of the implications. It was more than unusual. What Gay had suggested, or agreed to, lacked any consideration or knowledge of the process as a whole. Gay had managed to destabilise an already tense situation.

The days that followed did not bring any further clarity.

It was a worrying development, mainly because if it was true, it would undermine the entire selection process. As part of their draft contract, every KPC member who had been invited to join the KSF had 6 weeks in which to decide if they wanted to accept their place. Some newly appointed members of the KSF had already decided that the integrity of the process was so tainted they didn't want anything to do with it and had resigned. This latest twist would be a devastating blow to those who believed that they had been selected on merit. It appeared that direct action from the protestors had indirectly influenced a senior NATO Commander into making a rash and ill-thought-through decision. Mehmeti had finished by telling me that Thaçi promised the protestors would have an answer on this issue within 48 hours.

By the Friday afternoon, three days later, and without any formal response from the PM, the protestors were beginning to act with a greater degree of malice. Threats were made against individuals, specifically against Rama and his family. They were demanding resignations from Selimi and Mujota; and they were losing control. A former KPC General tried to join the organising committee, to act as a moderating influence, but he soon left when it was clear they were not listening. The atmosphere was no longer good natured; it had turned ugly.

With Kasper navigating the routine hazards of driving through central Pristina – pedestrians stepping off the pavement without warning, cars pulling out with little care for oncoming vehicles – I was deep in thought, trying to make sense of the last few days and thinking about what to do. I was on my way to see Brigadier Enver Cikaqi, a bright and capable senior officer who had been selected to run TRADOC. When I arrived in the communist era brick building, a dimly lit rabbit warren more suited to secret torture chambers than a place of learning, I found Cikaqi in good spirits but completely overwhelmed by the task at hand. I had called him to arrange the visit to see how his new command was taking shape. He explained that almost all of his new staff had never had a training role before. He was fortunate to have some very capable officers but it was going to be an uphill struggle in the near term. KFOR's lack of a mentoring plan to assist the KSF would be keenly felt in TRADOC. Cikaqi's story was not uncommon in those early days of the KSF. When I left his office to find my way back to the entrance and to Kasper, waiting outside, I was confident that whatever was thrown at him, Enver Cikaqi would make it work.

Only 1,500 or so personnel were going to be initially recruited from the KPC; the remaining 1,000 places would come from new recruits over a period of time. Back in the relative calm of MCA Division in Film City, I had been told that the Kosovo-wide recruiting programme, a task that started on the KSF's inaugural day, had been going well. These new recruits, men and women, would be drawn from across all ethnic groups. As some KPC personnel had indicated that they didn't want to join the new force, other names were being added from the unofficial reserve lists that were in circulation. However, there was no hiding the fact that all available slots in the KSF had already been allocated to the KPC through the selection process. The protestors were demanding places in the KSF that no longer existed.

While Rama wanted to protect the integrity of the MCA Division process, the KFOR Commander appeared to have driven a coach and horses through the middle of it. Rama repeated his desire to deal with the issue discreetly. However, the protestors' increasingly aggressive stance, General Gay's obsession with maintaining a 'Safe and Secure Environment', and politics being played by the Prime Minister, seemed to be driving decision making. The established NATO planning process that MCA Division had employed and which we, as NATO officers, were all familiar with, had been cast aside.

Away from the protestors in Pristina, Rama was becoming increasingly concerned about the way KFOR and MCA Division had left the KSF to get on with it alone. There were no mentors in any headquarters, KFOR troops were not engaging as they had done before and communications were beginning to break down as a result. Throw into the mix the potential impact of General Gay's change of plan, and morale was plummeting. It was the opposite of how Rama and I imagined the first few days and weeks to be like when we had sat together in the hotel in Vushtri.

At the end of the week Rama again met Colonel Von Andrian, who had asked Rama to draw up three lists. One of these lists included the names of the EOD and Search and Rescue personnel who, almost to a man, had been unselected for service in the KSF, reflecting their poor levels of overall fitness. One of the jewels in the crown of the KPC had been effectively wiped out by the objective application of the 'NATO Standards' mantra, which had long since been discredited. A special waver had been granted for these individuals but the MCA Division could not simply make up posts for them. The more people who were brought into the KSF as a result of these issues, the fewer spaces would exist for the new recruits who were so necessary for bringing fresh blood into the KSF. Rama was also asked by Von Andrian to make a list of people he felt were undeserving of being in the KSF (there were 60) and finally those he felt should have been selected (167). The numbers didn't stack up and Von Andrian and Rama were locked in discussion, trying to navigate a way through the mess.

By now, Von Andrian had mentioned to me that General Gay was soon going to make an announcement, probably at the weekend, relating to the content of the PM's message to the protestors a few days before. Von Andrian made a few quick calculations. From an original figure of around 1,000 KPC personnel, applying certain fairly arbitrary criteria on age and rank, Von Andrian suggested to Rama that the numbers Gay was referring to were approximately 145 officers who would need to be brought back into the process. At least this didn't sound too bad.

The problem remained that the KSF had already allocated its available slots during the selection process, leaving the remaining slots for new recruits. A certain percentage of positions were also being retained for ethnic minorities and these couldn't be touched. There was a fear that if all unselected KPC personnel were allowed back into the force, it would be a disaster for the health of the organisation. These KPC officers had been excluded for a reason; yet they were soon to be invited back into the process as part of a course of action dreamed up in isolation by the KFOR Commander. In effect, General Gay had acquiesced in the face of moderate political pressure from the Prime Minister. How could the world's foremost security alliance allow this to happen?

Rumours then started to spread that General Gay had unexpectedly been called back to Naples at the weekend, presumably to explain what was going on. I had been in regular contact with Lieutenant Colonel Chris Gunning in Naples, the Military Assistant to the Joint Force Command Deputy, General Pearson, ever since they had both visited Pristina with Admiral Fitzgerald in October. I often gave Chris a UK view of what was happening in KFOR HQ; having first-hand situational awareness was vital for him to be able to advise General Pearson on what was really happening in Kosovo. I had also heard from Naples that KFOR HQ had simply stopped sending reports to Naples because the situation was so out of control. As much as I couldn't believe this was the case, under General Gay's tenure as the KFOR Commander, nothing surprised me anymore.

Chris valued my insight. I was so ashamed of the way General Gay and his command team were behaving, to the detriment of KFOR's reputation and the KSF's ability to stand on its own two feet, I felt obliged to keep communication channels open to Chris. Whether it was the content of my reports that had finally alerted Naples that something was going badly wrong, I will never know. However, calling General Gay back to Naples to justify his actions made absolute sense.

The weekend was also significant for another reason. Major General Nick Caplin, the KPC Coordinator and *de facto* Minister for the KPC had come to the end of his tour of duty. He had looked out for the KPC's best interests at the highest level from the moment I had first met him back in August. The KPC had stood down and the final 6 months of its existence was now going to be looked after by a small legacy team, led by Colonel Roberts and a respected KPC Brigadier.

At his leaving function, Brigadier Kastrati, who had worked closely with Major General Caplin, had presented him with his personal side arm, de-activated and in a presentation box. It was a very personal gift and took General Nick completely by surprise. However, as soon as he thanked General Kastrati, he handed it back to him, asking how he would be able to get it in his luggage and on the flight home. The arrangements were left to a member of the Embassy. Major General Caplin was held in high regard and would be missed. For me, Caplin's imminent departure was bad news.

As my tour had progressed, there had been a regular flow of ill-considered orders and requests from Di Luzio and the KFOR headquarters regarding the KPC-KSF process; each one had been unpicked and side-stepped by Generals Selimi and Rama, guided by me and supported in the most part by Major General Caplin. I was increasingly aware that the way I had been advising the KPC team throughout the majority of my tour had frustrated Di Luzio and even Lieutenant General Gay, although I didn't know at that stage to what extent.

After the de-activation of the KPC, I simply persevered with what I had been doing throughout my tour, providing the vital connection between Selimi, Rama and the KFOR hierarchy. Common sense suggested this function should continue until my replacement arrived two weeks later. However, my role was becoming less effective. Selimi was located in the former KPC HQ, now renamed a KSF Ministry building, Rama was in Land Forces Command outside the city, and both men needed close support. I couldn't be in two places at the same time so something had to give. I chose to support Rama, mainly because that's where I felt my advice and guidance would have the greatest effect. It was a situation that needed to be resolved, one way or another. With the KSF formed up, the need for an LNO was stronger than ever, but I was very conscious that my job title was KFOR LNO to the Kosovo Protection Corps, not the Kosovo Security Force.

And I knew these details mattered in NATO circles, where pragmatism was often lost in the adherence to dogma. I expected there to be a transition in my own appointment before my scheduled departure.

CHAPTER FOURTEEN

'Too little, too late'

With rumours beginning to spread outside KFOR and the KSF, the situation was becoming grave for the reputation of the MCA Division selection process. Its integrity, in the eyes of the International Community, was coming under intense scrutiny. Bizarrely the NATO staff in MCA Division were unable to reach Lieutenant General Gay to clarify what he had agreed to, or even to understand his intent; and Di Luzio appeared to be unwilling to put his own career at risk by engaging the KFOR Commander over the current crisis.

General Gay alone was the man who should have stood firm against the pressure applied by Thaçi; he should have had the moral courage to take the matter back to his staff officers before offering his advice and committing to a course of action. Instead his pattern of indifference towards the 'New Tasks' throughout his time in command, and his lack of understanding of the detailed work carried out on his behalf by MCA Division, was about to have a dramatic impact on the KSF.

Knowing that General Gay would shortly fly to Naples, I started writing my report on the Saturday at my desk in the KIKPC building, a grainy TV showing British Premier League football my only company. The report was finished by Sunday morning and I sent it out straight away rather than waiting until 6pm. I wanted to try to stop this decision from being set in stone by describing the alternative solution suggested by Rama days before. It was almost the last throw of the dice to reverse a potentially damaging order from being given, with all the implications that it carried.

On the Saturday I had contacted Colonel Von Andrian and suggested that he stalled the process, to give Admiral Fitzgerald in Naples the chance to speak to General Gay. I felt strongly that we had to do everything possible to prevent further damage being done to KFOR's reputation and the whole selection process by Gay's unilateral decision. In fact it was clear that Gay had already committed KFOR to a new course of action before he was summoned to Naples. As I was sending the report out, I learned that General Gay had already written to the Office of the Prime Minister, agreeing to the demand for all unselected KPC personnel to be readmitted to the process through the training option. The only stipulation was that they were above 'the minimum standard', whatever that meant. The news broke later on Sunday, accompanied by a press statement.

The protestors would be delighted; despite my best efforts, I was too late.

I spoke to members of MCA Division who had conducted their own quick estimate of the situation and had crunched the numbers. The totals differed significantly to Von Andrian's initial calculations, suggesting it was closer to 500 personnel; in other words at least two extra training courses would have to be tagged on the back of the original training programme which was currently due to be completed later in the year. Not only was there an impact on NATO resources, every additional place offered to the unselected KPC personnel was one less new recruit from Kosovo's wider community. It was the worst possible outcome.

I also learned that General Gay had received a letter from the Prime Minister on the Tuesday of the previous week, the day of Thaçi's second meeting with the protestors, asking for the unselected personnel to be brought back into the process. General Gay had replied on the Wednesday confirming the plan in principle, without any recourse to his staff officers who had designed and overseen the process. Everyone's subsequent efforts had been in vain.

Gay had committed the MCA Division to pull a rabbit out of the hat, in the most public and strategically embarrassing way anyone could imagine. In a stroke Gay had made a hasty decision that was lacking any detail. With only 7 months of his command left, he had managed to kick the can down the road and had deliberately left the issue to be resolved by the next Commander of KFOR, a German officer due to arrive in August.

General Gay's lack of attention to detail had been exposed. Dragging out the planned training by adding up to 500 unselected KPC personnel onto unplanned courses, that had not been resourced, was going to extend the process beyond his period of command. The plan for training to be completed in time for the declaration of Initial Operating Capability, or IOC, in September was no longer going to be possible, needlessly harming the KSF's fragile reputation inside its borders and in the region.

The question of status was also raised immediately from within MCA Division. The KPC was due to be entirely dissolved on 14th June. After this time no salaries would be paid, the organisation would cease to exist, no uniforms could be worn. The status of the unselected KPC personnel beyond June was therefore anyone's guess. The spontaneous proposal lacked rigour and credibility; it was a long way short of 'NATO Standards'. And everybody knew it.

Of more importance from a brand perspective, General Gay had managed to upset NATO's key strategic partners in Kosovo. The International Civilian Office, the ICO, whose representatives had sat on all the selection boards and signed a document to verify the integrity of the selection process, felt that they had been compromised. The UNDP, who were tasked with bringing the unselected into a well organised resettlement programme, now had a huge gap in their numbers because Gay's decision had introduced uncertainty amongst those who would have been using their services. The unselected were going to be sitting around waiting to be invited to a training course at some point in the future, rather than engaging with the UNDP and moving on with their lives. They would be waiting to start training where they would need to perform above a 'minimum standard' that had not been defined. Pristina's leading diplomats were in disbelief.

By the Sunday evening I needed some fresh air and arranged to see Zija to explain what was going on. Meeting in a bar we had been to before, he was shocked that the PM had such influence over the Commander of KFOR. His observations were bang on. Zija and I had got to know each other well over the previous months. He was benefitting from my briefings; and KFOR was benefitting from having a journalist who knew what was going on. However, with General Gay going off on a tangent, I was beginning to wonder whether our joint efforts had been worth it.

It was quite clear that by the time the KFOR Commander had returned to work on the Monday, assuming he had made his trip to Naples, he would have read my weekly report. It included Rama's alternative solution, written before General Gay's press release was issued, that would have maintained the integrity of the original selection process. The question was whether anything could be done. I knew that my report had shaken things up. That morning Dave Finnimore got in touch with me to tell me that a team from Naples was being dispatched to find out what was really going on in Kosovo and they had asked to see me. I drove down to the old KPC building, to Selimi's temporary office. I explained everything to both Selimi and Rama, less some of the detail about Naples. They were bemused. There is no doubt that the Commander of KFOR had isolated General Selimi the week before and railroaded him into agreeing to a decision about bringing the unselected back into the process, without giving him the opportunity to check with anyone in the KSF, including me, whether it was wise. General Gay probably knew we would outmanoeuvre him again. I suggested to Selimi that he should go and talk to the PM, who was unlikely to understand the full implications of what Gay was telling him. It was inconceivable that General Gay had any grasp of how the decision would undermine the existing selection process or the implications for the resettlement of those unselected personnel who had accepted the decision.

After a very difficult conversation with Selimi and Rama, Simi and I drove to meet Nuredin Lushtaku in Collection. Nuredin had got in touch with Simi, saying he wanted to see me about his weapon. I wasn't in the mood for a protracted conversation about whatever agenda he was pursuing and I arrived with little enthusiasm.

I was sitting at a small table in the place that had become a second home, 5 minutes away from the KPC headquarters building, dressed in my British military uniform. With background music and the usual soundtrack of a busy café filling my ears, waiting staff taking and delivering orders to customers sitting around us, I took stock of my surroundings. This was where I had been sitting on Announcement

Day with Selimi, Gashi and Dreshaj; in only a couple of weeks events seem to have rapidly gone downhill. I was becoming increasingly disillusioned by what was happening and had I started to wonder whether I had made any sort of difference in Kosovo at all. I was flanked by two people who I had got to know during my tour; one for all the right reasons and the other because he was, in most people's eyes, a dangerous trouble maker with a lot of influence.

Wearing his ever present baseball cap, the conversation soon moved on from his weapon, which he was keen to know about since handing it in the previous month. Speaking through Simi, Lushtaku was complaining about the levels of dissatisfaction amongst the former KPC members who had been shut out of the newly launched KSF. Becoming increasingly militant in their words and actions, Lushtaku was clearly concerned about the influence they seemed to have. Protests had taken place in central Pristina, and the rhetoric was growing with further violent disruption promised. They had a point; the well planned process of establishing the KSF had been poorly executed by NATO, and it had just been further undermined by NATO's most senior officer in country, Lieutenant General Giuseppe Gay, the Commander of KFOR. It was a shambles.

I turned to Simi, my interpreter and by now a personal friend, and said that somebody had to do something. Lushtaku was chain smoking and looking menacing, an image he liked to cultivate. He had been a thorn in the side of many for some time, eventually leading to his recent 'retirement' from the KPC that he had served since 1999. I decided to explain to Lushtaku what had been going on, to fill in the blanks in his own knowledge. He was close to the Prime Minister and I calculated that it would be helpful for some of what I was saying to be passed on. I told him about my meetings with Adrian Mehmeti from the protest movement in a café in Pristina a few days before. It was clear that those who had not been selected for the KSF were determined to fight the outcome. The absence of an effective information campaign by KFOR over the preceding 6 months had contributed to the lack of preparedness amongst the KPC. The disruption to the KSF's attempts to organise themselves was getting out of hand and beginning to adversely affect those former KPC members who had been offered a place in the newly established security force.

I then brought him up to speed with the last few days, telling him about how General Gay, without warning or recourse to his staff, had unilaterally decided that the selection process for the KSF would be re-run, bringing back into the fold those who had been legitimately unselected by the NATO-led selection boards. I explained how the plan had been ripped up in front of our eyes; to everyone's astonishment the protesters now had hope. It was a dramatic turn of events and a decision that would have a profound effect on the whole plan to launch the KSF, in particular in managing the retirement of those members of the KPC who had not made the grade. It was all highly damaging. I felt uncomfortable explaining the story and from Lushtaku's body language I sensed that the conversation was going in a new and unexpected direction.

As Simi translated, Lushtaku expressed his view that someone needed to explain to the Prime Minister the damage being done by the KFOR Commander's most recent decision. I took another sip of my macchiato and asked who would be best placed to do that. The silence from both men answered my question and I realised the implications of what I was about to say next:

"OK, I will have to tell him then."

It was as simple as that. Lushtaku seemed completely at ease at the prospect of making arrangements for me to meet Hashim Thaçi, the Kosovan Prime Minister. And in that highly pressurised and stressful moment, coming at the end of an extraordinary 6 months, it felt that meeting the country's top politician was the only genuine course of action left open to me. I hoped I wasn't too late and that in some small way I could bring the whole process back on track and undo the considerable damage done by General Gay's decision.

Lushtaku confirmed that he would make the necessary phone calls. I only asked one thing from Simi, who also seemed a little intoxicated by the conversation; I must receive a guarantee that nobody would ever know that it had happened. I received Lushtaku's word, or 'bessa', which in the context of Kosovo's still relevant medieval honour system, was good enough for me. I sat back in my chair and contemplated what I had just signed up to; I was going to meet the Prime Minister at Vila Germia that night.

After leaving Collection I went back up to Film City and headed to the restaurant for a late lunch. I always ended up eating soup in the sandwich bar just round the corner from the main dining hall. There was something peaceful about eating there, especially after the rush had died down. I could gather my thoughts and watch members of KFOR aimlessly wander past, looking for an excuse to dive into one of the many cafés on the NATO base where they could sit down, have a cigarette and drink more coffee. Taking soup also made me feel better about myself compared to those who would regularly eat two or three courses for lunch. So I sat with my soup and my open notebook and began to think about what I was going to say to Hashim Thaçi that evening.

I started to jot down a few ideas. I noted things that the PM clearly did not understand about the process of selection for the KSF; issues that he should have been told about a long time ago by the Commander of KFOR but had either ignored or was ignorant to them. Why did it have to come down to a British officer to do something that should have been done by an Italian 3* General? That of course was the problem. While I was sitting at the table, I saw Migena walk past. She didn't stop; she just smiled and walked on. I watched her go, wanting to tell her what I was about to do but knowing that she would advise me against it.

I had met Hashim Thaçi twice before, both times with General Selimi; the first a private meeting between the two men, the second with the Minister for the KSF, Fehmi Mujota, Major General Caplin and Simi. I had spoken to him both times. So in a way, we were already on speaking terms but I could hardly describe the relationship any more generously than that.

As the time ticked away towards the meeting, I grew progressively more uncomfortable with the plan, but there was no backing out now. I sat in my accommodation, nothing more than a metal box, with a door, a window and small *en suite* bathroom, wondering what the hell I had signed myself up to. I tried to relax, but I still had the same illness that had struck early on in my tour and I was nervous. As I contemplated the next few hours, I received a text telling me that the PM was in a meeting with a group of overseas Ambassadors. It was suggested that I might meet the Deputy PM instead. When I read that message I almost felt relieved.

To distract myself from the impending meeting I called home and spoke to everyone, although my daughter was quite unsettled and we had to end the call prematurely. It was again so reassuring to hear familiar voices, but my mind was on my meeting later that evening; I could barely think of anything else.

At the pre-arranged time I grabbed the car keys, dressed in civilian clothes, and headed into town to meet Simi at a bar called Apartment 196, a regular haunt for me during my tour. As we waited it became increasingly clear that we would not be meeting anyone so late that night. Exchanging nervous conversation, Simi eventually got the message that it would happen the next day, with further details to follow. I drove back to Film City and went straight to my bed, in desperate need of sleep.

The next day was like any other day, except I knew I was going to be meeting the Prime Minister to tell him that the decision regarding the 'New Tasks' that the KFOR Commander had agreed to was going to be extremely damaging to his country and the KSF. No pressure then.

In the morning I had just returned from seeing Brigadier Cikaqi at TRADOC again and was heading back to Film City for lunch when Simi told me we were on for 1pm at Hotel Victory, which ironically was a stone's throw from the old KPC headquarters building. Sitting in the KFOR dining facility, looking around me that lunchtime, I really felt different from everyone else, mainly knowing that I was about to do something that was highly likely to result in my leaving Kosovo prematurely if anyone found out. I revealed my nervousness about this to Simi when we met but he had given me his 'bessa' and Lushtaku had also given his. I was reassured.

Hotel Victory was noticeable in Pristina for a miniaturised Statue of Liberty on its roof. It certainly wasn't a discreet location. Kasper was at the wheel as we sat there in a lay-by just short of the hotel, dressed in civilian clothes, waiting. I had chosen not to tell Kasper what we were going to do. That might have been an error on my part, but the fewer people who were aware, the better. Just before we drove to the hotel at the allotted time Simi got another message to say it had been delayed by an hour. The atmosphere in the car was not helping my mood so I immediately decided to drive back to Film City to drop Kasper off because he was clearly frustrated at not knowing our plans. It was understandable.

I then drove back to Hotel Victory. On the way Simi received a final text:

"It will be the Prime Minister."

The meeting had just been notched up a few degrees; I knew then I had one shot to make a difference. We drove up to the hotel and found a parking place out of sight. We were instructed to go through the lobby and into a large conference room, to order a drink and to wait. There were quite a number of large round tables, covered in table cloths, lined up along one side and at the far end of the room. We walked up to an empty table and sat down, remembering to leave a chair for the PM. We were not alone in the room, the Transport Minister was also sitting at a separate table with some other Government colleagues a few metres away. A waiter came across and took our drinks order, which quickly arrived; a glass of tonic water for me and a Coke for Simi. Making some small talk to pass the time, I was also checking my notes to be clear what I was going to say.

After about 20 minutes Thaçi appeared in the room and I sensed that familiar aura that accompanies people in positions of power and influence. He started walking over, briefly stopping to shake hands with the Minister at the nearby table. I felt the room suddenly get much smaller and it was as if the entire universe was focused on me; the Prime Minister; our table; and the impending conversation. I stood and we shook hands as he greeted me warmly, no doubt briefed by Lushtaku on who I was and what message I was delivering. He also greeted Simi and we sat down. With very limited time, I dived in. I explained why I was there and went into detail about the implications of the decision the KFOR Commander had made. I suggested he should go back to General Gay to ask him to reconsider.

Thaçi listened to what I had to say and we discussed the subject very amiably. He said he would not go back to the KFOR Commander, giving me the impression he was happy with the outcome to let the unselected personnel back into the process. He confessed that he was worried about the protesters and he needed to calm them down. But he was clear, there was no going back. He said that he wished we had met before the decision had been made. The last question he asked me was how long I would be staying in Kosovo and that we must stay in touch during my final couple of weeks.

With that he stood up, we shook hands, and he left us. As Simi and I walked out of the room a few moments later I suddenly said, 'Simi, we need to pay for the drinks.'

"The Prime Minister can pay," replied Simi.

I don't know why but I laughed out loud, the tension and relief instantly flowing out of me. I had done my best but I had been too late. He still had the power in his hands but in reality, both he and General Gay had too much to lose. At least I had tried to explain the implications of the decision to which he had been a part. There was nothing more I could do.

In fact, those words suddenly took on an unexpected meaning.

CHAPTER FIFTEEN

'11 Days'

The next morning I received an ominous message from Colonel Von Adrian, who wanted to see me in Film City. I half knew what he was going to say as I walked into the MCA Division building. When I found him at his desk we stepped away from other people and he came straight to the point; he explained that my post was no longer required after the de-activation of the KPC. With the establishment of the KSF now complete, and the KPC no longer the focus for MCAD and KFOR, on paper at least, my role had come to an end. In reality there had never been a greater need for my position.

This situation was something I had been considering for some time, but I had not had any formal conversations with anyone in MCAD or KFOR about it. Von Andrian said the decision had come from General Gay, the KFOR Commander, via Di Luzio. I had already warned off Colonel Duncan Hopkins, the most senior British Officer in KFOR, and my portal into the UK MoD, over what may happen. After briefing him, Colonel Duncan then spoke to Di Luzio to explain that it was unlikely that I would be replaced by London if the liaison officer role was no longer going to be supported.

I always suspected that once Major General Caplin was out of the picture, the KFOR command team would contrive a reason for me to return to the UK earlier than planned. I wasn't very happy but there was little I could do about it.

Feeling deflated, I headed over to see Selimi and Rama. This was going to be a blow to them; they didn't need the liaison officer function to be withdrawn at a time of need. While I was with them Selimi received a message and hurriedly left to see the Prime Minister. I spent a very nervous hour until he returned, wondering whether he would find out that I had met Thaçi in Hotel Victory the day before. My fears were in vain; judging by Selimi's face he had not been told and the 'bessa' system had worked. I mentioned the possibility that my post would be pulled by the UK MoD if KFOR no longer wanted a Brit in that the role, a suggestion Rama dismissed out of hand. The conversation had run its course and I had an appointment with the vetting team, so I left the two men to ponder life without a British Liaison Officer for the first time in 10 years. I was the 19th and last UK Liaison Officer with the KPC. What I did not expect was for KFOR to remove the post completely.

Over at the chicken hut, I had spent an hour with Migena discussing a number of KSF senior officers who were still undergoing vetting enquiries. While I was in the vetting unit I was sent a message and asked to see Di Luzio over in the KFOR headquarters building 10 minutes away. Migena and I wrapped up the vetting discussion and I walked round to Di Luzio's office in defiant mood. He explained that in the KSF era there needed to be a different form of support. I was intrigued what that would consist of. At that stage, KFOR had not appointed anyone to fill any mentoring roles with the KSF, even though I had flagged the issue up weeks earlier. There was not even a plan for it. It took all my self-control not to point out his flawed logic, but it would have been a waste of time.

Now that I had been directed to withdraw from the position there was an immediate vacuum. When I first met Di Luzio in September the previous year, he described my role as being a sensor for the command team; using his analogy, it looked as if the operator of that sensor clearly didn't like what he was hearing.

After seeing Di Luzio I called Simi to let him know the news. I called Migena, to speed up my remaining interviews with her as I didn't know how much longer I was going to be staying in Kosovo. I also spoke to Dave Finnimore to let him know what was happening. Whilst I was happy that I had always done what I felt was right for the KPC and for Kosovo generally, I knew the decision wouldn't look good. On paper it made perfect sense, but rumours were already gaining traction, although I was unaware of their source. I had no way to control what people were thinking and saying; frankly, I didn't care that much.

I went to see Colonel Hopkins again to discuss what was likely to happen about my departure. He explained that the decision on whether I leave early or as planned on the 23rd February was sitting at a high level in London. Colonel Duncan and I got on well, he was in my corner, particularly after having seen what I had been doing throughout my tour. I felt a profound responsibility towards Simi though. There was no dressing it up; Simi would not be happy doing any other job in Kosovo other than working with the British. In many ways, it was a personal disaster for him.

The next day, 5th February, I heeded Col Duncan's advice and stayed away from Land Forces Command while Di Luzio went in person to explain the decision to Selimi and Rama. I needed to see quite a few people as I had no idea how long I was going to be staying in Kosovo. I saw Terry and explained what was happening, I met up with Adrian Mehmeti to explain that I was going to hand him off to Terry, who, as the US Assistant Defence Attaché, could continue to keep in touch with the protestors' activities. I also visited Zija who by then had left the newspaper and had started in a new role at a Kosovo TV station, located in a nondescript residential area of Pristina near a small shopping centre called 'Green'. Zija and I were firm friends and it was great to see him moving on. I explained what had happened and we shook hands, perhaps for the final time before leaving Kosovo.

That evening I went out with Simi. He was sanguine about the turn of events. He confided that he didn't care about my role not being replaced because he had decided that he was going to leave KFOR in June anyway, when the KPC fully dissolved as an entity. He also explained that he had received calls from Lushtaku, and also from Agim Çeku, Kosovo's former Prime Minister, to ask if there was anything they could do. It seemed the rumour mill had already kicked into action, with people apparently saying I had been suspended. It was not the truth but I couldn't control gossip.

However, I was still in Kosovo and I was therefore able to add value, it would just have to be less overt. I decided to carry on seeing Rama and Selimi as long as they wanted me to. I wasn't going to allow the situation to prevent me from making a difference, even if I was now very limited in what I could do. It had been a very challenging time, both personally and professionally, in the last few days. I was effectively an officer without portfolio.

However, the one thing everyone in uniform likes about military life is the variety, so the next morning I drove down to Slim Lines to meet HRH, the Princess Royal, who was making a flying visit to Kosovo to meet the British military unit deployed in the country. I had been invited to meet her along with every other Brit in Kosovo. We were waiting in the combined Officers' and Sergeants' Mess when she arrived; I was in the last group to be introduced to her. HRH moved round the room in that all too familiar and highly choreographed way, which was so familiar to members of the military who had met royalty before. When she came to our group she was relaxed and enjoying herself; HRH and I briefly chatted about what I was doing, as well as having conversations with others in my group. I had met Princess Anne a few times before and liked her company. It had certainly been a week of extremes.

It was also a great opportunity to meet an old friend from Staff College, Lieutenant Colonel Dom Fox, who had just arrived in Kosovo for a tour of duty. Dom and I had produced the 'underground' course magazine at Staff College which had remained anonymous until the final week. Dom and I had spent many a happy hour standing by photocopiers late into night in the Defence Academy in an attempt to avoid detection. It was great to see a familiar face from my previous life. I also managed to catch up with the UK Ambassador, Andy Sparkes, who was very interested in the events of the last couple of weeks. He made it clear he wanted to have a briefing from me before I left. The Ambassador also relayed a conversation he had had with General Gay, who had apparently denied all knowledge of giving the instructions for the Press Release to be issued the previous weekend, which had effectively consigned the integrity of the selection process to the bin. I was bemused more than anything; how could the Commander of KFOR say that? How could he not have had a hand in releasing the news when he alone had made a decision so universally unpopular across the wider stakeholder community in Kosovo? If I needed any further evidence that Gay was unfit for office, this news confirmed it.

I soon excused myself from the event and drove back to Film City to change before taking the Landcruiser into Pristina to observe the protest that was planned for the afternoon. Even though the rhetoric from the protestors was building, and Adrian Mehmeti had confirmed the rising anger, the protest was completely uneventful, even boring, and afterwards I drove over to see General Rama in Land Forces Command. General Rama was beginning to struggle. He had been keeping a lid on everything in the first few days of the KSF, fired up and being decisive. However, the noise from the unselected KPC personnel was drowning out Rama's calls for support; the abject failure of KFOR to make any provision for mentoring the new force was a growing problem. I had heard that Rama had slept in his office for 4 hours earlier in the week; he was also drinking heavily and smoking in his office. Learning that the Liaison Officer position had been removed certainly wasn't the straw that broke the camel's back, but it was a contributing factor, a bitter blow to Rama. The worsening situation for him personally and for the health of the KSF, was serious. Rama was the key to a successful KSF, he was the force's barometer; he needed to be held close, not abandoned.

When I entered his office I didn't really know what to say to him; I felt strongly that I had let him down, even though the decision had been out of my hands. I stayed for 20 minutes but it was uncomfortable being with him, and soon left. This was not how I wanted to finish my tour in Kosovo, I was certain of that. General Selimi was also as unhappy as General Rama. I had earlier drafted a letter for Selimi to send to Admiral Fitzgerald, expressing his disbelief at the decision Gay had made about unselected personnel, which suggested he had not really had much say in the key meeting between the KFOR Commander and the Prime Minister the previous week. He also wanted to do something about my role. I suggested he write to General Gay to demand an explanation, to appeal to him to change his mind about removing the liaison officer post. So I drafted another letter for General Selimi, this time to General Gay. It was delivered without response.

Under the circumstances I was holding it all together pretty well. I was increasingly accepting of my situation as each day passed. I played things around in my head a lot though; could I have done anything differently? Was it my fault that the post had been cut? I spoke to Group Captain Andy Omerod, General Pearson's Executive Assistant in Naples who I had worked with in Baghdad a few years earlier. In his view the role had naturally run its course, and it was not difficult to agree. It just felt to me that it had been personal.

The abrupt nature of the decision suggested there was more to it. Turning off the tap of news that did not fit with the Italian Command Group's own narrative was something they had been looking forward to ever since Major General Nick Caplin had left Kosovo. The stand down of the KPC gave them the excuse. However many times I looked at the situation, as objectively as I could, I always came back to the same conclusion. Removing the LNO role and cutting adrift the KSF was a failure of KFOR to apply common sense, flexibility and pragmatism to the situation. I should not have been surprised though; these qualities were consistently in short supply in Film City.

I was starting to look beyond Kosovo to what was coming next in my life. I was becoming desperate to get home and see my children, who were happily living their young lives, blissfully unaware of what Dad was going through hundreds of miles away in Kosovo. I learned in Baghdad in 2004, at the height of the insurgency, that when things don't quite go to plan, it is better to be philosophical about events. That's where I was on that Friday afternoon; I was passing my days seeing people for the last time, people who I respected and had become friends, not knowing exactly when I was going to be leaving.

It was a bizarre situation but there were worst things in life, so Terry Anderson and I decided to go out and celebrate. We were also joined by Migena for dinner in a jazz café called Sokoli e Mirusha, owned by my good friend Adrian Koci, whom I had met back in October during a Hallowe'en party. The name of the café came from a ballet, written and composed by Adrian's Father in the 1970s. It was a great place to while away the hours.

Terry, Migena and I ended up in the Depot nightclub where we bumped into Magnus Brydal from the NATO Advisory Team, a hard-living Norwegian lawyer who was great company, if slightly crazy at times. In the packed club, deafened by the music and almost choking in the smoky atmosphere, I told Migena what I had been doing that week, specifically the meeting with Thaçi. Her look said it all but I knew she was also proud of what I had been trying to do. She knew I was standing up to an Italian 3* General, and even though there was only ever going to be one winner, my conscience was clear. After too many drinks I got back to my room at 2am, but there was little time for sleep. Somehow I had been talked into going Skiing with Terry with the bus leaving at 6.30am.

Going to Brezovica, the ski resort I had visited back in October with Migena, Dave and Dean, was going to be a lot better than hanging around Pristina under the circumstances. After travelling for two hours we finally arrived, managed to find some boots that fitted and signed for some skis and poles. The place looked so different to my last visit before the snow had fallen, back in October.

It was a clear, sunny day and the crowds were out. This was not a standard ski resort though. Normal protocol seemed to be put to one side and I was unprepared for the pushing and shoving to get on the main, slightly rusty, chairlift. Once at the top of the lift though, I felt that familiar sense of freedom wash over me that goes hand in hand with standing in the mountains. I soon learned that skiing in Kosovo was unlike anywhere else in the world that I had experienced. There were normal skiers, snow boarders, people on toboggans and ski-doo riders, all using the same slopes. Both Terry and I were very tired from the night before so after a couple of runs from the top, we withdrew from the crowds and sat for much of the day in a café overlooking the main slope. We watched the crashes as they happened from a safe distance. It was entertaining if slightly awkward. Sitting together, drinking hot chocolate, trying to keep warm in the weak winter sun, was just what I needed; in fact we both enjoyed it so much we repeated the experience the next day.

On the Monday morning I was invited to brief the British Ambassador on what had been going on in my world. By now I was permanently wearing civilian clothes and a scruffy Barbour jacket wherever I went. Wearing uniform seemed to be pointless and I had already packed up a large container with a lot of my gear to be shipped back to the UK that day. In the Ambassador's office were Jonathan Mitchell on the Embassy Staff, Anna Jackson the Ambassador's deputy, Colonel Hopkins' replacement Colonel John Whitby, the Military Liaison Officer Lieutenant Colonel Jules Carmichael and Colonel Stuart Roberts from MCA Division. We went through events thoroughly and it was clear that there was little genuine comprehension of what had been happening to the Kosovans, whom I had been working so closely with. Colonel Stuart filled in the gaps from an MCA Division perspective.

After finishing with the Ambassador, I drove across to see Generals Selimi and Rama who were in the restaurant, Collection. They were meeting Adrian Mehmeti that afternoon, my contact in the protestors group, and a couple of others who I didn't know. I was invited to join them and I felt like I was sitting in Vrani Do all over again with Potera and Maloku, listening to their complaints and watching Maloku try to rip up the pension law document. Different time and different people, but the message was the same; I was again invited to speak to the group by Rama. I repeated the lines that I had said back in October at the Protection Zone 5 headquarters. I tried in vain to inject a degree of perspective and common sense into the discussion but there was an intransigence that was not easily going to be overcome. Mehmeti said they were still not happy and the press release from KFOR had done nothing to change people's minds. I smiled at the irony of that comment; the hasty and ill-thought-through actions of General Gay, under pressure from the PM, had resulted in catastrophic decision making and it had not made any difference at all. Nobody was happy apart from Gay. The total lack of detail behind the announcement was the issue, a fact not lost on Colonel Roberts and those of us who cared so deeply about trying to get the establishment of the KSF right.

The next morning I met Terry for lunch at ANA restaurant downtown and we reminisced about the last 6 months. Spending time with Terry was good for morale; we had done our best and we had shared some good times. We had established a strong bond. I also phoned the British Embassy because General Selimi had asked to see Andy Sparkes, the British Ambassador. I left lunch later than planned and decided to blue light across Pristina so that I could collect Selimi in time. We were told to meet the Ambassador at his residence. The house, downtown Pristina, was entirely surrounded by high-rise buildings. It reminded me a little of images I had seen of the colonial buildings in Hong Kong, the huge skyscrapers bearing down on the Queen's representative. Selimi was in his KSF uniform, the Ambassador was in a suit but I was again in scruffs. I really didn't have any smart clothes with me. It was a most civilised meeting, drinking tea, sitting on a very comfortable UK Government-funded sofa in a bright and airy room, looking out at the buildings on all sides.

We were there for an hour and it was primarily a conversation between General Selimi and Ambassador Sparkes; only they were talking about me and the removal of the liaison officer post. I was feeling quite awkward at the level of praise I was receiving from Selimi. I was taken aback. I think Andy Sparkes sensed my discomfort. We all knew it was too little too late, which seemed to be a theme in those final few days.

Eventually, Selimi and I left the Ambassador's residence and walked round to a local bar, on Selimi's insistence. We sat down and ordered a Peja beer each and chatted in English. After all the tension and stress of the last few weeks it was as if we had put everything behind us. Our relationship was affected by the fall out over his personal weapon, much to my regret. Selimi was a hard man to really get on with day to day and he was even harder to read. But sitting at that table in that café at that time, trying to explain the reality of the new UK-Kosovo relationship going forward, I felt we had re-established our friendship. When I eventually got back to Film City, Colonel Stuart told me that approval had been received for me to leave theatre, all I needed to do was choose which flight to take. I decided that even though I was only really marking time I said I would go on the following Monday, which would allow me time to see everyone, throw a leaving party and then escape to Macedonia at the weekend for a bit of decompression before flying back to my life in the UK.

On the Wednesday I booked my flight, something I had been looking forward to doing for quite a number of days. I also press-ganged Colonel Stuart into letting me use his apartment for my leaving party on the Friday evening. I busied myself sending out the invites and hoped that my reputation had not been too badly damaged by events, so people would still want to come. I also dropped off some things that Agim Çeku had asked for at one of our earlier meetings. I was due to see Çeku again the following day for a one-to-one. That evening, with snow flurries making driving hazardous and the tell-tale precursor to more persistent and heavy snowfall, I went out for dinner at a restaurant called Pure just outside Pristina. Normally excellent in Pristina, the food and service in Pure were not up to the normally high standards I had come to expect; and being served a bowl of soup but without a spoon seemed to be the perfect metaphor to describe the challenges faced by the KPC and latterly the KSF, in the face of KFOR indifference.

The next morning I drove to the KSF Ministry building, the scene of so many meetings with Selimi, Caplin and Minister Mujota. I wanted to see Dr Syla whom I had got to know well, but when I arrived he was double booked. I stepped out, dressed in my walking boots and Barbour jacket, to find Minister Mujota and an aide walking past. We talked for a few minutes, we shook hands and wished each other well. My final meeting with Çeku followed at his political party offices in town. I found him to be on good form. He wanted the best for his country and the KSF. I explained the events of the last couple of weeks and he was shocked at what had happened. This reaction was becoming commonplace.

As I was leaving Simi called me to say that the journalist who had been secretly meeting Major General Caplin, Ali Cenaj from the newspaper Zeri, wanted to meet me because he had heard about the LNO's office closing; the issue was becoming national news! I agreed to see him and later on met up with Simi. We met initially in Apartment 196, then drove to a bar I had never been to before to meet Cenaj. Like many he was surprised to see the liaison officer post close. With the three of us hunched over our coffees, sitting around a small table, I explained to him the chain of events over the previous two weeks, apart from the Naples connection, which he didn't need to know about. Cenaj didn't take any notes or record the conversation and I trusted him. After all, he had been discreetly meeting General Caplin for a number of months, trusted with accurate information about the KPC – KSF process that would help his readers understand what was going on, giving him the inside track. He was fascinated by what had been happening, however we had to cut the meeting short because I had a leaving dinner at the restaurant R2 with the KSF and I didn't want to be late. We agreed that we would meet again the following afternoon.

Being in R2 brought back many memories. I had always eaten well there and many key decisions had been taken over a glass of wine and a slow-cooked meal. Ilhe, the owner, once again greeted me after I knocked on the heavy wooden door at the entrance, and he led me to the table at the rear of the dining room, which felt like it actually belonged to us. The dinner was well attended and went well, with both Dr Syla and General Rama generous in their praise for me. And as previously promised, Rama gave me his uniform and a personalised flag that had been made for him whilst serving in the KPC. The end was now in sight.

The next morning I rolled off my bed and staggered in bare feet to my desk, which was pushed up against the only window in the room. I stretched across to draw back the flimsy curtain and stared outside, knowing that the frozen Balkan winter scene would soon be replaced with the fields and trees of southern England. Most of my personal possessions had been shipped back to the UK, so I was in a sleeping bag each night, on a NATO-issued mattress, which conspired to make those last few days feel as if I was in transit, which in many respects I was. After a hot shower, and changing into civilian clothes, I walked across to the KFOR HQ, via a long breakfast, to see Andy Lennard for a mid-morning meeting. The entrance to the headquarters was next to the coffee area and barber shop, so the place was packed with uniforms, mainly Italian personnel, standing around, talking loudly and laughing with each other, drinking their espresso coffees. The meeting followed a familiar pattern; swapping stories about the incompetence of the current KFOR leadership and laughing at some of the more notable examples. After saying goodbye to Andy, on my way out of the building, Colonel Adriano Graziani, the head of KFORs media team, quietly pulled me to one side. My day was about to get a lot worse; but then it was Friday the 13th.

Graziani said that he had been told that a young journalist in Kohe Ditore, who used to work for Zija, was about to run a story on me, saying that I had been suspended and was leaving early. I thanked Graziani for letting me know and walked out of the headquarters, head held high, to call Simi who immediately gave me his word that my name would not appear in the paper. I was paranoid that an inaccurate and wildly exaggerated story in a Kosovan newspaper featuring a British Army Officer was likely to be picked up by the British press with all the unnecessary attention that would bring. I had to stop that from even being a possibility. Before leaving Film City I saw Graziani briefly again, where he suggested some 'lines' for me to take to the meeting.

Knowing that Simi was on to it, and that he had spoken to Zija, who had recently left the newspaper, to have a word with the young journalist about not running the story at all, Simi and I left to have a final meeting with Ramush Haradinaj. I was thoroughly looking forward to seeing Ramush as I had begun to enjoy our encounters. He was a force to be reckoned with but he was also good company.

It seemed fitting to see him. Back in the same room, with coffees delivered, glasses of raki poured and small Cuban cigars gently smouldering, we spoke briefly about my family and our future plans in the UK. He ended the meeting by giving me a couple of gifts and we departed on very good terms. As I stepped onto the footpath outside the building, the reality of the earlier news suddenly hit home.

Zija had said that he would get in touch with me when he was with the journalist because I had insisted that I wanted to meet him, to explain that whatever he was proposing to write was untrue. After leaving Ramush's offices, Zija called and suggested I go over with Simi. I had also received a text telling me to report to KFOR headquarters because Di Luzio wanted to see me before he left for a meeting away from Film City. Dealing with the journalist though was far more important and I chose to ignore Di Luzio's request. I had more important things to deal with.

So after receiving the call, I drove with Simi over to the 'Green' shopping centre where I had met Zija only a couple of days earlier; we did not expect to meet again so soon. The journalist was called Kastriat and as I arrived they were sitting at a table. Zija had already given his word to me that the situation would not get out of hand but I felt I needed to quash the story face to face. As I arrived, with Simi waiting in the vehicle, I shook hands with both of them and sat down. I was asked some very direct questions about the alleged suspension, which I answered robustly, keeping within the agreed lines to take. I wanted to save my own skin and I didn't want to put my reputation at risk.

He then asked me about a rumour that I had contacted Naples about the selection issue. I had not heard this accusation before and I instantly felt a deep sense of shock. I had to concentrate hard to keep my expression as neutral as possible; I flatly denied it, maintaining eye contact with him throughout. He then turned to Zija:

'He says everything's cool.'

Zija had given me his word and in that short but intense conversation I had snuffed out any potential article and perhaps even saved my own career back in the UK; those were the stakes I felt I was playing. What he hadn't seen was my brain kicking into action, asking very difficult questions; how the hell did he know about Naples and who from KFOR could possibly have let that slip? And why? This situation had suddenly taken a sinister turn.

All I could think was that there was a sophisticated smear campaign underway, with information being passed out of KFOR into the hands of journalists and others who were now busily spreading rumours about me. I didn't know what to think; I was absolutely exhausted and was only really functioning in low power mode. Even though I didn't have time, I asked Simi if we could go and meet Lushtaku straight away. I believed he was behind the 'suspended' story getting in the media in the first place. It was irrational, I had no evidence to back up the assumption but I was still reeling from what the journalist had said to me.

I regretted the decision to meet him almost immediately.

It was late in the day and I still had my leaving party to attend that evening at Colonel Stuart's apartment. I should have been relaxing and writing a speech. Instead I was meeting former KPC senior officers who had an axe to grind and wanted to make a point, one I believed they were making at my expense in the most public way possible. Lushtaku was with Naim Bardiqi, an officer who had not been selected for the KSF. Bardiqi had been in touch with me several times asking me to meet him so that he could complain about the unfairness of the selection process. The truth was hard for some to accept, but on the whole, the selection process did actually select people who were better than others, however flawed it had become. Bardiqi was one of those who was clearly deeply affected by his rejection.

When we arrived Lushtaku immediately started talking about the process. He was in no mood to be interrupted. Nonetheless, I told him what I thought. It was an uncomfortable meeting. I made it clear how damaging it would be to me for these allegations to be swirling around the media, like flurries of snow in the car park outside. I was absolutely drained; emotionally, physically and mentally. I only had a few days left yet I was sitting in a café on a cold, dark night in Kosovo's capital city trying to protect my own personal reputation. It was madness. I simply didn't understand what was happening. If it was a local agenda I was pretty disappointed that my dedication and hard work appeared to have counted for nothing; if the rumours were coming out of KFOR I was very concerned. But I couldn't think straight; I was running on empty and the sooner I got on my flight, the better for everyone. I left before Bardiqi had a chance to kick off and, with Simi, headed back to Film City.

I got back to my room and lay on my sleeping bag, my head spinning by what had happened in the last few hours. I was disturbed by a call from Colonel Stuart Roberts to tell me that Andy Michels, an American security representative from the International Civilian Office, had received a report via various sources that Zeri, the newspaper that Ali Cenaj worked for, was going to run a story which would be potentially even more damaging to me. I messaged Andy Michels, someone who I had never spoken to during my 6 months, and we arranged to talk the following morning.

I changed and headed out to Colonel Stuart's apartment. Pretty much everyone who had been invited came to the party, including former Prime Minister Agim Çeku. I was showered with gifts of cigars, speeches were made, and many of my colleagues and friends, those I respected most, said some very complimentary words about my efforts in Kosovo. I was determined to enjoy myself and try to relax. I got drunk to block out the looming issue of the newspaper article. At least I was surrounded by people I cared deeply about and with whom I had shared some unbelievable times whilst in Kosovo.

Towards the end of the evening, as a plan started to form to go clubbing in Gračanica again, I was called by my wife. It was completely out of context and totally unexpected. I walked out of the main reception room into a quieter corridor as she started talking about where we could all go on holiday after I got back. But I could hardly string two words together; I was tired, drunk, emotional and feeling extremely vulnerable. It was all I could do to politely end the call. I felt terrible, but my differing worlds had come crashing together. And I couldn't cope. I returned to the party and after declining the opportunity to go 'Serb-side' again, we took taxis into town for a final visit to the only half-decent nightclub in Pristina, Depot, notorious for its B52 shots, sticky floor and lack of emergency exits. I didn't stay long but it had been a good night.

I woke up on the Saturday morning and remembered that I had to call Andy Michels from the ICO. When he answered he explained that a source at the Kosovo Police had heard that I had uncovered irregularities in the KSF selection process and had revealed them outside the chain of command to Naples. Although it sounded similar in nature to the issue raised by Kastriat the previous day, I hadn't mentioned Naples to anyone, so it could only have come from inside KFOR.

I had to act on it quickly to avoid something coming out after I had left Kosovo when I would be unable to defend myself. Michels said that the article was due to be printed the following week after the anniversary of Kosovo's independence, so we had some time. He also suggested I speak to Andy McGuffie, a British comms specialist working for the ICO. I called Andy, we arranged to meet and after quickly changing, I drove down to the entrance of Slim Lines, five minutes from Film City. Standing next to our respective vehicles, I explained what had happened from my perspective. Andy advised me to write everything down as an insurance policy just in case something came out later. He also said that he would make some phone calls to try to quash the story. He didn't rate the Kosovan press and reassured me that everything would be fine.

Unable to do any more I drove back to Film City and packed a few things. I had decided to stay in Skopje for the night in an attempt to decompress a little before flying back into the heart of my family on the Monday afternoon. I drove south out of Pristina and tried to do my best to block out everything that had happened in the past 24 hours. I was rapidly becoming immune to my own tiredness and I knew I needed some head space.

Skopje gave me the environment I craved. I walked, I ate and I slept as much as two days would allow. I reflected on the imminent closure of one chapter of my life and the opening of another. By the time I got back to Pristina on the Sunday evening I put my things together ready for the following day. There was nothing more to say to anyone. As Monday morning dawned, the previous 72 hours felt like they hadn't happened at all. After grabbing some breakfast I ambled onto the 'walk of shame' to meet Migena for a final coffee. Back at my accommodation, I packed my things into the Landcruiser, reunited with Kasper one last time, and drove out to the airport.

It was the 16th February 2009.

Almost one year earlier the Prime Minister of Kosovo, Hashim

Thaçi had declared Kosovo's independence from Serbia. That decision on 17ᵗʰ February 2008 had kickstarted a process for the KPC that I had been intimately involved in during my 6 months. All along the route to the airport, flags had been tied to every lamp post in preparation for the celebrations the following day. As we drove along the road, that needed a 4x4 to navigate in places, it was clear that the flags signified a new start. It was a real sign of patriotism and pride; a small part of me hoped I had added to that feeling in some small way.

I was missing the anniversary but, to be honest, I had given enough to Kosovo and I now needed to try to get my family life back on track again. I didn't know how I was going to be able to come down from the pressure, the intensity and the stress that I had been exposed to in the 6 months since driving to Gatwick back in August, especially in the last couple of weeks. Kosovo had got under my skin and I had loved being there. I had met people who had changed my life and who I would miss. I knew I would come back again. For now though I needed some normality, some calmness and I had a lot of preparations to make before taking command of my regiment.

My tour in Kosovo was over; I was going home.

PART TWO

CHAPTER SIXTEEN

'Going Back'

22nd April, 2018

I am standing in a long queue at the airport, snaking my way around barriers, designed to maximise space in the departures area but unwittingly allowing me to study the other passengers as we pass each other time and again. I find myself drawn to the faces, the body language and the behaviour of others. I cannot stop myself studying how people behave, what they wear, the way they conduct themselves. The way people interact says so much about who they are and where their motivations lie. In the queue I see people who appear to be new to flying, looking slightly overwhelmed as they shuffle anonymously towards the check-in desk. I see tired children, with even more tired parents, trying to keep the family's mood light while we are subjected to the tiresome ritual of shuffle, stop, wait, shuffle, stop, wait.

Standing here in this line, clutching my cup of coffee, listening to the people around me talking in recognisable Balkan accents, I feel myself drawn back into distant, yet vivid memories; their voices conjuring up images of Kosovo that I thought had been long buried. I am recognising words and remember how I spent 6 weeks attending evening classes to learn basic Albanian. A phrase sends me back to a time and place I had forgotten long ago. I am looking at faces that remind me of walking on the streets of Pristina. There is a growing familiarity accompanying these memories. And they are having an unexpected effect on me; to my surprise I am feeling nervous.

It's just after 5 o' clock in the morning and I am about to fly to Skopje in Macedonia. But that is not my final destination; I am returning to Kosovo for the first time in 9 years.

I had been waiting for the right opportunity to return to Kosovo for some time. With the tenth anniversary of the formation of the Kosovo Security Force fast approaching, I am very keen to reconnect with the many people I spent such a tumultuous period with during the birth of what remains the youngest security institution in the Balkans. I want to discover whether the Kosovo Security Force has grown into an organisation that is truly professional, respected by its people, and which will in due course be ready to transition into an Army. These were the hopes of many of the people I worked so closely with in the KPC and latterly the KSF. When I walked out of the departure lounge in Pristina to return to the UK back in the winter of 2009, I was battered and bruised but defiant over my contribution to the formation of the new security force and the decisions I had made. But there was no hiding it, the KSF was in a mess when I left.

So my return is long overdue. It has been clear to me for some time that I need to return to the country that had left such a profound impression on me 9 years earlier. Kosovo is seared into my heart; I spent 6 months in the newly independent country, during which time I made friends for life and experienced some of the most extreme range of emotions any person can safely endure. There may not have been any bullets flying (actually there had been a few), but Kosovo drew out of me reserves of moral courage that I did not know I had; Kosovo had tested my core values like no other period in my adult life. And, despite what had been thrown at me, I hoped I had left my mark on the country's fledgling security sector.

I was about to find out whether others shared this view and to understand whether it had all been worth it.

When I finally decided to go back to Kosovo a couple of weeks earlier, the first message I sent was to my old friend Simi. I told him I was planning to return and asked whether he would be willing to act as my fixer, as he had done all those years ago, when I was living and working in Pristina. I initially asked him if he would be able to arrange some meetings for me. I wanted to sit down with people who I had spent time with 9 years earlier. I was keen to see several important individuals: General Rama, who was now the Commander of the KSF; Brigadier Enver Cikaqi, the newly appointed Land Forces Commander whom I had last seen at the Royal College of Defence Studies in London; Agim Çeku who was now in Government as the Deputy Minister for the KSF; and Ramush Haradinaj, an MP and political party leader when I knew him, but now the country's Prime Minister.

I wanted to know that I would be able to maximise my time back in Kosovo and fixing the meetings was important to me before I booked my flights. Instead I smiled as I read Simi's messages; I had completely forgotten how Simi works. In his indomitable way he confidently told me that everything would be fine. When I suggested he should confirm the meetings before I book my flight he turned it around.

'You book then tell me when the trip is confirmed.'

And that is precisely what happened. I did what I was told, which was normally the case with Simi.

Leaving behind a cold, misty rain in the UK, I arrive in Skopje to unseasonably hot weather. It is similar to the first few weeks I had spent in Kosovo in 2008. In a quiet airport, an hour's drive south of the Kosovo border, I pick up my hire car keys and walk out with my bags, it's just after lunchtime and nobody is around, the sky is blue, there is no wind, it is silent, the car park almost empty of people. I am sitting in the car, adjusting the seat and the controls and quickly realise that I need to buy a map. I am confident that I remember the layout of this part of Macedonia from my earlier visits in 2008 and 2009, so I set off following road signs, something I am not used to with satnavs dominating driving habits back home. I stop at a service station, not far from the airport, to buy an ice cream and a map of the region. I sit for a moment to orientate myself; the last time I was in this part of the world it was a freezing Balkan winter, snow was lying on the ground and the temperature was hovering around zero degrees.

I check the map and remember the names of places long since forgotten. A wave of nostalgia washes over me as I start the car and head west on a near empty motorway. I am travelling for 30 minutes when I finally see what I have been looking forward to for a long time; the road sign indicating the junction for Pristina. I turn off the motorway onto the familiar single-track road that winds its way north to the Kosovo border at Hani Elezit.

The road I am taking hasn't changed at all in the intervening years. It twists and turns following a very steep-sided valley, covered in dense woodland, that was the route into Kosovo for British troops when they entered the country in 1999 after the ceasefire with

Serbian forces had been signed. The road has a special meaning for me and my mind drifts back to what it must have been like during those extraordinary times 19 years earlier. Sooner than expected I see the signs warning me of the approaching Macedonian border, followed shortly beyond by the Kosovo customs post. I am quickly doing a check in my mind; do I have my passport? Did I check to see whether I needed a visa? What will happen if there was some message tagged against my name when I left last time?

As it turns out, my thoughts are unnecessarily alarmist. I glide through the Macedonian border with ease and join the queue to enter Kosovo. With the traffic stopped, and the anticipated levels of disorganisation in evidence, I am hoping I am in the lane that moves forward quickest. Nearly all the cars around me have Kosovan number plates; it is Sunday afternoon so perhaps the occupants have been shopping in Skopje for the day, or maybe they have been enjoying a weekend at one of the many tourist locations in Macedonia.

The cars also demonstrate the wealth gap that has always existed in Kosovo. Relatively new Mercedes Benz coupés, clean and looking every bit the symbol of success, contrast with dirty older vehicles, driven by people with little outward sign of anything approaching a reasonable income. My observations are cut short as the car in front starts to move and I too creep forward cautiously, inching my way to the customs officer, seated in a scruffy-looking booth, to present my British passport. I have a long list of reasons rehearsed in my mind why I am crossing the border in case I am asked, but they remain unused. My passport is returned to me, I say thank you in Albanian, and drive into Kosovo.

I can't quite believe I am back.

The feeling of relief and excitement is immediately replaced by a very strong memory of being in Hani Elezit, the border town I am driving into. I am taken aback by the familiarity of the huge cement factory that dominates the valley floor in the centre of the town. This image immediately makes me return to an episode that took place during my tour.

I am in the town where Major Rufki Suma prevented his men from signing up to the KSF. We visited many times to try to get him to change his mind, often without success. He courted the media and his behaviour was a portent for what was to transpire elsewhere in the KPC's ranks. Driving alongside the factory, passing underneath huge conveyor belts that span the road and travel hundreds of metres away across the valley floor into the distance, something catches my eye that immediately makes me laugh.

On the path, on the opposite side of the road to me, I notice a large pile of stones next to what looks like a hole. I look closely and remember how I made the journey to this town on my own to see Suma in the hope that I might be able to change his mind, to appeal to his better judgement over applying for the KSF. As it turned out I wasted my time but when I arrived that day in October 2008, the men under his command and influence were working on the path next to the road at what appears to be exactly the same spot as the pile of stones and the hole. Is it possible that the two events are connected? Can the unfinished hole on the path be related to the KPC's work in the town 9 years earlier? Is it the same hole?! It seems highly unlikely but I smile to myself at the thought and keep driving north.

Whilst the single-track road I am driving on is as poorly maintained as I can remember, I know there is a major road-building programme ongoing in Kosovo which is already improving the country's infrastructure and making a huge difference to travel times between Kosovo and Albania in particular. The evidence is clear to see. High up on the hillside on the Macedonian side of the border I have already noticed a dramatic grey scar cutting through the trees just below the crest on the opposite hillside to me, the tell-tale signs of a new road beginning to take shape. Once I am across the border in Kosovo the reason for the height is clear; there are huge supporting columns, standing hundreds of feet tall, being constructed along the valley floor parallel with the old road I am driving on now, ready for a new motorways to link the capitals of Kosovo and The Republic of Northern Macedonia. It's an impressive sight.

Leaving behind the motorway construction, the Kosovo I am seeing now appears at first glance to be much the same as I remember. The road I am travelling on links Kosovo's southern border to the capital, Pristina, and extends up to the country's most northerly town, Mitrovice, and beyond to the border with Serbia. It's a Sunday afternoon so the roads are not very busy. Under a clear sky, I am leaving behind the steep-sided valley and the ground is becoming flat as far as the eye can see. As the valley's forested walls taper away, I notice a snow-topped mountain beyond the ridge line to the west, standing majestically against the hazy blue sky.

Within a few minutes I see the road sign indicating the left-hand turn for Prizren, the oldest and most attractive city in Kosovo a couple of hours' drive away. Along that road is the Kosovo Serbian enclave of Brezovica; a dilapidated ski resort, home to a derelict communist-style hotel, ageing ski lifts and a café on the top of a converted double-decker bus. I am tempted to turn left and make an unplanned visit; surely it can't still be in the same condition as it was 9 years earlier. The potential to redevelop the area and turn it into a winter playground seemed clear to me in 2009. I spent the weekend skiing there with Terry Anderson, the United States Assistant Defence Attaché at the time, on one of my final weekends in

Kosovo. Skiing in Brezovica easily goes down in my memory as one of the most dangerous sporting experiences of my life. I am left to ponder its current condition as I press on north towards the capital.

The Kosovo I remember was home to so many international organisations that it felt like every other vehicle was from the UN, OSCE, KFOR or EULEX, plus any number of well-meaning transnational institutions. The country was awash with international staff, spending their time and tax-free salaries in the bars, restaurants and cafés in Pristina. At the time there were 16,000 KFOR troops deployed. It felt like Kosovo was being crushed under the weight of the international presence.

I notice there seem to be more commercial premises that have been built, strung out along the roadside selling building supplies and new cars; that's a good sign. I am driving through an area that is home to over 650 US Army reservists who are deployed in Kosovo to contribute to KFOR's mission to maintain a safe and secure environment. The number of KFOR troops in Kosovo has reduced significantly since my last visit, with just over 4,000 now deployed. Many of the international organisations have also left or scaled back their presence. During the whole journey from the border to the outskirts of Pristina, I only see one US Army truck. On the whole, the vehicles passing me on the road seem to be predominantly Kosovan; it's a clear indication that a degree of normality appears to have returned to Kosovo and it is a welcome sight. I am looking forward to seeing Pristina more than ever.

Close to the southern town of Giljane I am given the opportunity to join one of the newly built motorways, and, as it's a novelty for me, I take the slip road and follow the signs north. The motorway is practically empty. The idea to join the new road seemed like a good one at the time but entering the built-up suburbs of Pristina I realise that by taking the motorway I am arriving from a different approach to what I remember. To my surprise I barely recognise the buildings and roads. How has the last 9 years managed to blank out the sights and sounds of a city I knew like the back of my hand? It is unnerving.

Following the signs to the centre I finally see a junction I remember and pull over to speak to a taxi driver parked in front of me. It's hot when I step out of the air conditioning, the sun's heat taking me by surprise as I walk up to the driver. Although I am a little embarrassed, I ask him if he knows the name of the hotel I am staying at. He does. I ask him whether he would drive there with me following behind in my hire car. He will. I ask him how much it will be. He replies €3. I have forgotten my Albanian but my sign language skills remain good.

And so I am once again driving through the city that has a set of rules all to itself. I had forgotten that people step off the curb and expect cars to stop, wherever they are and whatever speed they are travelling at. I remember how the likelihood of coming into contact with other road users is high; I had been in a minor accident last time I was here. I am on heightened alert following the taxi looking out for pedestrians, other cars wanting to use the same bit of tarmac as me, and avoiding the many pot holes in the road. I get a flashback to when I drove at speed through the city in my official car, with blue lights on and siren wailing, an experience that was both exhilarating and terrifying in equal measure, paranoid about hitting a pedestrian who had chosen to exercise their right to cross the road regardless of the traffic conditions.

And then, as I pull up to a set of traffic lights, I am hit from behind. Swearing loudly, I get out of the car and walk to the rear where the other driver has also got out to inspect the damage. Fortunately the dent to the hire car's bumper doesn't look too incriminating and I tell the other driver, in English, to forget it. There is nothing I can do so I get back in. The lights change to green and I am once again moving slowly in the Pristina traffic, following the taxi driver for the final couple of turns to my hotel. I find a dusty car park on the opposite side of the road, turn off the engine and let out a deep sigh. It is as if I have never been away. I am back in Pristina.

I have a very busy week ahead. I am hoping to meet many people, including the country's Prime Minister, to gauge the success of the KSF, to share memories and to discuss the rights and wrongs of NATO's influence over the security sector transition 9 years earlier.

My hotel is ideally located close to the centre of the city and, after checking into my spacious room, I am eager to walk into the afternoon sunshine and to taste the capital's atmosphere once again. The nerves I was experiencing have subsided and the sense of belonging is already growing inside me. The traffic looks less intimidating from the lopsided pavement I am walking along and I quickly remember to look down as much as look up in case I come across an unguarded hole. Another memory appears in my mind; I am running outside the KFOR base one evening in 2008, following the road down the hill from the base and I narrowly avoid a manhole, normally protected by a metal cover, which is missing.

I consider stepping into the road, knowing that the approaching cars will stop, but at the last second I hesitate and remain on the pavement to wait for a break in the flow. I decide to get my bearings in the city before putting my old theory to the test; I don't want to find out that the practice has slipped out of use.

I am meeting Simi later on, my friend and fixer extraordinaire, at the prominent Skenderbej statue that stands proudly overlooking Mother Teresa Boulevard in the shadow of Kosovo's Government building. It was here that I stood in bemusement, 9 years earlier, watching as many of the unselected members of the KPC expressed their anger in front of the symbolic seat of power in the newly independent Kosovo. It seems fitting that we are meeting at the same spot.

A short distance away I sit down and order a drink and some food. There are hundreds of people walking in either direction along the main pedestrian thoroughfare. They are mostly Kosovan families and young people, laughing and joking, enjoying the warmth, taking exercise. I also see the occasional group of older people who are clearly tourists on an organised visit. I don't remember seeing this before. It is another positive sign of how Kosovo seems to be changing for the better; attracting a growing number of foreign visitors is going to be crucial for Kosovo in its aim of achieving what many refer to as normalisation in the eyes of the international community. I remember how much I enjoy people watching in this city.

When I finally meet Simi in the early evening it is as if we had only seen each other the day before. He never seems to change and we shake hands without much fanfare. We had last seen each other a couple of years earlier in the UK and, after the normal preamble of checking on our respective families, we get down to business. We order a drink and chat about the week ahead, Simi explaining what he has managed to arrange. We both shared some intense experiences during my 6 months in his country and I think he is quietly very pleased that I am back. We don't talk for long though as it is a Sunday evening and he has a family waiting for him. We agree the plan for the week and he drops me off at the hotel.

The key meeting with the Prime Minister is loosely scheduled for Thursday, once he is back from an overseas visit to Slovenia. In between the formal visits that Simi has arranged I also want to spend some time with Zija Miftari, the journalist I met clandestinely when giving him background information on the KPC-KSF process, all fully approved and authorised by the KFOR chain of command. Zija knows I am coming and simply asked me to let him know when I am in Pristina; I send him a text that I am here. Finally I want to see Migena, who is still working in Film City and who was such a source of strength and friendship in those final, dark days of my tour of duty. I really don't know how the week will unfold but I am hoping that everything slots into place.

I wake up to a bright, warm morning in Pristina. My window is open and the curtain is gently moving in the breeze. I can hear the city waking up outside. My appointment with Brigadier Enver Cikaqi is not until a little later so after breakfast I walk the short distance to the same restaurant where I ate the day before on Mother Teresa Boulevard, carefully waiting for a break in the traffic before crossing the road, stepping off the pavement with more intent, trying to make eye contact with the drivers going past. With time on my side I choose a seat in the sunshine, I move the chair so that it is sitting evenly on the ground, and I order a macchiato. It is the same waiter as the day before and we exchange greetings. I am already making friends.

From the moment I set out on this journey I questioned whether I was making a mistake by coming back out to a place that held so many mixed emotions for me. 'Never go back' is a mantra I tend to live by. However I had well and truly ripped that principle up by getting on the flight at Luton Airport. I had felt an unexpected nervousness when I was queueing to check in over the wisdom of making this trip. Those feelings had lingered into last night. Even though my meeting with Simi had been fine, I still wonder how I will be received by others. I take a sip of my first coffee of the day, listening to the sounds of the street and think about my imminent visit to the KSF.

When I arrive by taxi at the main entrance of Land Forces Command, I explain that I have a meeting with the Commander and I am not waiting long before a smart Land Rover Discovery pulls up to drive me to Brigadier Cikaqi's office. The journey takes 30 seconds and I could have walked, but I acknowledge the gesture and feel pleased that it has been made. At every opportunity I practice my very rusty Albanian and start to make friends again, following the approach I took 9 years earlier; the gate guard, the taxi driver, I am thirsty for engagement with people. I am taking everything in. The barracks is smart and well kept, it looks organised and there are both men and women in uniform. Inside the headquarters, which is spotlessly clean, there are civilians and uniformed personnel going about their day with what looks like real purpose. The building is fresh and pristine, without any trace of cigarette smoke. I smile at the satisfaction that smoking appears to have been consigned to history, a rare thing in Kosovo. As I wait to see the Brigadier I talk to a couple of the KSF personnel in his outer office. They seem intrigued that I was last in the same building on the day their force was formed, so many years ago in their young eyes.

I am being hosted by a Lieutenant who graduated through the KSF's University Study Centre, a programme which takes young graduates through a degree and military training to eventually be commissioned as officers in the KSF. It is similar to the US officer training programme at West Point. He is now serving in a media role in the headquarters. He is a bright, motivated and engaging young man. He talks about what he has done so far, with enthusiasm and passion. I am already feeling impressed; it seems to me that a career in the KSF is an attractive option for Kosovo's youth and he is a fine example of what is possible.

Brigadier Enver Cikaqi was appointed as the Commander of Training and Doctrine Command (known as TRADOC) in central Pristina when the KSF was established in January 2009. I went to see him a few days into his tour to find a man almost overwhelmed by the task in front of him. This time, we greet warmly and I am invited to sit on a large leather sofa in his airy office, a photograph of his President, Hashim Thaçi, framed on the wall behind his desk. I smile at the irony.

We talk about the months that followed his tenure. I am interested to know how the KSF coped with effectively starting from scratch. He is in a reflective mood. He explains that the KSF was keen to establish their own education programme whilst receiving training from NATO, which at one time included over 150 instructors from various nations. He explains that the quality of the NATO nation providing support was variable and each platoon of recruits was assigned a different NATO trainer. He said that as a result each basic training course was conducted over the same course length and syllabus but were influenced by different cultures and doctrine. The results were inconsistent and unhelpful. To emphasise this point, he recalls a joke that did the rounds about punishment given out during the training, with some KSF instructors, who were being mentored at the same time, asking the recruits if they wanted Bulgarian push-ups (only moving the head) or American push-ups (proper push-ups). It was light-hearted but it was at the heart of the problem. I laugh when he tells me this story, but I sympathise with him as well.

Brigadier Cikaqi explains that over the years he recognised that the KSF needed to forge its own path and generate its own standards, which in turn would give the KSF a sense of its own identity. Amongst all the well-intentioned support they received, Cikaqi was full of praise for Croatian troops who had deployed to Kosovo. As a new country themselves they were able to share their own experiences of creating an effective security organisation; he emphasises how invaluable their contribution has been. I am enjoying hearing these stories and I am reassured that Cikaqi is continuing to create a distinctive identity for the KSF.

He describes how the retirement of former KPC personnel over the years, and the introduction of younger people from across Kosovo, including the country's ethnic minorities, has already begun to change the culture and feeling within the organisation. The KSF's University Study Centre, designed to produce young officers, together with others who are trained in overseas military academies such as the UK and the US, are beginning to make their mark.

History has already shown that Kosovo's young people are the best of their generation. At The Royal Military Academy, Sandhurst in the UK, Kosovo's young KSF officer cadets have been awarded Best International Cadet, a significant accolade by any measure. I ask the Brigadier how some of the older KPC diehards enjoyed being led by young officers who had never served in the KPC. He replies that despite some early challenges with those unfamiliar with how modern military forces operate, over time it became less of an issue. I sense a better balance to the KSF from what he is saying. As if reading my mind, Cikaqi explains that at present over 60% of the KSF never served in the KPC.

Brigadier Cikaqi returns to the subject of NATO personnel who serve in Kosovo for 6 month tours, as I did. The early days of variable support through NATO seem to be over; he heaps praise on the current arrangements through the NATO Advisory Liaison Team, headed up by a German General and based in Film City. He adds that he still feels disappointment when some NATO troops deploy to Kosovo to further their own national agendas rather than working within the NATO mission to make a positive difference to the KSF.

We are immediately distracted by a knock on the open door. A Turkish liaison officer is standing uncertainly and clearly wishes to talk to the Brigadier. Speaking in English, the Brigadier gets up and walks across to him to deal with the matter. He soon returns to our conversation. Cikaqi explains his visitor is working in the KSF Ministry building and is assigned to him as a Liaison Officer. Although I could hear the brief conversation between them, I didn't understand a single word that the Turkish officer said. It occurs to me that having a foreign officer supporting the KSF who is indecipherable in English is unlikely to add value to the highly astute Brigadier General Cikaqi, a former lawyer.

My time with the Brigadier is over too soon and he has another appointment to attend to. I think we have run over time quite significantly. I walk out of the office with him and while he deals with the appointment I am taken on a brief tour of the barracks with the Lieutenant who is hosting me so attentively. Back in the waiting area, the Brigadier returns and we line up for a formal photograph in front of a large KSF plaque. Brigadier Cikaqi asks whether I have any plans for lunch, which I don't, so he tells me we are going out to a restaurant to eat some chicken. I know this is imposing on his diary and I am deeply touched. We walk downstairs while the Close Protection team goes ahead to get the vehicles ready. Outside the building and at the foot of the entrance steps the door is already open and I jump into the back of the Discovery. Amid barked orders and the slamming of doors, we are off, sweeping out of the barracks and turning into the busy Pristina traffic. It is just like the old days.

The journey to the restaurant is short but it provides me with a very strong memory of my many journeys across Kosovo in official vehicles. After an enjoyable lunch, reminiscing about days gone by, telling stories about life in the KSF, Brigadier Cikaqi drops me off in the city centre, a short walk from my hotel. It is kind of him to go out of his way for me and we say goodbye, with the promise to see other again soon.

The remainder of the day is free so I change in my hotel and explore the city once more, retracing my steps. I am starting to notice that the skyline has changed over time, new buildings have appeared and there is a density about the streets that I do not remember. The streets themselves are similar to what I recall; walking on the pavements is an accident waiting to happen with holes appearing without warning. I remember how health and safety is less of an issue here. Most roads are entirely normal but some streets are under excavation, deep holes in the roads are marked with warning signs and dust is kicked up by the heavy machinery involved in the construction. I feel completely safe though and at home on the streets of Pristina. That night I go out for some food close to the Sokoli e Mirusha café I visited so many times during my tour of duty. Afterwards I walk aimlessly along the streets that seem to be where the night life is at its best and I drop in to a bar. Writing in my diary, drinking a beer outside, the evening surprisingly warm, I feel at home.

The following morning I have an early appointment. I again walk into town, this time I step into the road with greater confidence and for the first time a vehicle slows at the sight of me leaving the pavement. It works; inwardly I am elated and am not really sure why. It feels like a small victory as I cross the road, like I have been accepted by this city once again. I am beginning to notice the same people opening their stores and going about their day. The sense of belonging is incredibly strong. I reach the end of Mother Teresa Boulevard and walk to the front of the taxi rank.

'Can you take me to Film City please?'

I am meeting Migena, who is still working in KFOR. She has agreed to sign me into the camp as a visitor so that I can take another look around the place. I am dropped off in the car park and walk through the outer security and up the short hill to the main entrance. I am living every step, alive to the significance of making this trip.

Migena is standing waiting for me and it is great to see her again after so long. After handing in my passport I am given an ID badge and allowed to walk in unhindered, relieved that I am not flagged up on a KFOR black list. Migena and I wander along the 'walk of shame', tripping over memories as we go. I am keen to see some of the old places again: the bars I went to; the cafés that were so often filled with Italian troops; the shops full of KFOR soldiers bussed in from across Kosovo on a Saturday; even my old accommodation block. As we walk past the old MCA Division office I see a familiar face. Adnan, who was General Caplin's interpreter throughout the period of my tour, seems happy that we have unexpectedly met.

I am struck by how few people are around. I wonder whether KFOR is on a holiday, but they are not. The drop in troop numbers across the country has had a knock-on effect on the numbers in Film City, even though they appear to be constructing more accommodation units. We stop in the same café where we had last seen each other on my final day. We sit down, order a coffee and take it all in. It feels very strange being back in Film City; my mind is overflowing with flashbacks and faded memories. It is deeply nostalgic to be here.

I leave Migena and my memories of Film City and choose to walk the short distance to the new KSF Ministry building, situated adjacent to the old Slim Lines barracks. I have an appointment with Agim Çeku, the Deputy Minister for the KSF, and also with General Rama. Underestimating the heat and my rusty navigation skills, I get slightly confused by the location of the newly constructed building. I am standing on the wrong side of a busy dual carriageway, with cars driving past at speed between roundabouts. Behind me is a huge new building under construction, in front of me is the disused main entrance to Slim Lines. I know I need to cross the road and still feel slightly wary about simply walking out into traffic, now moving much faster than in the city centre.

It's hot and I am carrying my suit jacket with my business case. I wait for a few minutes and manage to get across one carriageway unscathed, then wait for a few moments on the central reservation. I spot a gap in the traffic behind a car that is approaching in the outside lane doing at least 50mph. To my amusement rather than my surprise, the driver jumps on his brakes and stops his car to let me cross. I wave my thanks and quickly dash across the final two lanes before I cause an accident.

I find myself standing outside the camp that had once housed the British and Portuguese Battalions in Pristina. I had attended a Remembrance Service here in 2008, a formal and poignant ceremony conducted with military precision on a cold November morning. Whilst it is clear I am not in the right place, seeing the empty barracks fills me with an unexpected sense of regret at the loss of a British presence in Pristina. I quickly bring myself back to the present by the sound of airbrakes and the revving of a diesel engine; a coach has pulled up behind me and it looks like the driver is having the same issue as I am. He asks me a question and, judging by the age of the people on the bus, I am guessing the driver wants to know where the Land Forces Command barracks is. By now I work out I need to walk further down the road towards the city centre. I give him directions in sign language and then ask whether he can give me a lift. He opens the coach door and I get in. I am sitting at the front of a coach, next to the microphone, full of either KSF or potential KSF troops, to drive 250m up the road to the correct location. The temptation to make an announcement is strong.

As we pull up at the main entrance I hop off and walk through security and into the Ministry building. I am a little hot and bothered, smiling to myself at the circumstances of my arrival. I see Simi again and he leads me into a huge atrium in the newly built KSF Ministry. I know there is a British Liaison Officer who is working with Simi and I soon meet Lieutenant Colonel Paul Stainthorpe in their large shared office; together with the Turkish officer I had seen the day before with Brigadier Cikaqi. Simi explains that General Rama is busy and we are due to have lunch the following day. We quickly walk across the mezzanine to the office of the Deputy Minister for the KSF to see Agim Çeku.

It is good to see Agim Çeku, who I had last seen at my leaving party a few days before I left Kosovo. We talk a lot about how the new force has established its reputation in the country and he outlines the progress that the KSF had made, in particular he dwells on the next stage of Kosovo's security journey, transforming the KSF into the Kosovo Army. He laments the obstacles that seem to be laid in front of this goal but he remains positive. We also talk about Kosovo supporting international operations overseas, it is a conversation we first had in the rustic charm of the Pellumbi Restaurant, close to where we are sitting now. Seeing Kosovo take its rightful place in the world is not only Çeku's ambition, but one shared by many in the KSF and beyond. He reiterates his hope that Kosovo can become a security provider rather than a security consumer.

His phone is constantly ringing throughout our conversation so I leave him to it; we shake hands warmly and agree to keep in touch. It is clear that I am welcome in Kosovo and the doubts I had at the start of the week about how I was going to be received are proving to be groundless.

I leave his office and see Simi; he tells me we are going into Pristina with Lieutenant Colonel Stainthorpe for lunch. In town, Stainthorpe and I sit outside at a large and wobbly wooden table that can easily fit 6 people. He is wearing British uniform but we do not attract any attention. Simi has other errands to do so it is just the two of us, asking questions and finding common ground from our separate careers. Over lunch, shaded from the sun by a large parasol, we are both interested in each other's experiences in Kosovo; I ask him about what life is like for him as the British liaison officer in Kosovo in 2018. The role he describes is very different to my own experience. He spends less time with General Rama and much more time organising UK-supported military training activities. It is clear he is enjoying himself and that pleases me.

In my last few days in Kosovo in 2009, KFOR had recognised that they had made a mistake by not replacing me and had placed my former boss, the Swedish Air Force Colonel, into the liaison role with the KSF. But the Kosovans were not happy. The British Liaison Officer role was reinstated a few months after I left; the folly of the original decision by KFOR quickly reversed. Simi eventually joins us and we pass a very amiable hour together over lunch, the atmosphere supplemented by lively conversations drifting across from nearby tables.

When I get back to the hotel after lunch I leave my things in the safe and walk out to find a taxi. I decide, very much at the last minute, to make a pilgrimage. I head off in the general direction where I need to go. I find a taxi rank and approach a battered old Mercedes. I reach out to open the back door and the driver beckons me in. I explain to the old man at the wheel that I want to go to

Germia Park. While I was in Kosovo the first time, I used to escape the city and go for walks there, an area of parkland to the East of the city set across a number of hills that contain countless trails for walking and cycling. It was a place of solace that allowed me to gather my thoughts and escape the madness of my daily routine. It is also where I met Alexandra when I first arrived.

It's warming up and the windows are open. I try to fit the seat belt but it resists my attempts to comply. I let it flop back onto the backseat as I watch people and shops passing by, the warm wind filling the vehicle with sounds and smells from outside. We carve through the traffic at a fair rate of knots and soon start to leave the narrow, claustrophobic city streets behind. I pass landmarks that I had forgotten about; the Lido currently devoid of water, a large play area for children next to a car park at the foot of the hills. We continue, deeper into the forest, until I see the sign for the café car park on the left. I have this spot in mind as my start point, as suggested by Alexandra nearly a decade earlier. I pay the driver and as he drives away I realise I probably should have made some arrangements for a pick-up. I start walking with only my memory to guide me. I soon remember where I am and realise why I liked coming to Germia Park. The forest is alive with birdsong, shafts of light filter through the canopy forming shapes in the haze that change as I take each step; it's magical.

A few minutes into my hike, after a particularly steep climb, I realise I do not have any water with me. I press on, passing the occasional walker and cyclist, heading deeper into the hills. Eventually I leave a track and find myself on an old tarmac road. Left leads up to the top of the hill; right leads down to a second restaurant I have already decided will be my venue for an early dinner. I turn right.

There is one place I do want to see and as I walk down the road I notice a huge concrete structure on the left, set back and deserted. I do not remember this complex, built in the middle of the forest and which now seems to be abandoned. It is ugly and needs to be demolished. I make a note to ask Zija about it when I see him. What I want to see is on the opposite side of the road.

Nine years earlier this area was still cordoned off, with signs indicating a minefield. The UN's inability to clear this site following the 1999 conflict, so that families could let their children fully enjoy the park, always struck me as a failure of the UN's post-conflict efforts to return Kosovo to normality. I notice that the signs have gone and there is a plaque on a stone wall away from the road. Drawn to it, I step onto the grass verge and make my way across what used to be the minefield and clamber up onto the stone structure, set 30m back, so that I can read its words. I discover that the KSF and the Swedish Contingent in KFOR cleared the area in 2013. The fact that the Kosovans ended up clearing this site, with their Swedish colleagues, claiming back its land, seems appropriate. I am so happy to see this area restored to the people of Kosovo. I cover the final few hundred metres to the restaurant with a spring in my step.

The natural hospitality of the Kosovans is evident later in the evening. I walk into town again for a quiet drink to reflect on my day, taking some back roads to reach the area with the bars. As I am walking through a small tunnel underneath a building I see a couple of locals wearing Liverpool shirts; I ask them where they are going to watch the match, having forgotten that it is on. In excellent English, they invite me to join them and I walk with them to a bar. I explain why I am in Pristina and discover that one of them is the bar's owner. I am invited to stay and have a drink with them. They find me a seat and that is where I remain throughout the match. When I get up to leave they wave away my attempts to pay.

The following day I arrange to go over to Zija Miftari's office at the Klan Kosova TV studios on the outskirts of the city towards the airport. When I last saw Zija we had met in his local café close to the original location of the studios where he had just started working. That day I had asked him to arrange a meeting with a journalist who was going to write a potentially harmful article about me. Today, thankfully, everything is very different.

I let him know when I arrive and he quickly appears. It is genuinely great to see him. We sit outside and discuss events from 2009. I then ask him if my earlier request to go up to Mitrovice with him is still going to be possible. He confirms that arrangements are made for us to drive up to the northern town on the Friday, where we will also meet his friend, the Deputy Commissioner of the Kosovo Police. While we are sitting outside drinking a coffee, Zija asks if I would like to have a tour of the new studios. Before we go in, I ask him about the building that lies abandoned in the forest; he explains that it was a Government initiative to create a space for meetings outside the city. I can't help thinking it needs to be removed and the area returned to a natural habitat.

We then walk into the building. Inside the studio area different sets stand next to each other, each one created for the channel's live programmes. It's fascinating and very impressive. We reach the main editorial office and I am introduced to his boss. I notice one wall in the large open-plan office is made of brick. The architectural design really stands out. Zija sees me looking at it and explains that they are reclaimed bricks from abandoned houses, burnt to the ground during Serbia's campaign of ethnic cleansing in 1999. As we leave, with the promise to meet again on Friday for our visit to Mitrovice, Zija also explains the significance of the wooden pathway we are walking along between the building and the car park. It is constructed using sleepers taken from the railway lines along which thousands of Kosovo Albanian families walked, driven out of Kosovo by Serb forces in the full glare of the world's media. The nod to the past in the studio's design is deeply moving. I am looking forward to my trip to Mitrovice with Zija on Friday.

I leave the studio and am driving in a taxi towards my lunch appointment with General Rama at a restaurant that played such a key role during my tour, Collection.

Seeing General Rama again after such a long time is a highlight of my visit. As the Commander of the KSF I am delighted that he is now in the top spot; it's well deserved. I ask him about the current situation and his story so far. When I last saw him he was handing me a flag and his old KPC uniform at my leaving dinner, and, despite the formation of the KSF, Rama was struggling. What I am not prepared for is being able to communicate with him directly. In the 9 years since we had last seen each other, Rama has learned to speak very competent English. I know he has spent some time in York and the United States studying the language, and I am impressed. It is odd not having to talk to him through Simi for the first time.

After lunch, the first question I ask him is what he remembers of the 'NATO Standards' mantra that was so often quoted at us. Rama laughs deeply as he recalls the constant refrain coming out of Film City which made the manning of the KSF so objective that cultural clan balance was ignored and vital capabilities were nearly lost to the new force. Rama explains his shock when General Gay re-opened the selection process for those who had been rejected under the watchful gaze of the international community. We don't linger on the past though, and Rama draws a line under the conversation when he says, 'Anyway, we survived the situation.'

I learn that the KSF has recruited 34 Kosovo Serbs from Mitrovice, an astonishing fact under the circumstances. I ask about the security of their families in that highly sensitive and unpredictable town and he explains that a lot of effort goes into keeping everyone safe. I ask why they want to join a force that is predominantly Kosovo Albanian in its ethnic make-up. He says they want jobs and they want to make something of themselves; to them the politics is secondary. The story has a familiar ring to it. However he adds that the Serbian authorities have said that if any Kosovo Serbs who are serving in the KSF cross the border into Serbia, they will be arrested for war crimes. It seems extreme but under the circumstances, not at all surprising. The pressure must be intolerable from within their communities. It is clear that the KSF is inclusive, with over 10% of the force now recruited from ethnic minorities. Rama emphasises this fact by telling me that his own military assistant is a Kosovo Serb. He adds that for the last 6 years the KSF has been voted the most trusted organisation in Kosovo. It is great to hear that the KSF has managed to grow into such a respected part of Kosovo's public life.

I mention my conversation with Çeku about overseas deployments and he points out that the KSF has already deployed beyond its borders, into Albania and that there was soon to be a multi-national exercise taking place in Kosovo involving 12 nations under Rama's overall command. He is proud of the reputation the KSF has earned; they are the first security organisation in the Balkans to promote a female to the rank of Brigadier. In the male-dominated world that is the Balkans, that is no mean feat. I am impressed with the progress he describes.

My journey here to understand the KSF finally seems to be vindicated; the KSF has not simply survived, it has flourished over the intervening years.

I do have one last question for him; whatever happened to the officer who had been so disruptive towards the stand down plan that Rama had written, and who had led the protests in Vrani Do, but had still been selected for the KSF? Again, my question draws that deep laugh. He explains that Lieutenant Colonel Potera left the KSF and is now an active member of Vetevendosje, the political organisation that regularly holds large-scale street protests against Serbia's influence in the affairs of Kosovo. It is my turn to laugh at the irony.

I also ask him about Rufki Suma. He was the officer who had such an influence over his men that he prevented them from applying to join the KSF until the last safe moment. His complaints and constant briefings to the media drew visits to his ramshackle base in the south of the country from a range of senior and influential figures. He always struck me as someone who was vain, even narcissistic; someone who loved the limelight and who craved the power that being a KPC commander in a small town drew. Rama explained that he was on his third term in office as Mayor of the same town. I exhale deeply and we exchange a wry smile.

It is time to leave and Rama's driver appears at the table to take him back to the Ministry. We stand up together and I shake his hand, grateful for his time and telling him how good it is to see him again. With that he leaves. Now alone on the restaurant terrace, I reminisce; it was here that I spent many hours with both Rama and Selimi. I had agreed to meet the Prime Minister to try to convince him to change the KFOR Commander's mind about the re-opening of selections while sitting inside this restaurant. Collection holds a special place in my memory and it has been good to be back.

On a whim, I decide to walk the short distance to the old driving school, which was both the KPC HQ and then the KSF Ministry Annex when I was in Kosovo before. Walking past newly built apartment blocks which have completely changed the feel of the place that I remember, I stand on the sloping approach road where the President inspected the Kosovo Guard on the KPC's final day in uniform. I walk further up and stand in front of the building, now the headquarters of Kosovo's Customs organisation, remembering where my office had been, briefly reliving my upsetting conversation with my son on Skype, which I now know he doesn't even remember.

It is a building that holds mixed emotions for me, like so many in this country. As I am standing there one of the officials comes over and asks me whether I want any help. I explain why I am there and he suggests that I go back into the building to have a look at it again. I even walk up the stairs to where Generals Selimi and Rama had their offices, as I did every day during my tour. However, things feel very different now and I have a strong urge to leave. I walk out of the place for the last time, knowing I will never go back.

Outside on the road he asks me how I am getting back into town and when I say on foot he insists I get in his car with his wife and young son, who seems to be shocked into silence by my presence and his parents' excellent English. We talk politics, Serbia, the state of the country and everything in between during the 20-minute drive. They drop me at the end of Mother Teresa Boulevard and I thank them for their spontaneous kindness. This is becoming a theme of the week.

That evening I go out for dinner knowing I will be seeing the Prime Minister in the morning at 8.30am.

The next day, I follow my usual route into the city centre, crossing the dual carriage way with local confidence before stepping onto Mother Teresa Boulevard once more. This time I have a walk of about 100m to complete before arriving at the Government building. I fall in step with some local staff as I pass a couple of police officers manning the outer gate, then once inside I walk up to the security desk and explain I am there to see the Prime Minister. I look like a diplomat and that is what they assume. A phone call is made and I am asked to wait.

In that time I watch the steady flow of staff who are arriving for a normal day in the office, putting their bags through the airport-style screening machine and walking through the scanner before disappearing into the building's corridors. The occasional beep as a mobile phone is forgotten in a pocket makes me smile; some things are the same the world over. I am not waiting long before the desk phone rings and I am invited to go upstairs. It is 8.25am. As soon as I arrive I am shown into an anteroom and asked to wait. I speak briefly with the young lady who meets me and after a few minutes I see a familiar face again. I stand up and we exchange a warm greeting, addressed like I was 9 years ago, as 'Colonel'; he had met me on every occasion that I had visited Ramush Haradinaj in his party offices. He is now the Chef de Cabinet and the man who Simi has made the arrangements with for my visit. To be given 20 minutes with the Prime Minister, at short notice, is an extraordinary privilege.

I am sitting on a comfortable leather sofa in the area outside the Prime Minister's private office. It is 9 years since I was last here. Nothing has changed. I watch as a large number of people walk out from a meeting, presumably with the PM, chatting excitedly and only glancing at me when they catch me in their peripheral vision. And I do not have to wait long to hear those very familiar tones of Ramush Haradinaj coming closer, asking where I am; we greet each other warmly and he invites me into a large reception room. Chairs are lined up along both sides of the room to facilitate dialogue, with two chairs at the end, separated by a small table with a British flag placed alongside a Kosovan flag. It is clear this is the PM's seat and I am invited to sit next to him. It has a similar feel to his party office reception room. I notice the flags and remember his attention to detail. The same young lady from outside brings coffee although I am disappointed there is no cigar or glass of raki; I would have fallen off my chair if they had made an appearance.

I explain who I had seen during my visit and I ask the Prime Minister about the KSF and his view of its progress since 2009. He is measured and seems to consider his words carefully. He explains how the KSF represents the spirit of freedom, modelled very much on the UK military. Ramush sees the KSF as a great achievement but makes it clear that in his view it is ready for a transition, to make the next step towards becoming an Army, with complementary capabilities that can support Kosovo's allies in NATO. He is passionate that to be successful, the KSF has to be inclusive; it is a great achievement that Kosovo Serbs from the north in Mitrovice are serving in the force. Ramush believes that this integration is not new, that trust has existed between communities over time; with understandable pride the PM points out that with this level of integration evident in the KSF, it proves that it can happen elsewhere in society.

The Prime Minister is convinced that the KSF has managed to make itself a home for every person in Kosovo, whether Serb or Albanian. He repeats the now familiar ambition to deploy its forces overseas as part of an international coalition. We are enjoying a very open conversation, it is a joy to be sitting with Kosovo's most powerful politician. He is confident and optimistic about the country's future and he declares 'Kosovo is sustainable'; it is a strong message on which to draw our meeting to a close.

In no time my 20 minutes is up. The lady reappears and we pose for some photographs. The Prime Minister gives me a small Kosovan lapel pin and we once again shake hands warmly, remembering his vice-like grip in the process. We say goodbye and I walk out of his office, down the stairs, past security and back onto the street. It's not even 9 o'clock. I immediately head towards the restaurant I have been drawn to since returning to Pristina and sit down in the early morning sunshine, aware that I have just had my second meeting with a Kosovan Prime Minster in 10 years. My adrenaline is flowing and I wonder whether I should order the macchiato after all. It is a remarkable way to start the day.

I am sitting on a plastic chair on the grass in front of the restaurant, just set back from the umbrellas and beyond the main pedestrian thoroughfare. I am on a high, watching the world go by. The sun is hot and it is warming on my skin. I take stock and consider what I have achieved this week, mainly down to Simi's incredible reputation and black book. I never dreamed I would have managed to fit in so much. I soon head back to the hotel to change into more comfortable clothes and decide, at the last minute, to drive to the ancient city of Prizren in the south west of the country for lunch. I had only ever visited Prizren once in my 6 months and I owed it a second, flying visit. Forty minutes out of Pristina I drive past the junction for Stone Castle Vineyard, the scene of the final KPC gathering in January 2009. A celebration that is remembered by all who attended it. The new motorway makes driving very straight forward. I soon turn off at the Prizren junction, knowing that Tirana lies a couple of hours further south; it's quite a difference to my 9-hour journey via exposed mountain roads in the middle of winter on my way to watch a graduation ceremony in Albania's Military Academy.

2018. I meet Lieutenant General Rama for lunch at 'Collection', 9 years after I left. We reminisce about the KPC and KSF, talking together in English, reflecting his newly acquired language skills.

Standing in ethnic Serb-dominated north Mitrovice, with national flags flying and murals on the walls, Serbia's influence in this part of Kosovo is hard to miss.

Alongside my friend, Zija Miftari, the journalist who I met clandestinely during my tour.

Meeting the Kosovan Prime Minister on my return to the country after 9 years; Ramush Haradinaj and I discuss the health of the KSF and its impact on the people of Kosovo.

By the afternoon I am back in Pristina and once again walking across the city, this time hoping to meet one of the original members of the KPC and now the most senior female officer in any security organisation in the Balkans. In 5 Senses, a smart café close to Film City, I meet Brigadier General Spahiu, the female officer currently leading the Training and Doctrine Command, TRADOC. I explain what I am doing and I find a kindred spirit over the way the establishment of the KSF was managed. It is clear she remains troubled by what happened at the time and it is evident that she has not had a chance to speak freely about the subject for many years. We share a fascinating hour together.

That evening I meet up with Adrian Koci, the former owner of Sokoli e Mirusha, the jazz café that I visited during my time in Kosovo, including on one of my last nights out in the city. We share a great evening together discussing how we can make Kosovo a wealthy and prosperous country in its own right. Just as I am starting to renew old acquaintances in Kosovo it is nearly time for me to leave.

I check out of the hotel the following morning and collect Zija for our drive to Mitrovice, the scene of two significant events during my 6-month tour, and Zija's home town. On our journey north in my Macedonian registered hire car, Zija starts to open up to me about what happened to his family in 1999. I ask him whether he had ever considered joining the KLA. He explains that he and his friends were approached by someone, a so-called KLA recruiter, but they suspected that he was a Serb sympathiser and chose not to sign up. It was a decision that may have saved his life. As a teenager living with his family in Mitrovice at that time, someone simply knocked on their door and told them they had to leave. Zija's father was a journalist and they had family ties over the border in Albania, so they packed what they could and drove south to safety. They were lucky. They stayed in Albania until the end of the conflict when it was safe to return. It is a story I take a while to digest.

Approaching Mitrovice I recognise a very prominent, tall brick tower with red and white paint that indicates our arrival on the outskirts of the town. The tower is the legacy of a battery factory that is long since abandoned. I am listening to Zija as he gives me directions; 'Left here, right at the roundabout, go straight.' His instructions are a little late so I am having to react quickly; 'Right here and then over the bridge.'

I am driving without realising where I am until he says, 'We are now in North Mitrovice.'

When I was in Mitrovice in 2008 and 2009 it was forbidden to cross the bridge and go into the ethnic Serb-dominated northern part of the city and beyond. It was considered unsafe and subject to sudden changes in security. I had only seen the ground from the open door of a helicopter flying at 500 feet when I had taken a flight with the French Army during my tour. Looking out of the car now, what I am not prepared for, and which takes me by surprise, is an Albanian enclave immediately over the bridge. The trees along both sides of the road are adorned with red and black Albanian flags, many threadbare and flapping about in the wind, they have seen better days but the message is irrefutable; we are Albanian and this is Kosovo. I keep driving ahead and after about 100m the Albanian flags disappear, the trees once again bare. After a short distance the trees are this time decorated with Serbian flags. And the flags do not stop, they keep going as far as the eye can see. It feels as if I am in Serbia; it is an eerie sensation. As if to emphasise the point that I am no longer in an area of Kosovo, governed by Pristina, very few cars have number plates, they have been removed. It seems a petty protest, but it makes an impact.

We park in a side street adjacent to a secure police station, with high wire fences and look-out towers. There is an old UN building across the road that used to be a courthouse. We get out and, under a baking sun, walk round to the entrance. My decision to hire a car in Macedonia proves to have been a good one, the number plates failing to attract any attention from the local Kosovo Serbs who are on the streets. Zija's friend soon emerges and we walk together up a short hill and then along a main road towards a large statue and pedestrianised street. We stop and choose a table outside, in full view of countless murals painted on the walls of a building across the road from where we are sitting.

I am trying to compute where I am and who I am sitting with; we are in north Mitrovice, drinking a coffee that was paid for in Serbian dinar, Zija's friend is the Deputy Police Chief for North Mitrovice and he is a Kosovo Albanian. He talks a lot about how life has changed, how it is so much more calm now compared to even three years earlier. He says that in 2015 it would have been impossible to have been sitting outside like this. It remains a delicate situation though; one word from Belgrade, Serbia's capital, and the atmosphere in the northern part of the town can change quickly.

I ask Zija's friend how he is supporting those who have joined the KSF. He explains that he and his team work closely with the Kosovo Serbian community and a lot of effort is made to ensure the families of those serving in the force are protected. This week I have talked to General Rama and the country's Prime Minister about the recruitment of ethnic Serbs in the KSF and what an achievement it is; seeing the nationalism on display in this part of the town, getting first-hand experience of the challenges they and their families face, makes me respect those who have joined even more.

Throughout our time sitting at the table a steady stream of locals make a detour to shake the policeman's hand. Serbian is spoken. Backs are slapped. It is the epitome of community policing and I get the impression from what I am seeing that the people here are enjoying their peaceful co-existence. The damaging nationalism that has undermined efforts at integration over the years doesn't appear to be very evident in the people who I see this morning. When we finish our coffee, an experience I will never forget, we walk over to the murals and I ask whether I can take some pictures. I am told to go ahead. The three of us also pose together as a memory of our meeting. We are in the heart of Serb-controlled northern Kosovo and I am feeling as relaxed as I do on any street in the UK, if not more so.

As we finally make our way back to the car, out of nowhere, two British soldiers in uniform and floppy military hats casually walk past in the opposite direction, carrying sidearms and looking relaxed. I double take and look back to be sure what I have just seen. Our host explains that they are always on the streets.

It seems that every time I visit Mitrovice, British soldiers are never far away.

By the time I drop Zija off at the TV studios back in Pristina it is after lunch and he needs to get home. I am deeply indebted to him and I tell him so; he shrugs it off, perhaps thinking that the many favours we have done each other over the years have all balanced themselves out. We quickly say goodbye and I pull out of the car park and take the road south to Skopje; for now, my time in Kosovo is at an end.

Driving on the new motorway again, I think about the warmth with which I have been greeted during the week. It has rekindled strong feelings of respect and fondness for the country and its people that have lain dormant. At times this week it was a humbling experience; people had put themselves out for me so that I could make the most of my visit to Kosovo. The hospitality and natural kindness I have experienced reassures me that despite the difficulties faced by the country's politicians, its military leaders and the people, who have to manage the many day to day challenges of living in the country, Kosovo has a positive future.

When I finally return to my home in England, I sit down and once more open my Kosovo diary from 2009. I turn to the entry I made on my last day. I read the words I had written somewhere over Switzerland on that British Airways flight, cruising over the Alps on my way back to the UK and the life I had put on hold for 6 months.

"I am deeply proud of what I have done here. I believe I have made a difference and helped the forward progress of this country. I have put myself into situations I never thought I would have to. I have taken risks and I have dug into my reserves of moral courage; perhaps more than I ever have done before. But after everything, even if the shit hits the fan in the papers this week, I am content with my contribution and everyone's kind words have reinforced this feeling. Perhaps I have allowed my idealist approach to get in the way of prudence, but I have been honest and truthful and I could not just stand by and watch things go wrong with the KSF. My conscience is clear and I am happy."

ACKNOWLEDGMENTS

There are many people I would like to thank.

To my publishing team, for believing in this project and for turning it into reality. My gratitude goes to John White and Erica Fitzpatrick, who both offered to read early versions of the manuscript. Their positive comments and combined wisdom helped me take the next steps on my journey. To Stephen Bywater, a successful author of two novels, for his encouragement and advice, and for unwittingly sowing the seeds for my next literary project. To Stuart Roberts, who was always so patient with me when I would randomly get in touch to ask him obscure questions about the KPC stand down plan. Our conversations always ended up on the same subject, which never failed to make us laugh. We may have seen events unfold from different perspectives back in 2008/09, but he has since become a dear friend. To Dave Finnimore, who showed such strong moral courage to help the KSF start life in as good a shape as possible, but who is sadly no longer with us to read of his exploits. I would like to thank Nick Caplin, for his wise advice and support, both during the events in this book and more recently. To those members of my family who let me use their properties in Northern Portugal, in Norfolk, and to Jamila and Stefan, my Airbnb hosts, in Lagos, the Algarve, where I broke the back of the manuscript. I will always hear the sound of the sea when I think of this book. It is ironic that I spent so much time by the coast writing about a landlocked country. I would like to thank all those people who showed me such support and kindness when I went back to Kosovo, via Skopje in Macedonia, in March 2018; they know who they are as they all feature in the final chapter. Going back to Pristina was one of the most emotional journeys I have ever undertaken. And there is one person who deserves a special mention, and without whom this book would never have happened. Arsim Rexha, aka Simi, has served the UK's military representatives with loyalty, integrity and dedication since 1999. He offered me a unique insight to Kosovo and its people and continues to open doors to this day. I will always be deeply grateful to him. When I deployed to Kosovo my children were very young, yet they were present in my thoughts throughout the original tour. When I was writing this book, the same feelings came back to me all over again. Seb and Tilly are grown up now and, thankfully, have no memories of my time in Kosovo. They have turned into independent and mature young people and I am incredibly proud of them. Finally I would like to thank Alex, who has given me so much support and encouragement during the latter stages of writing *Under A Feathered Sky*. Her patience and strength at times of need will never be forgotten. Her highly tuned editing skills have helped make this book what it is today.

ABOUT THE AUTHOR

Ade Clewlow MBE served in the British Army for over 25 years. Having deployed across the world, from Belize to Baghdad, he arrived in Kosovo as a Lieutenant Colonel looking forward to a routine six month operational tour of duty. What Ade found in newly independent Kosovo was a population determined to grow into a respectable, and respected, member of the international community. The events during his tour inspired him to write *Under A Feathered Sky*. Ade lives in the UK and works in the security industry.

This is his first book.

Printed in Great Britain
by Amazon